S0-BZK-508

The Evaluation Interview

The Evaluation Interview

RICHARD A. FEAR

Senior Consultant with the Selection Systems Division of Mainstream Access, Inc.

Past Vice President of the Psychological Corporation

Third Edition

McGraw-Hill Book Company

New York St. Louis San Francisco Auckland Bogotá Hamburg Johannesburg London Madrid Mexico Montreal New Delhi Panama Paris São Paulo Singapore Sydney Tokyo Toronto

Library of Congress Cataloging in Publication Data

Fear, Richard A.
The evaluation interview.

Includes index.
1. Employment interviewing. I. Title.
HF5549.5.I6F4 1984 658.3'1124 83-14955
ISBN 0-07-020218-4

4567890 BKP/BKP 898765

ISBN 0-07-020218-4

The editors for this book were Bonnie Binkert and Stephan O. Parnes, the designer was Jules Perlmutter, and the production supervisor was Sally Fliess. It was set in Caledonia by Black Dot, Inc.

Printed and bound by The Book Press.

"Observe what a man does; listen to what he says; how then can you not know what he is"

Attributed to Confucius

Contents

Preface xii

PART ONE Prologue

CHAPTER 1 The Changing Scene 3

Foreign Competition 3
Equal Employment Opportunity 4
Employment at Will 6
The Trained Interviewee 9
The Changing Technology 10
The Staggering Costs of Poor Selection 13
The Importance of Training Interviewers 16

CHAPTER 2 Equal Employment Opportunity 17

Major Federal Laws and Executive Orders 17
Title VII of the Civil Rights Act of 1964 20
Affirmative Action 21
Why EEO Regulations Came into Existence in the First Place 22
Why Companies have Overreacted to EEO Regulations 24
EEO Makes Good Business Sense 25
Why Interviewers Are Required to Observe Certain Important Aspects of EEO Regulations 26
It Is Still Possible to Select the Best Qualified Applicants 33

CHAPTER 3 How to Handle the Trained Applicant 34

Outplacement Services Provide Valuable and Much-Needed Assistance to the Average Job Seeker 35
How to Identify the Trained Applicant 36
How to Use to Advantage the Skills of the Trained Interviewee 38
How to Cope with the Trained Applicant 39
Trained Interviewers Need Have No Fear of the Trained Applicant 45

CHAPTER 4 Worker Specifications 47

Management 50
Research and Development 52
Production Supervision 55
Sales 57
Finance 59
Employee Relations 61
Matching the Applicant with the Job 64

CHAPTER 5 Preliminary Selection Steps 66

Recruiting 69
Application Form 70
The Preliminary Interview 72
Aptitude Tests 77
The Reference Check 80
Physical Examination 81
Preliminary Selection Steps Provide Valuable Leads for the Final Interview 82

PART TWO Developing Relevant Information

CHAPTER 6 Nature of the Evaluation Interview 85

Essential Aspects of the Final Interview 86
Philosophy of the Interview 87
Functions of the Interview 88

CHAPTER 7 Developing Rapport and Helping the Applicant to Talk Spontaneously 90

Small Talk 92
The Calculated Pause 94
Facial Expressions 95
Voice 97
Lubrication, or Reinforcement 99
Playing Down Unfavorable Information 100
Comprehensive Introductory Questions 102
EEO Considerations 105

CHAPTER 8 Probing More Deeply for Clues to Behavior 107

Interviewing as Conversation 108
Function of Follow-up Questions 111
Kinds of Probing Questions 116
EEO Considerations 124

CHAPTER 9 Techniques of Control 125

Why Control Is Necessary 126
Techniques of Control 132
Other Factors of Control 136
Effective Control Requires Judicious Pacing 139
EEO Considerations 140

PART THREE Interpreting Information Developed

CHAPTER 10 Interpretation, An Introduction 143

Complexities of Interpretation 144
First Considerations 145
Process of Interpretation 149
What to Interpret 153
How to Interpret 154
Trait Constellations 161
Trait Description 172

CHAPTER 11 Interpreting Work History 175

How to Structure Discussion of Work History 177
Relevance of Prior Jobs 178
Duties 179
Likes 181
Things Found Less Satisfying 183
Conditioned to Work? 185
Level of Earnings 187
Reasons for Changing Jobs 190
Leadership Experience 193
Number of Previous Jobs 193
Achievements 194
Development Needs 197
Factors of Job Satisfaction 201
Type of Job Desired 204
EEO Considerations 206

CHAPTER 12 Interpreting Education and Present Social Adjustment 208

Structuring the Discussion of Education 209
Best and Poorest Subjects 211
Grades 213
The Overachiever 215
College Boards 215
Extracurricular Activities 218
Effort 220
Special Achievements 221
Training beyond Undergraduate Level 222
How Was Education Financed 224
Present Social Adjustment 227
EEO Considerations 233

CHAPTER 13 Mental Ability, Motivation, and Maturity—A First Consideration 235

Mental Ability 236
Motivation 241

Maturity 245
Implications for Selection of College Students 248

CHAPTER 14 Terminating the Interview and Writing the Interview Report 250

Terminating the Interview 250
Completing the Interview Rating Form 255
Futher Uses of the Completed Interview Rating Form 278

CHAPTER 15 How to Train Interviewers 279

Learning by Doing 280
Physical Facilities 281
Qualifications of the Trainer 282
Composition of the Training Group 283
Interviewees for Practice Interviews 285
The Training Week 288
The Bottom Line 296

APPENDIX 1 Interview Guide 297

APPENDIX 2 Interview Rating Form 301

APPENDIX 3 Illustrative Reports of Interview Findings 307

Index 321

Preface

The third edition of *The Evaluation Interview* marks the 25th year of publication. During this time, many changes have of course taken place in business and industry, changes which now make it more important than ever to hire highly qualified people at all levels of an organization. With five completely new chapters, this third edition treats the more important of these changes, such as increased foreign competition, Equal Employment Opportunity (EEO) regulations, the new challenge to the common law doctrine "employment at will," the implications of outplacement and the training of interviewees, and the impact of the new technology on the hiring function.

For the first time since its publication, this book includes a new chapter on the training of interviewers. In this chapter, the author has decided to share what he has learned about training interviewers over a lifetime of performing this consulting service. Built on the philosophy of "learning by doing," this chapter points out the importance of practice interviews with bona fide interviewees, how to obtain such interviewees, the electronic equipment which enables the trainer to communicate with the interviewer during each of the practice interviews, and the specifics of the training week.

This third edition includes a greatly expanded discussion involving the selection of minorities and females. In addition to an entirely new chapter on EEO, specific EEO considerations are included at the end of several chapters.

Those familiar with previous editions of this book will note that the chapter on early home background has been omitted from this edition. This omission involved a very difficult decision, a decision made primarily on the basis of the fact that some people without appropriate training have nevertheless been including the early home background in their interviews, despite the fact that they do not have sufficient background adequately to interpret the data. Since inappropriate interpretation can be unfair to the applicant involved, the chapter has been omitted altogether. Prior to making this decision, however, the author carried out some research with twenty different interviewer training groups. In each training group, half of the interviews included the early home background and the other half omitted this section of the interview. The results of this research indicate that although the early home background does help to understand behavior, the omission of this area does not appreciably affect the overall employment decision.

The techniques for developing information and interpreting data do not, of course, change. The chapters devoted to these techniques, however, include new insights as well as new probing questions. The book is still an essentially practical how-to-do-it work—one that spells out detailed procedures for handling applicants from the time they walk into the room until the interview is terminated. Readers are provided with a "track to run on" which guides tham step-by-step through a discussion of the applicant's work experience, education, present social adjustment, and self-evaluation. Detailed intstructions for writing the report of interview findings are also included.

In arriving at the philosophy and techniques here expressed, the author has drawn upon his practical experience as the principal source. At the same time, he is deeply indebted to colleagues past and present who have contributed valuable ideas along the way. In particular, the author is deeply indebted to James F. Ross, formerly director of the Career Continuation Center, Bethlehem Steel, now managing partner of J. Ross Associates, Ltd., for many valuable ideas and for help with the manuscript. He would also like to thank Dorothy D. Christian, Organization and Staffing Manager, Aircraft Engine Business Group, General Electric Company, for bringing to his attention the statement attributed to Confucius which he has chosen as the epigraph for this book.

Richard A. Fear

PART ONE

Prologue

CHAPTER 1

The Changing Scene

During the 25 years since this book's first publication, many changes have, of course, taken place in business and industry—changes which make it more important than ever to hire highly qualified people at all levels of an organization, from hourly workers all the way up to top management. These changes have brought a steady decrease in productivity and have made it difficult for many companies to compete successfully with their counterparts in Germany and Japan.

FOREIGN COMPETITION

Many companies—particularly those involved with the manufacturing of steel and automobiles—have found it increasingly difficult to show profitable earnings. This is because their competition in such countries as Germany and Japan have learned to produce their goods at less cost and with higher quality.

The steel and auto industries, largely through the pressures of powerful unions, have allowed labor costs to get out of hand. It is now estimated that the hourly cost (including benefits) of producing automobiles and steel in this country is $8 to $10 higher than the average wage in U.S. industry in general.

U.S. buyers have been quick to perceive that some foreign built automobiles have a rather substantial quality advantage over cars they can buy in this country. This has resulted in a steady increase of auto imports and a corresponding decrease in cars manufactured in this country. Although some of the factors involved are beyond our control, such as a lower standard of living in some foreign countries, other factors are well within our control. For one thing, we can focus more attention on the hiring function, to the extent that we select people who are better qualified and more highly motivated to turn in a quality performance. If properly done, this alone could substantially reduce Japan's competitive advantage.

EQUAL EMPLOYMENT OPPORTUNITY

The enactment of the Civil Rights Act of 1964 has had a profound and disastrous effect on hiring practices in this country. The record shows that industry, for the most part, has not yet found a satisfactory method of hiring minorities and females within Equal Employment Opportunity (EEO) guidelines. Most large corporations have been the target of myriad charges of discrimination. As a matter of fact, it is not unusual for a large corporation to have as many as several hundred separate charges of discrimination at any given time. The cost of case preparation, involving the time of important people for conferences and court appearances, average as many as 40 expensive hours per case. And, when outside legal assistance is necessary, another $10,000 to $20,000 per case is involved. It can be argued that industry has brought this enormous burden on itself through past inequitable practices. But, be that as it may, the staggering costs of processing discrimination charges has had a remarkable and predictable effect on U.S. industry. Managers in many companies have panicked, taking the stance that former methods of selection are no longer possible. They have become so sensitive to the possible charges of discrimination that they have given up employment tests, downgraded the function of interviewers, and in many cases reverted to hiring at random. In so doing, they have surrendered an important management prerogative—a prerogative that they very much need in order to make a profit and stay in business. The day is long gone when most companies have such a competitive edge that they can afford to resort to indiscriminate hiring.

As will be seen from a subsequent chapter, however, hiring at random is never justified. It is still quite possible within the legal confines of EEO regulations to select the best qualified persons available. It is still possible to give aptitude and dexterity tests and to train interviewers to select the best qualified people from among those available. There is nothing in the regulations that specifies that one cannot *reject* those minorities and female applicants who do not measure up to the requirements of the job. At the same time, it must be emphasized that proper selection within EEO guidelines cannot be accomplished without knowledgeable people. Since most charges of discrimination occur because of ignorance of the law, interviewers must be carefully schooled in terms of what they can and cannot do. This means that modern selection techniques must incorporate another dimension—EEO regulations.

EMPLOYMENT AT WILL

Employment at will has historically been recognized as a state common law doctrine that permits an employer or employee to terminate a work relationship at any time, without notice and without cause. Thus, if employers discover that they have totally unqualified individuals in their work force, they have normally been able to fire such individuals without risk of recrimination. But this is no longer necessarily so. There is a growing trend in this country to limit the doctrine of employment at will. Fourteen states have already adopted laws which recognize *abusive discharge* (or *wrongful discharge*) as a basis for a possible court action that can be brought by an employee against an employer. Courts of several other states have indicated that they would also recognize abusive discharge in appropriate cases. As a consequence, we are now witnessing a rash of cases wherein former employees are suing their previous management for wrongful discharge. Many companies now view this trend so seriously that they are undertaking every means at their disposal to rectify this situation. They take the understandable view: "How can you run a company if you can't fire your incompetent people?"

Undoubtedly, there are people who are terminated without due cause—people, for example, who after many years of loyal service have been unfairly terminated by their managers because of some relatively inconsequential action. It seems only right that such individuals should have some recourse. But this is not the problem that faces industry today.

The Marginal Worker

The real problem in this situation is the marginal worker, the individual who is just good enough to "hang on" but not good enough to make a real contribution. When conditions become difficult, as they are now in this current recession, companies are forced to "cut back" and quite naturally try to eliminate the nonproducers. While the marginal worker can be fired without cause in the vast majority of the states in the United States, employers increasingly run the risk of court action *because their records concerning their marginal workers are not good enough to stand up in a court of law.*

Many supervisors suffer from a lack of mental toughness. They are inclined to give questionable workers the benefit of the doubt, assigning a satisfactory rating to a marginal worker's performance when they should have faced up to the fact that that individual is unqualified and therefore should be terminated early in his or her career with the company. The sooner it becomes evident that an individual is unqualified for a given job, the quicker a termination should be effected, both for the good of the individual and for the good of the company. In the early stages of a career, it is far easier for a young person to get another job, perhaps a job where the competition is not quite so great. But, if individuals are permitted to remain with the company for 10 years or more, they have a right to believe that their work has been satisfactory and are therefore surprised and angered if they are subsequently terminated. A member of a recent interviewer training group, a director of research, recently reported that he was forced to terminate a Ph.D. chemist. Before taking this action, he asked a previous supervisor about the individual's competence. That supervisor replied: "Actually, he was no good at all during the time he worked with me." The director of research replied: "But you gave him a very satisfactory rating." The supervisor rejoined: "Oh, you know how it is. One hates to ruin a person's career; there is always the chance that he will do better somewhere else." The director of research then checked with the individual's supervisor two steps removed and got the same response. This is a classic example of how marginal and even unqualified workers are protected in industry because nobody has the courage and mental toughness to face up to their incompetence and do something about it before it is too late.

The recent trend, involving the challenge of *employment at will* doctrine, has important personnel implications. More than ever before, it now becomes vitally necessary to select good people at the very start of their employment, people who are capable of making measurable contributions and who therefore merit long years of employment with an organization. And that, of course, is what this book is all about.

Supervisors Need Training in Performance Appraisal

Lack of effective supervisory training represents one important reason why industry harbors so many marginal people. Some of the more sophisticated companies, of course, have been training supervisors in the techniques of performance appraisal for many years. But, even in many of those companies the results of such training leave much to be desired. For the most part, the training is not sufficiently intensive to help supervisors become more *objective* about the people reporting to them. More serious still, supervisors get far too little training in the techniques of giving back information to the people they have rated. Because they really do not know how to handle feedback interviews, they understandably feel awkward and generally do a bad job.

It is easy for supervisors to tell subordinates about their strengths but, again, due to lack of training, they have a very difficult time discussing shortcomings—those traits and abilities that need improvement. As a consequence, they often omit discussions of shortcomings altogether or, if they do discuss them, they phrase their comments in such innocuous statements as: "You need more experience with our product line." This completely undermines the entire purpose of the feedback interview, which should be designed to stimulate the individual's growth and development. Unless a supervisor documents the individual's shortcomings, the person's work performance is not very likely to change.

Because supervisors realize that they will have a difficult time communicating shortcomings, they often tend to disregard them and, in so doing, rate subordinates higher than they deserve.

As pointed out in subsequent chapters, interviewer training can be of enormous help in preparing supervisors for the feedback discussion. They learn how to develop rapport, how to document their findings with hard data developed from the work experience, and how to soften the impact of negative information by means of appropriate introductory and qualifying phrases. This is one reason why companies involve so many managers in interviewer training sessions.

THE TRAINED INTERVIEWEE

It has been estimated that as many as 15 percent of persons now out of work and looking for jobs have been professionally trained with respect to their performance in the interview situation. Some corporations, faced with the need to lay off employees with appreciable seniority, willingly pay professional consultants rather sizeable fees to help these individuals get another job. This is known as *outplacement* and has become very big business indeed in the United States.

The outplacement program, as valuable as it is to those in need of finding another job, presents the interviewer with a new set of problems. These problems stem from the fact that some graduates of outplacement are trained to take control of the interview away from the interviewer, resist discussion of earnings on previous jobs, and to exaggerate past achievements. Suggestions for coping with trained applicants appear in a subsequent chapter.

THE CHANGING TECHNOLOGY

The computer and other aspects of the new technology are transforming the jobs and lives of millions of Americans. Many have already lost their jobs to the computer and a larger number still are in jobs that are becoming increasingly obsolete. It seems clear that the emerging economy will demand higher skills and special abilities in a high technology workplace. Demographic analysts point out that dramatic shifts in the population and work force are taking place.

In an article written by Thomas W. Lippman that first appeared in *The Washington Post* and was reprinted in *The Albany, (N.Y.) Times-Union* on August 29, 1982, the author points out:

> The population in rural counties after decades of decline, grew in the 1970's at a rate equaled only in the 1850's. At least 3.5 million Americans moved out of urban and suburban communities into 'non-metropolitan areas' in the 70's, and the rural population experts expect the trend to continue. Interstate highways, electronic communication, the community college system, low land cost and a paucity of unions are making the rural areas attractive to industry

and factory work is supplanting farming as the employment of much of the rural population.

There is general agreement also that there will be a continuing shift of jobs from manufacturing to services as foreign competition and the new technology take away millions of jobs. As Frank J. Prial notes in an article that appeared in *The New York Times* on October 17, 1982, "There are more jobs available in the New York area right now than there have been for a long time. But few of them are for those who need them most: the thousands of unskilled and undertrained workers left behind in the headlong flight of manufacturing from the metropolitan region."

In view of the fact that many of the jobs associated with the new technology will require higher-level skills, it seems abundantly clear that the United States needs a retraining program of huge dimensions. Happily, some of this training is already underway. Many automobile workers, for example, are being retrained for other careers through the joint efforts of the United Auto Workers (UAW) and the automotive giants, General Motors and Ford. Ford has also developed a totally privately funded retraining initiative at the company's new National Development and Training Center. Available to any laid-off UAW/Ford worker or any UAW/Ford hourly on-roll employee, the retraining program is meant to provide counseling help in assessing job and career interests and to help direct individuals to appropriate training and development resources.

Many of the jobs associated with the new technology will draw upon a higher level of intelligence than was previously required for many entry-level jobs. As a consequence, the poorly educated, unskilled high school dropouts may very well become permanently displaced. Whereas many such people could formerly be absorbed on routinized assembly operations, these same individuals may not be able to qualify for higher-level positions. Functional illiteracy represents a far greater problem in this country than most people realize. In a comprehensive study carried out by the author many years ago, lack of a sufficiently high IQ represented the single most important reason why teenagers drop out of school. Many high school dropouts, therefore, will find it difficult to qualify even for the new entry-level *training.* They will simply be unable to pass the aptitude and dexterity tests which should be required for acceptance in many of the more complex retraining programs. Unemployment among the unskilled and poorly educated is already a most serious problem in this country. And, when young adults cannot find work, a growing number turn to alcohol, drugs, and crime.

On the positive side, though, people of normal intelligence—and fortunately a very high degree of unemployed people fall into this category—can be retrained for jobs that are far more interesting, and even more exciting, than some of the routine, mindless jobs in which they formerly found themselves trapped.

The Success of a Retraining Program Depends First of All upon Appropriate Selection

During the next few years, the federal government, state governments, and private industry will spend millions of dollars on retraining programs. Unfortunately, some of these funds will be largely wasted because of insufficient attention to the quality of people accepted on these programs. Individuals should not be accepted for retraining unless they possess the capacity to learn, mechanical aptitude, finger and hand dexterity, or whatever other abilities may be required to graduate from the program. The successful applicant should also have an appropriate degree of maturity and motivation. Hence, a carefully designed selection program, including aptitude tests, and comprehensive interviews, is just as important here as it is in selecting people for jobs in manufacturing or services. Individuals who are forced to drop out of a retraining program because of inability to learn or failure to put out the required effort not only find the experience humiliating but often suffer a serious blow to their basic self-confidence. Unsuccessful students are also extremely costly to the retraining program. If a training program has space and equipment for forty students but only graduates twenty, that program is obviously inefficient and unnecessarily costly.

THE STAGGERING COSTS OF POOR SELECTION

In spite of the fact that changes in the fabric of society have made companies increasingly vulnerable because of the presence of incompetent, disruptive, and disgruntled employees in their organization, most companies have given far too little attention to corrective action. Even though effective means of personnel selection have been available for years, the vast majority of companies in this country entrust their selection to personnel and management people who are still largely untrained. The results are predictably haphazard and indiscriminate. One recently retired professional personnel man describes the situation thus: "It never ceased to amaze me that 'scientific' chemists, engineers and managers were perfectly willing to accept and to participate in sloppy, unthoughtful, slovenly selection procedures."

That haphazard selection still exists is largely due to the fact that management has so little understanding of what this is costing their companies. If management would take the time to study the situation in an objective manner, top executives would be amazed at the staggering costs—costs which can run into millions per year at a single plant. The cost of hiring and maintaining a poorly qualified entry-level worker over a probation period that may last as long as 3 months ranges between $5,000 and $7,000.[1] In view of the fact that many companies lose 40 percent or more of the people hired in a given year, the cost is enormous indeed. A study carried out in one of the large manufacturing plants of the Bethlehem Steel Company involved two sample groups of more than 900 employees. Each group was tracked for the first 24 months of employment. Group A, the control group, consisted of employees who had been hired *before* the new selection procedures were installed, and group B involved employees who had been hired *after* the new selection program was inaugurated. The results were astonishing indeed. The new selection procedures reduced the turnover rate by a remarkable 28 percent, while absenteeism dropped 42 percent, tardiness 38 percent, grievances filed 82 percent, accidents reported 25 percent, and compensation cases 33 percent. When these results were translated into dollars, it was discovered that the new selection procedures resulted in the saving of more than a million dollars per year in that plant alone.[2] This is an excellent example of the extent to which many of industry's problems can be solved by a carefully designed and executed selection program.

If it costs between $5,000 and $7,000 per hiring mistake with hourly people, the cost is obviously much higher with higher-level applicants—applicants that normally require

[1]See Richard A. Fear and James F. Ross, *Jobs, Dollars and EEO*, McGraw-Hill, New York, 1982, pp. 3–6.

[2]Ibid, pp. 11–14.

at least 1 year to prove themselves. And it is with this population that this book is primarily concerned. The cost of hiring an ineffective recent college graduate can be broken down as follows:

Salary	$21,000
Benefits (usually one-third of salary)	7,000
Recruiting	2,000
Training	2,000
Administration (employment, medical examination, etc.) minimum	1,000
Total	$33,000

The cost of $33,000 probably represents a minimum, since these costs run appreciably higher in some companies. Moreover, the costs listed above only include *tangible* expenses, omitting such intangible items as greater demands of the supervisor's time, loss of productivity that might have resulted from the employment of a more effective person, and possible contribution to poor morale. When tangible costs alone are considered, however, hiring mistakes in the case of only fifteen college educated people would involve a cost of some $500,000 and many large corporations make more hiring mistakes than that. If one considers that many so-called marginal workers are not terminated at the end of the normal 1-year trial period, the total costs of indiscriminate selection are enormous indeed. Certainly, the bottom line—the extent to which income exceeds expenses—can be greatly improved with the installation of a cost effective selection program, a program that ranges up the line from the lowest paid hourly worker to people who make the important management decisions.

THE IMPORTANCE OF TRAINING INTERVIEWERS

The changing scene of today's industrial society places ever increasing emphasis on selecting the right man or woman for the right job. As complex as this has always been, it is even more complicated today. In addition to searching an applicant's background for clues to behavior, today's interviewers must concern themselves with EEO regulations, regulations involving the handicapped, and the occasional candidate who has been professionally trained as an interviewee.

Yet, by and large, interviewers receive less formal training on the job than any other important people in industry. Financial people often come equipped with a degree as a certified public accountant (CPA); most labor relations people have prior training in labor law and labor negotiations; and even typists and stenographers come equipped with substantial preparation. But what kind of formal training do interviewers receive? Very little indeed! They are expected to learn from experience, by trial and error. As bad as this has always been, it has become almost *dangerous* in today's world. Ignorance of important aspects of the law alone can get interviewers into the kind of trouble that could conceivably cost their companies a great deal of money.

The cost of training interviewers is very modest indeed in the light of potential savings. A well-trained, intelligent, perceptive interviewer can save the company literally hundreds of thousands of dollars over a period of time. Interviewers assume the key responsibility for handling a delicate, complex function in business and industry. But they cannot be expected to do the job without specific and comprehensive training.

CHAPTER 2

Equal Employment Opportunity

This chapter is devoted to a better understanding of Equal Employment Opportunity (EEO) regulations—why they came into existence in the first place, why companies have overreacted to these regulations, and why an effective EEO program makes good business sense. And, because most charges of discrimination stem from an ignorance of the law, we will highlight the eight most important areas of the regulations which are likely to give interviewers the most trouble.

MAJOR FEDERAL LAWS AND EXECUTIVE ORDERS

At the very beginning, let us point out that interviewers can be guided by two basic precepts:

1. An employer must not discriminate in any manner against an individual on the basis of that individual's

race, sex, age, religion, national origin, handicap, or veteran status.

2. Whenever an employer has fewer minority or female employees in its work force than are available in the area work force, that employer must take affirmative action to recruit, hire, and promote such minorities and females.

Before we expand more fully on these two concepts, it may be helpful to review briefly the major federal laws and executive orders concerning EEO.

1. Title VII of the Civil Rights Act of 1964
2. The Equal Pay Act of 1963
3. The Age Discrimination in Employment Act of 1967
4. Executive Order 11246
5. The Rehabilitation Act of 1973
6. Vietnam-Era Veterans' Readjustment Assistance Act of 1974

Title VII of the Civil Rights Act of 1964

Title VII of the Civil Rights Act bans all forms of discrimination in employment based on consideration of a person's race, color, religion, sex, or national origin. It covers all terms and conditions of employment and holds a company and its supervisors responsibile for any discriminatory acts which occur in the workplace. Title VII is administered and enforced by the federal Equal Employment Opportunity Commission (EEOC).

The Equal Pay Act of 1963

The Equal Pay Act prohibits pay differences between male and female workers who are performing equal or substantially equal work, the performance of which requires equal skill, effort, and responsibility and which is performed under similar working conditions. The Equal Pay Act is enforced by the EEOC.

The Age Discrimination in Employment Act of 1967

The Age Discrimination in Employment Act bans discrimination because of age against anyone at least 40 years old but less than 70. Certain state laws prohibit age discrimination against any adult *regardless* of the person's age. Simply put, it is illegal to base any personnel decision on age or otherwise adversely affect a person's status as an employee because of the person's age. This law is enforced by the EEOC.

Executive Order 11246

Executive Order 11246, issued by President Lyndon Johnson in 1967, applies to all employers with government contracts or subcontracts. The executive order and its implementing regulations prohibit a contractor from discriminating on the basis of race, color, religion, sex, or national origin, but also obliges each contractor to take affirmative action in hiring and advancing in employment qualified minority and female personnel. The contractor's commitment to affirmative action must be set forth in a written affirmative action compliance program at each of its facilities. These programs include goals for hiring and upgrading minorities and women and must be revised annually. Enforcement of Executive Order 11246 is carried out by the Office of Federal Contract Compliance Programs (OFCCP), U.S. Department of Labor.

The Rehabilitation Act of 1973

The Rehabilitation Act requires federal contractors to take affirmative action to hire and promote qualified handicapped persons. A contractor must have a written affirmative action program at each of its facilities which is designed to ensure that qualified handicapped persons are employed, upgraded, and provided reasonable accommodation to facilitate their employability. The OFCCP enforces this law.

The Vietnam-Era Veterans' Readjustment Assistance Act of 1974

The Readjustment Assistance Act very closely parallels the Rehabilitation Act in that it requires affirmative action by federal contractors in hiring and upgrading Vietnam-era veterans and disabled veterans.

TITLE VII OF THE CIVIL RIGHTS ACT OF 1964

Some 19 years ago, a sufficient number of fair-minded people concluded that something must be done to correct past inequities. With the passage of the Civil Rights Act of 1964 all forms of discrimination in employment based on consideration of a person's race, color, religion, sex, and national origin were banned. Although this was a major step in the right direction, the overall effects fell far short of the hopes of the original sponsors. Although the Civil Rights Act of 1964 presumably assured everyone equal opportunity, this objective could not be put in practical operation because people were not all on equal footing. Because they had been denied equal opportunities in the past, blacks and females were not able to compete with white males. To cite one example, there were not enough blacks and females in our engineering schools to afford appropriate representation for these two minority groups in professional engineering jobs. Nor were there enough blacks and females "in the pipeline" to assure eventual representation in highly skilled jobs and managerial positions. To aspire to such positions, one must not only receive appropriate training but must also be given gradually increasing relevant responsibility over a period of time.

AFFIRMATIVE ACTION

Because earlier attempts to provide equal opportunity proved insufficient, President Johnson issued Executive Order 11246 in 1967. This applies to all employers with government contracts or subcontracts, and its implementing regulations prohibit a contractor from discriminating on the basis of race, color, religion, sex or national origin. This order also obliges each contractor to take affirmative action in hiring and advancing in employment qualified minority and female personnel. The contractor's commitment to affirmative action must be set forth in a written affirmative action compliance program at each of its facilities. These programs include goals for hiring and upgrading minorities and women and must be revised annually. In effect, this executive order was designed not only to insure equity but also a program that would compensate for the historic lack of equal opportunity. As a consequence of this executive order, all companies with government contracts must show good faith efforts to promote minorities and females into all levels of an organization.

Affirmative action is therefore more than nondiscrimination. Affirmative action requires the employer to make *positive efforts* to recruit, employ, train, and promote qualified minority members and females when it is clear that they have been excluded from jobs in the past, even though no overt or traceable discrimination is evident. If minority members or women have not been employed in numbers that reflect their availability in the work force, affirmative action is required to recruit and employ proportionately more qualified minorities and women. Thus, if the area work force contains 15 percent minorities, any hiring done on an annual basis must be made up of that percentage of minorities.

As a result of the cutbacks put into place by the Reagan administration, there are far fewer compliance agents and officers available than was the case previously. Those that remain appear to be prioritizing their efforts and concentrating on target companies. One observer sizes up the current situation as follows: "True, it may be easier to get away with something today but God help the people that get caught because the compliance officers will throw the whole book at them, in the form of costly fines, loss of government contracts, and even consent decrees."

WHY EEO REGULATIONS CAME INTO EXISTENCE IN THE FIRST PLACE

One has only to inspect the ranks of management in most companies—even at the lowest level—to note that blacks and females have not been afforded the same opportunities as white males. In one Fortune 500 corporation, it was recently noted that the top management group involving some 200 people did not include a single minority and had only one female. Sad to say, moreover, this situation is quite typical of the ranks of management in many large U.S. corporations. In another study conducted in a shipyard many years ago, a large group of blacks and whites hired in 1958 were tracked for 15 years. Members of these two groups were basically unskilled people who had not graduated from high school. After 15 years, it was discovered that the black workers were earning $1.50 per hour less than the white employees. During this period, moreover, many of the white employees had been promoted to some aspect of supervision while almost all of the black employees remained laborers. When one realizes how many years qualified blacks and females have been available in the marketplace, one must recognize that blacks and women have historically been *held* back. The historical impediments still exist in this country—and will someday cause a new revitalization of EEO regulations.

That blacks and females have not been afforded the same opportunity as white males stems from a number of factors, such as denial of equal educational opportunities, inadequate counseling, insufficient training, lack of guidance, and adherence to stereotyping, to name a few. Many women and blacks find it difficult to advance in an organization because no one has taken them "under his wing," so to speak. A young, attractive white male on his way up often finds someone in an organization who takes a special interest in him, acquaints him with the politics of the organization, and provides much needed counseling. Because prejudice and assumed social barriers still exist in many organizations, blacks and females are less likely to receive this kind of guidance.

Stereotyping represents another barrier to upward movement. Because women have been stereotyped as secretaries or some type of administrative assistant, it is difficult for many people to conceive of them in the role of a manager, particularly in those cases where men might be reporting to them. Minorities and women also suffer from predetermined role models. The effective salesperson, for example, has often been thought of as a "blond, blue-eyed, 6-foot 2-inch male." In view of this, the employment of blacks and women in the sales force represents a major readjustment of attitudes and thinking in most sales organizations.

WHY COMPANIES HAVE OVERREACTED TO EEO REGULATIONS

In the previous chapter, we have called attention to the fact that many companies have given up in the attempt to hire *qualified* minorities and females, at least at the entry level. More serious still, this general attitude has, in many cases, been extended to the selection of nonminorities as well. What this frequently amounts to comes very close to selection at random or indiscriminate hiring. As noted earlier, this is costing industry untold millions of dollars a year—dollars that could be restored to the bottom line by means of an effective, cost efficient selection program.

Industry's overreaction to EEO regulations is, of course, understandable. Failure to comply with certain of these regulations has resulted in the loss of multimillion-dollar federal contracts in some cases. In other cases, violation of the regulations has produced a negative public image—an image that could conceivably affect the overall sales of the organization. On February 1, 1983, *The Wall Street Journal* carried an article by David T. Garino which called attention to the fact that the Reverend Jesse L. Jackson has been promoting a boycott of a number of companies he accuses of not hiring, promoting, or doing business with enough minority members. Mr. Garino notes: "Not many companies care to tangle with the charismatic Mr. Jackson, who has negotiated concessions to black businesses worth a total of $275 million from Coca-Cola Company, R.J. Reynolds Industries, Inc.'s Heublein unit and Philip Morris Inc.'s Seven-up unit." This, of course, provides tangible evidence as to the extent to which companies will go to protect their public image. In all cases involving charges of discrimination, the administrative burden of defending such charges has been enormous. Small wonder, then, that so many companies have decided to "play it safe" by resorting to indiscriminate hiring rather than risk violation of the law.

Careful scrutiny of the EEO regulations, on the other hand, reveals that industry does not have to assume a defeatist attitude. It is entirely possible to develop an effective selection program that not only satisfies all requirements of the law but also results in the selection of highly qualified employees at all levels.

The great problem we face today stems from the fact that so few personnel people, managers, and even those directly involved with EEO have actually read the EEO guidelines and hence operate on the basis of what they have learned secondhand. Because it coincides with their own prejudices, moreover, some of these people are even willing to believe some of the "horror stories" that are floating around. They look at the regulations as something negative, something that will not allow them to do what they would like to do. These people fail to realize that the spirit and intent of the regulations proclaim that an employer can still be selective. The regulations also make it possible for an employer to be creative in the design of an effective selection program. The regulations simply give rights to some people who have been treated unequally in the past. As one EEO manager puts it, "The regulations allow for a considerable amount of latitude; an employer can even be a son of a bitch if he wants to so long as he is a son of a bitch to everyone."

EEO MAKES GOOD BUSINESS SENSE

In the past, many good, potentially productive people have been rejected for employment because of prejudice and inflexible stereotype. When, as a result of EEO regulations, companies are forced to hire people on the basis of merit and objective qualifications rather than previous stereotypes, they discover that the *quality* of the work force improves. This improvement in the quality of the work force is particularly noticeable in those cases in which the company has a well-designed selection program in operation. Interestingly enough, the addition of better qualified employees to the work force often has a "ripple" effect in the sense that current employees seem to "catch fire" and become more productive.

Regulations protecting minorities and females force a company to review its selection methods and to evaluate its entire work force. In so doing, many employers have found that such a review of employees has resulted, among other things, in the discovery of employees with a great deal of potential for movement within the organization. For example, such an audit frequently turns up women in secretarial jobs who have acquired appreciable relevant training for higher-level positions. And some minorities working as laborers are found to have acquired skills which would qualify them for a much more demanding job.

WHY INTERVIEWERS ARE REQUIRED TO OBSERVE CERTAIN IMPORTANT ASPECTS OF EEO REGULATIONS

Since most charges of discrimination result from ignorance of the law, the eight areas most likely to give interviewers trouble are discussed below. The discussion not only highlights the regulation but points out the reasons behind the regulation.

Marital Status

There are three questions that often trap interviewers in the sense that they result in charges of discrimination:

Are you married?
Do you plan to be married?
What kind of a job does your husband have and where does he work?

In the past, these have been considered bona fide questions and even today could be of concern to the interviewer. If a woman's husband has a job and could conceivably be relocated from time to time, she might be expected to move along with him. Under EEO regulations, however, it is illegal to ask these questions because one would normally ask them only of women and this of course represents *sex discrimination.*

But, other than the fact that a married female *might* not stay with a company for as long as a single person, what other relevancy do such questions possess? If a company has the kind of selection program in place that produces top candidates, any applicant—whether married or single—should be sufficiently productive to justify that person's employment, even though personal factors may require the individual to leave within 2 or 3 years. In other words, if a company can get 2 or 3 years of solid production from a top candidate, the original employment of such a person would certainly be justified. Many studies have shown that one highly qualified worker can produce as much or more than three marginally qualified people.

Children

It is illegal to ask women whether they have children, plan to have children, or what arrangements they may have for taking care of children while they are working. This is a violation of regulations on *sex discrimination* because such questions are only asked of women—almost never asked of men.

Today most interviewers know enough not to ask questions about marital status and whether or not women have children but they sometimes drift into the habit of casually discussing such questions after the interview has ended. This is, of course, just as illegal as addressing these questions in the interview proper.

The evaluation interview is designed to promote a great amount of spontaneous information and, as a consequence, some women may volunteer information concerning their marital status, number of children, and arrangements for taking care of the children while they are at work. There is a great temptation on the part of interviewers to ask additional questions about such arrangements, but this, too, is illegal. Interviewers may listen to this information and interpret it as indicative of some personality trait such as maturity or reliability, but they cannot regard it as a reason for rejecting the individual for employment and must be very careful not to include it in writing up the results of the interview.

Religion

Everyone is quite aware by this time that it is illegal to ask an applicant's religion or even to consider it. This has been incorporated into the laws because religion has no relevancy at all to anyone's ability to perform satisfactorily on a given job.

There are cases, however, where religious beliefs prohibit people from working from sundown on Friday to sundown on Saturday. If the job for which the individual is being considered requires weekend and shift work, certain accommodations must be made. Interviewers cannot reject such applicants on this basis alone because arrangements can usually be made for other people to work those hours in exchange for a Sunday assignment. In order to reject applicants who have a problem working on weekends, interviewers would not only have to prove that appropriate accommodations could not be made but would also have to prove that accommodations for changes in the work schedule were never made for other reasons—to enable an employee to attend certain university classes that might be held during the late afternoon, for example.

Race and National Origin

As obvious as this question is, some interviewers still fall into a trap. It is so easy to become careless and make such a comment as: "You have an interesting last name; what nationality is that? Is it Armenian?" Of course, such a question is completely illegal and could invite charges of discrimination.

Some other interviewers assume that an applicant may be black on the basis of such application information as school attended, neighborhood location, and social affiliations. As a consequence, they may not even invite such an individual in for an interview, judging in advance that the candidate may be "different and therefore not as good." In today's world, interviewers must rid themselves of such stereotypes and make every effort to base selection decisions on such objective criteria as relevant experience, education, basic abilities, and personality traits.

Age

Interviewers who reject applicants on the basis of age alone lay themselves and their employers open to possible charges of discrimination; charges that could cost the organization a great deal of money.

When interviewers conclude that a given applicant is "too old to work here," they are often guilty of such stereotyped thoughts as: "He does not have enough energy," or "She would not be willing to work long hours," or "He wouldn't be sufficiently flexible," or "She may not want to work many more years." Even if some of these thoughts may be valid, there are often compensatory factors. For example, many older persons bring years of relevant and important experience to a new job as well as a higher degree of maturity and judgment. Moreover, if we know anything at all about people we know that there are vast individual differences. Some men and women of 55 have more energy, more stamina, and a greater willingness to work than some other people 10 or 15 years younger.

Confronted with the question of age, interviewers are on safe ground when they hire or reject on the basis of such objective criteria as appropriate experience, relevant education, adequate level of basic abilities, and personality traits suitable to the job in question.

There are some situations, however, where age can be discussed. For example, in some jobs such as police officer or security guard where the applicant will be required to carry a weapon, one must be 21 years of age in order to be considered.

Interviewers must be very careful in answering direct questions such as, "Do you hire people over 65?" Obviously, one should never answer such a question with a flat, "No." It is much more appropriate to say: "Of course, providing the individual possesses the necessary overall qualifications for the job under consideration."

Health

The Rehabilitation Act of 1973 requires federal contractors to take affirmative action to hire and promote qualified handicapped persons. A contractor must have a written affirmative action program at each of its facilities which is designed to insure that qualified handicapped persons are employed, upgraded, and provided reasonable accommodation to facilitate their employability.

In the past, people have been rejected because of such medical problems as high blood pressure, history of cancer, diabetes, amputation, partial paralysis, and loss of any part of the body, such as having only one eye, one kidney, or one lung. Such medical problems can no longer be used as a basis for rejecting an applicant. Rather, organizations must make reasonable accommodations to employ the handicapped when other qualifications are appropriate. The current law, moreover, makes it illegal to reject the handicapped person because that person's history of medical problems makes him or her a poor risk with respect to insurance and workers' compensation cost. Today, there is only one criteria where the selection of a handicapped person is involved: "Can the applicant—with proper accommodation—do the job?" And that is the way it should be!

Interviewers should be aware of the fact that it is illegal for anyone other than authorized medical personnel to discuss the specifics of a medical problem with a candidate. In the event that applicants bring up such a question, they should be asked to postpone that particular question until they get together with the company physician. Interviewers, of course, are neither trained nor licensed to make a selection decision based upon a medical problem. It is for the company physician to decide whether or not an applicant possesses the physical ability to perform a given job.

Veteran Status

The Vietnam-Era Veterans' Readjustment Assistance Act of 1974 very closely parallels the Rehabilitation Act of 1973 in that it requires affirmative action by federal contractors in hiring and upgrading Vietnam-era veterans and disabled veterans. In processing such individuals, moreover, it is now illegal to ask about the type of military discharge. This is because a higher percentage of blacks receive "general" and "dishonorable" discharges. But it has been discovered that some such less-than-honorable discharges have been made as a result of prejudice and hence are not justified. Interviewers are on safer ground when they confine their questions to periods of service and type of work performed. In connection with the latter, however, it is permissible to ask about the individual's likes and dislikes, accomplishments, and leadership experience.

Reference Checks

Many interviewers do not realize that it is now illegal to get reference information by telephone. This is because such information can be unfair to the individual concerned. The informant might not remember correctly and, more seriously, the individual involved does not have an opportunity to tell his or her side of the story should any negative information be divulged. The current laws specifically state that individuals must be given an opportunity to tell their side of the story where any negative information is brought to light. Finally, oral information does not mean anything anyway. In cases of discrimination, negative information must be *documented* and this means it has to be in writing.

All of this should not be taken to mean that reference checks should not be made. Quite to the contrary, reference checks can provide valuable information, information that can be checked with an applicant's statement during the preliminary or employment interview. But reference checks *should be carried out by mail only* and should be confined to such questions as dates of employment, positions held, attendance record, and reasons for termination.

IT IS STILL POSSIBLE TO SELECT THE BEST QUALIFIED APPLICANTS

In spite of the "dos" and "don'ts" discussed in this chapter, there is no reason at all to assume a negative attitude. Many companies have put too much emphasis on what EEO regulations prohibit employers from doing. As a matter of fact, any company can build an effective selection program within the framework of EEO regulations, particularly if that company adopts procedures designed to reduce vulnerability to government intervention.[1]

[1]See Richard A. Fear and James F. Ross, *Jobs, Dollars and EEO*, McGraw-Hill, New York, 1982, pp. 27–50.

CHAPTER 3

How To Handle The Trained Applicant

Outplacement has become big business in this country. Many corporations, faced with the necessity of reducing their payrolls, now provide consulting services to those discharged individuals with substantial number of years of employment. These services provide training in such factors as (1) how to research the company where application for work is being made, (2) where to look for possible places of employment, (3) the most effective manner of handling telephone conversations, (4) how to dress for the interview, and (5) how to put one's best foot forward in the interview itself. Outplacement services have grown by leaps and bounds during the past few years, due in part to the fact that they provide help in a time of great need. These services also gain from the fact that corporate management understandably experiences appreciable concern when it is forced to terminate people with long years of experience. Even when times are difficult, therefore, management readily agrees to pay several hundred dollars per terminated individual in order to help such individuals obtain other positions.

Nor is outplacement likely to disappear with the end of the recession. As noted in Chapter 1, a dramatic change in the U.S. work force is taking shape, a change that will surely extend throughout this decade and perhaps into the next one. As a result of the expected exodus of people from manufacturing into services and from cities into rural areas, workers will continue to lose their jobs and find it necessary to search for new ones. Many such people will seek help with this transition, not only in terms of how and where to look for another job but also how to present themselves more effectively in the interview. This means that outplacement is here to stay.

An increasing number of colleges and universities also provide instruction in effective ways of interview presentation to those about to graduate. This training, while valuable in telling students what to expect in an interview and generally how to handle themselves in this situation, is far less intensive and specific than the training received as a part of outplacement. Informed college students, then, represent no problem at all to the trained interviewer.

Outplacement programs teach such specifics as (1) how to take charge of the interview, (2) how to postpone completion of the application form, (3) how to evade discussion of previous earnings, particularly when they have been relatively low, and (4) how to provide narrative discussion of accomplishments.

OUTPLACEMENT SERVICES PROVIDE VALUABLE AND MUCH-NEEDED ASSISTANCE TO THE AVERAGE JOB SEEKER

Many people—particularly those who have spent a number of years with one company—have had very little practice with respect to seeking another job. Many do not know how to write an effective résumé, organize their background for effective presentation, or how to sell themselves in the interview itself. Hence, the training they receive as part of the outplacement program is not only timely but exceedingly valuable.

Unfortunately, most job seekers will be interviewed by people in industry who have had little or no formal training in the interview process. In most companies, applicants for jobs are interviewed by employment personnel without formal training or by department managers who know even less about conducting an effective interview. Many of the latter, in fact, are often so uncomfortable in the interview situation that they resort to talking too much about the job and the company, and consequently give applicants too little opportunity to tell what they can do. Outplacement services teach applicants how to extricate themselves from such situations, in effect by subtly taking over control of the interview in such a way that they have a genuine opportunity to tell what they are capable of doing. Department managers usually react positively to this approach since it accomplishes what they, because of lack of training and experience in interviewing, are unable to accomplish through their own questions.

Untrained interviewers are a pushover for the trained applicant. Since they really do not know what they are doing anyway, they readily go along with the applicant who *does* have a plan. This means, however, that they too frequently learn *what the applicant chooses to tell rather than what they need to know.* To put it very bluntly, the trained applicant is frequently able to do a "snow job" on the untrained interviewer.

HOW TO IDENTIFY THE TRAINED APPLICANT

In order not to be taken in by an applicant with outplacement training, interviewers should be able to identify such individuals within a few minutes of the start of the interview, or perhaps even before the applicant arrives. In that way, they will be able to obtain the *complete* picture of an applicant's background, including a discussion of the shortcomings as well as strengths.

The first clue that interviewers may have a trained applicant on their hands will occur when the latter tries to postpone completing the company's application form by stating that they prefer to find out whether or not they are interested in the job before they go to the trouble of completing the application. They note that they would prefer to work from their own résumés, which, of course, have been designed to highlight the positives and conceal the negatives.

Trained applicants will make a subtle but immediate attempt to take charge of the interview by paying some sort of a compliment to the interviewer or the company and then launching the discussion with some such comment as: "Since I've already learned a considerable amount about your organization, I suppose you would like to have me tell you about my previous jobs and how my past experience might best help me to make a contribution here." The interviewees then proceed according to plan, discussing their jobs in logical order and highlighting their major accomplishments.

Trained interviewees will be relatively well informed about companies with whom they hope to make a new association. They will work into their discussions comments about the company's earnings, research activity, and possible future prospects. They will also ask the interviewer what happened to the last person who held a job for which they may be applying.

HOW TO USE TO ADVANTAGE THE SKILLS OF THE TRAINED INTERVIEWEE

Applicants with training actually make the job easier for the trained interviewer. For one thing, they have taken the time to organize their background material and hence will require less time to tell their story. This means, too, that many of the specifics of their previous vocational and educational history will be on the tip of their tongues, since they have recently brought all of these facts to light in their preparation for the interview.

In most cases, interviewers find it difficult to get applicants to discuss their strengths, strange as that may seem. This is because most individuals do not take the time to think much about their major ability and personality assets. But this is not the case with the trained applicant. Such individuals have had specific training not only in how to identify their strengths but also in how to present them in the most effective manner. This is a big help to interviewers because they not only get confirmation of strengths which they have already perceived but also may learn about an additional strength or two, clues to which have not completely crystallized in their minds. As soon as the strength is mentioned, however, they can often see immediate documentation in terms of hard data supplied earlier in the interview.

Because trained interviewees will have researched the company, they will normally be genuinely interested in the job in question. Otherwise, they would have eliminated the company from consideration. And the fact that the interviewee has had the initiative to go through the outplacement program is in itself a positive factor, in the sense that it provides a strong clue to such important elements as judgment, maturity, and motivation.

Although, as indicated above, interviewers will normally

benefit from the training and preparation undertaken by trained interviewees, they should guard against a possible tendency to become overly impressed. Since the average applicant comes to the interview with very little in the way of preparation, trained interviewees often look very good indeed in contrast. Every effort must therefore be made to be completely objective. Do not be overly impressed, for example, with well-organized résumés. Some professional probably developed the résumé for the individual involved. In like manner, do not be overly impressed with the fact that the applicant has so much knowledge about the company. This is not *necessarily* an indication of judgment and maturity since they probably did not do this on their own. This is part of their training. Finally, do not be overly impressed with the extent to which they are able to document their strengths. This is, of course, also part of their training.

HOW TO COPE WITH THE TRAINED APPLICANT

Although interviewees who have been trained make the interviewer's job easier in some respects, they also present a different set of problems. They obviously cannot be permitted to take control of the interview; nor should they be allowed to concentrate solely on their accomplishments. Interviewers must therefore restructure the conversation in such a way that they obtain the entire story, which of course includes both positive and negative factors.

As soon as interviewees attempt to take control, interviewers must step in and take control themselves. They can do this by authoritatively introducing their lead question, perhaps utilizing a vocal tone which assumes consent: "Actually, I would prefer that you discuss all aspects of your background in logical order, including your work experience, education, and present interests. Suppose you start with your jobs, going back to the first job and working up to the present. I will be interested in how you got each job, what you did, your likes and dislikes, your level of earnings, and any special achievements. Where do we start? Did you have any jobs in high school?"

The Trained Interviewer's Plan Counters the Applicant's Plan

With this first question, interviewers completely upset the trained applicant's plan. In the first place, applicants become immediately aware that, contrary to their coaching, interviewers have a plan of their own. Secondly, they have been taught to expect a "question and answer" type of interview where interviewers ask a whole series of short direct questions such as:

"What are the reasons why we should hire you?"
"What traits do you have that make you a leader?"
"How good are you in working under pressure?"
"What are the reasons that you did not make better grades in college?"

Trained interviewees have come prepared to answer questions such as those listed above, in a sense to spar with the interviewer. When permitted to discuss their backgrounds in a situation where they will be expected to do some 85 percent of the talking, they are forced to discard their prepared "game plan" and accept the interviewer's plan. As the interview unfolds, moreover, most applicants feel that they like this type of interview better, because it does not "put them on the spot" to the same extent as the more direct "question and answer" approach they had anticipated.

Trained interviewees come prepared to ask many specific questions about the company and about the job for which they are applying. But experience has shown that applicants become so engrossed in discussing their life's story that they completely forget to ask questions about the job and the company. The questions they are taught to ask, however, are all legitimate. Interviewers should therefore invite them to ask any question they may have *at the end of the interview.* By that time, interviewers will know whether or not they are interested in the applicant and this will govern the amount of time they spend answering these questions.

Once they have established control, interviewers can maintain control by drawing upon suggestions discussed in Chapter 9, "Techniques of Control." Thus, should individuals attempt to revert to their own game plan, the interviewer may subtly and tactfully interrupt them, bringing them back to the subject under discussion. Since interviewers are in the power position—they have the job to offer—the establishment of control should not be difficult. And, once interviewees realize that they will have ample opportunity to talk about all of their experiences, they normally "fall into line" and become completely responsive.

Even in cases where trained applicants seem somewhat resistant to relinquishing control of the interview, do not permit an adversarial relationship to develop. Rather, control unobtrusively and utilize all of the rapport-building techniques discussed in Chapter 7, such as reinforcement, or "lubrication"; facial and vocal expression; and playing down unfavorable information. Compliment applicants on their well-organized discussion as well as their ability to fortify the discussion of their strengths with appropriate documentation.

As noted earlier, trained interviewees prefer to use their

résumés as a basis for discussion and thus try to postpone the completion of the company application form. In order to circumvent this ploy, send the company application with the letter that sets up the interview. State that it is company policy not to interview anyone who has not completed the application form carefully and accurately.

Many job seekers have been trained to developed narrative discussions of accomplishments. Obviously, this is one of the important aspects of their background so the interviewer should listen attentively. But try to differentiate between true accomplishments and embellishments. Such a question as: "How was this accomplishment reflected in increased earnings?" flashes a signal that the interviewer is not about to be taken in. Avoid lengthy discussion of accomplishments. By judicious use of questions, make applicants stick to the facts and eliminate any tendency to overelaborate. Occasional use of "why" questions (discussed in Chapter 8) also helps to keep the discussion honest.

"Why" Questions Help Maintain Control

Many trained applicants will gloss over reasons for leaving a given job, quickly launching into the discussion of the next one. In such a case interviewers should interrupt, utilizing the appropriate timing and reinforcement discussed in Chapter 7, with such a question as: "Tell me a little more about the things you found less satisfying on your last job." If this does not provide reasons for leaving, say: "What prompted your decision to leave that job?" Do not be satisfied with a superficial response. Say: "What were some of the other factors that contributed to that decision?"

When asked to respond to such a question as, "What traits did you demonstrate that caused your supervisors to promote you?" interviewees realize that they are being given ample opportunity to reveal their strengths. Questions such as this, together with the reinforcement that takes place throughout the interview, help to take the blunt edge off of why questions and to maintain rapport.

In discussing education, be sure to ask why individuals chose their major in college and how they expected to be able to use that specific major when they graduated. Also ask why they decided upon the college of their choice and why they found certain subjects to their liking.

Why questions represent a most effective means of destroying an applicant's prearranged plan to discuss his or her background and restore control of the interview to the interviewer.

Insist upon a Frank Discussion of Earnings

Since it is important to get a history of financial progress, make every effort to get starting and ending earnings on every job. If interviewers insist on getting salary information on all important jobs *from the very beginning*, it is normally much easier to get this information on the last or present job. Interviewers are, of course, aware of the fact that some applicants try to inflate earnings on their most recent position with the thought that this will give them more leverage in their salary negotiations for a new job. Hence, it is important to look for little telltale signs of possible exaggeration when earnings are stated, such as avoidance of eye contact, squirming in the chair, or added color in the face. As might be expected, though, interviewees are not trained to lie about their earnings. They know that the interviewer may ask to see a payroll stub from the present employer, a W-2 income summary form, or may run a reference check with a previous employer.

Make every attempt to get *ending* earnings on one job

and *beginning* earnings on the next one. This not only provides useful information on salary progress but also makes it a little more difficult for applicants to distort the true facts. When beginning earnings on a subsequent job do not compare favorably with ending earnings on the previous job, interviewers begin to wonder why the job change was made and probe further with such a question as, "How did you feel about taking a new job that paid only slightly more money than what you were making previously?"

Probe for Shortcomings as Well as Assets

Although trained interviewees get considerable coaching in how to identify and present their assets, they do not always expect to have to discuss their shortcomings. Interviewers, on the other hand, must develop information about both assets and shortcomings if they are to make appropriate job placement or appropriate assignment to a retraining program. An individual who has a genuine dislike for and lack of ability to handle detail, for example, should not be assigned to a highly detail-oriented retraining program such as that involving computer programming.

Hence, as discussed in Chapter 11, interviewers must make every attempt to get shortcomings as well as assets. When applicants seem unable to come up with any meaningful shortcomings, press them a little by such a comment as: "What are some of the other traits you would like to improve? No one is perfect, you know; we all have some shortcomings and persons who know themselves well enough to recognize what they need to improve are far more likely to grow and develop." Follow this with "double-edged" questions (Chapter 6) as a means of introducing possible shortcomings observed during the interview. If this is done shrewdly and accurately by bringing up a shortcoming that applicants recognize immediately as one of their genuine development needs, they will gain new respect for the interviewer and become more cooperative. For example, the interviewer might say: "What about self-discipline? Do you have as much of this as you would like to have or is this something you could improve a little bit?" Now, if the applicant knows that his self-discipline is weak, he will immediately become aware that the interviewer knows him better than he had realized and will subsequently become even more cooperative.

Since the discussion of shortcomings is preceded by a very thorough discussion of strengths, applicants are normally quite willing to admit to a few shortcomings, since they do not want to give a completely unbalanced picture of themselves.

TRAINED INTERVIEWERS NEED HAVE NO FEAR OF THE TRAINED APPLICANT

Rapport-inducing techniques described in Part Two of this book are so powerful that most trained applicants will soon become very cooperative and tell interviewers what they need to know. They will soon realize that they are dealing with a professional interviewer, that they will be given ample opportunity to discuss their accomplishments, and that the interviewer will only insist on getting the facts—*all* the relevant facts. Rapport-inducing techniques, combined with why questions and double-edged questions give interviewers a big advantage over any applicant, no matter how well that applicant has been trained.

More insightful interviewees, moreover, will be quick to realize that they are being given a much better opportunity to discuss their entire history than they would have under their own game plan. They sense that interviewers are interested in optimal placement and that this is as good for them as it is for the company. This is why a skillfully conducted, comprehensive interview can do so much in itself to sell a candidate on the company in question.

CHAPTER 4

Worker Specifications

It is surprising that so few people recognize the seemingly obvious fact that intelligent selection is predicated on the knowledge of what to look for in the applicant. How indeed can we evaluate a person for a job if we do not know what abilities and personality traits are necessary for success? Yet so many company employment departments are "playing it by ear" in this respect. Now it is true that many companies have developed job descriptions as a result of their job evaluation programs. But most job descriptions tell what must be done rather than what abilities or personality traits are required. Thus, the job description, while certainly very helpful, is not wholly satisfactory for hiring purposes. In addition to job descriptions, *worker specifications* are needed. The latter involve a list of those traits and abilities required for successful job performance, thus enabling the employment interviewer to compare the applicant's qualifications with the specific demands of the job. Worker specifications, moreover, should provide the basis for developing the application form, the preliminary interview, employment tests, and the final interview itself.

Interviewers should spend enough time in the plant or office to familiarize themselves with the jobs for which they are selecting new employees. This gives them an opportunity to assess working conditions, physical demands, promotional possibilities, occupational hazards, and other factors of the work setting. Even a day or two a month spent in this kind of activity will not only enable interviewers to become more knowledgeable but will help them gain the respect of the supervisory force.

As a first step in building worker specifications for a given position, interviewers should study the job description. As a second step, they should study applicant data and other background information of several incumbents on that job, in an effort to determine unique experience, training, and specific skills. As a next step, they should develop a questionnaire providing space for a notation of required aptitudes (verbal, numerical, mechanical, manual, and the like) level of mental ability, preemployment training required, type of supervision, responsibility for the direction of others, working conditions, and other required characteristics. Armed with such a questionnaire, interviewers can then contact appropriate supervisors as well as those individuals holding the job in question.

A word of caution is in order. Items appearing on worker specifications should be regarded as *factors favorable to success* and nothing more. Worker specifications represent a synthesized list of subjective opinions. And, valuable as these are, they cannot be quantified. For example, because everyone involved has said that a given job requires superior mathematical ability, interviewers cannot insist that every successful applicant for that job obtain a score that ranks him or her in the top 10 percent on a test of numerical ability. As will be seen later, aptitude tests can only be used where such tests have been appropriately validated and cut off scores determined.

In developing worker specifications, interviewers should concentrate first on those jobs for which the most people from outside the company are selected. As time permits, they can then develop worker specifications on those jobs which they are less frequently called upon to fill.

Before embarking upon the task of developing worker specifications, interviewers should have in mind the *general idea* of the qualifications normally found in successful employees on a wide variety of jobs. This permits them to ask about the relevance of a given trait, should the supervisor or subordinate fail to include it. If interviewers are able to give the impression of having some understanding of certain jobs, they will gain quicker rapport with supervisors and subordinates alike.

With these objectives in mind, we have prepared a series of general worker specifications for a number of key higher-level jobs, based upon knowledge gained from evaluating candidates for these jobs over a period of many years. It should be emphasized that the specifications that follow are *general* rather than *specific.* Hence, they cannot be expected to represent the requirements for any one job in any given organization. On the contrary, they are designed to give the interviewer a general overview and to be used primarily as background information. Specific job demands vary widely from company to company, depending upon job content, organizational setup, and company atmosphere. In developing the following worker specifications, we have omitted certain common denominator traits that are important in practically all jobs, traits such as honesty, loyalty, willingness to work hard, and the ability to get along with others.

MANAGEMENT

Qualifications for executive positions vary with respect to level of responsibility and the kind of people to be supervised. The chief accountant, for example, need not have the same degree of dynamic, tough-minded leadership normally required in the plant superintendent. In general, however, the qualifications for the executive may be broken down in two categories: leadership and administrative ability.

Leadership	*Administrative Ability*
Assertiveness	High-level mental ability
Production-mindedness	Good verbal ability
Tough-mindedness	Good numerical ability
Self-confidence	Ability to think analytically and critically
Courage of convictions	Good judgment
Ability to take charge	Long-range planning ability
Ability to organize	Good cultural background
Decisiveness	
Ability to inspire others	
Depth and perspective	
Tact and social sensitivity	

The ideal executive is a happy blend of a leader and the administrator. As a leader, executives must be able to influence their subordinates so that they will willingly carry out their wishes. On the one hand, they must be forceful, dynamic, and willing to take charge. Since they are dealing with the human element, they must at the same time use tact and social sensitivity in their general approach. Social sensitivity, or awareness of the reactions of others, plays a big part in the development of good human relations. Leaders who understand their subordinates and sense their reactions know which ones need forceful direction and which ones need a pat on the back in order to obtain optimal job performance.

True leaders must have decisiveness, born of self-confidence and courage of convictions. They must believe implicitly in their own abilities and, once they have set their course, they must follow through without any waivering of purpose. In this connection, too, they should be tough-minded, in the sense that they must be willing to make difficult decisions that may tread on the toes of a few but work for the good of the many.

In the final analysis, industry rewards those who are able to get things accomplished. Thus, leaders must be able to organize and inspire their subordinates so that they accomplish their purpose in the shortest period of time. This ability is often referred to as "production-mindedness."

As a behind-the-scenes administrator, executives are faced with day-to-day as well as long-range planning. Since this is an intellectual function, it requires a rather high degree of mental ability. Executives are called upon to think in the abstract and to integrate a large number of complex factors. To do a top job as a manager, then, the individual's mental level should be appreciably above that of the average college graduate. This also holds for verbal and numerical abilities. The former plays a big part in one's ability to communicate, to express oneself orally and on paper. Executives who cannot establish good lines of communications are handicapped indeed. Although numerical ability may not be quite as important as verbal ability in many executive positions, it nevertheless plays an important role in such functions as setting up budgets, analyzing statistical reports, and the like. And, with the increasing role of automation in the plant and office, managers without a fair amount of sophistication in quantitative analysis will be lost in the shuffle. The administrator is constantly faced with the task of analyzing various problems and breaking them down into their component parts. In working out solutions to these problems they cannot afford to take things at face value. They must examine each factor critically, looking beneath the surface to explore any hidden meaning.

If they are to exercise good judgment, it logically follows that managers must have depth and perspective. They must see every item in relation to the whole picture. Otherwise, they will find themselves in the position of not being able to see the forest for the trees. Experience has shown that a good cultural background adds appreciably to one's ability to see the overall picture. Some knowledge of the arts and some understanding of the cultures of other people normally produce a body of knowledge that contributes to intellectual maturity and judgment. This is a factor to which many industrial leaders refer when they characterize someone as "broad-gauged."

The executive qualifications discussed above are, of course, not all inclusive; there are obviously many other traits and abilities that make a contribution. We would like to emphasize again that no single executive is likely to possess all of the above qualifications. None of us is perfect; we all have some shortcomings. For the most part, we carry out our jobs as well as we do because certain of our assets are strong enough to compensate for our shortcomings. So it is with executives; they may possess certain traits in such abundance that they largely make up for what they lack in other areas.

RESEARCH AND DEVELOPMENT

Jobs in this category spread over a wide scale as far as job content is concerned. At one end of the scale we have the "blue sky" research worker who is searching for truth for truth's sake. At the other end of the scale, we find the practical pilot-plant operator who is principally concerned with getting the "bugs" out of some process that others have conceived and developed. The vast majority of research and development people, however, fall somewhere between the two extremes of the scale. Their general qualifications can be summarized as follows:

Superior mental capacity
Superior numerical ability
Good verbal ability
Good mechanical comprehension
Ability to think analytically and critically
Tendency to be reflective
Intellectual curiosity
Creativity
Carefulness
Methodicalness
Ability to handle details
Patience
Good academic training

There can be no substitute for top-level mental and mathematical abilities if one is to operate with a high degree of productiveness in a research and development job. In fact, this type of a position probably places more demands on intellect than any other industrial assignment. Much of the work involves thinking in the abstract and using current knowledge as a springboard to new and uncharted fields. In many technical jobs, moreover, mathematics and physics are requisite to obtaining the desired objectives. Thus, the best people invariably possess numerical facility as well as an understanding of mechanical principles. As a group, they are also remarkably analytical and critical in their thinking.

The ability to conceive new ideas is, of course, an important requirement in a research and development person. Here again intellect plays an important part. Although all brilliant people are not necessarily creative, one seldom finds really creative people who do not have a relatively high degree of intelligence. Such persons are usually reflective, in the sense that they have a strong theoretical drive. They are the kind of people who have so much intellectual curiosity that they are motivated to dig to the bottom of a problem and find out what makes things tick. Their curiosity leads them to forsake the status quo in quest of new and better ways of doing things.

Because the job requires reflective individuals and those who can adjust to a somewhat confined work situation, research and development people usually display some degree of introversion. For the most part, they are not the kind of people who require contact with large numbers of people in order to find satisfaction on the job. On the contrary, they are usually content to work by themselves or as a member of a small group.

Technical experiments are of such a precise nature that one minor slip may completely invalidate the results. Consequently, research and development people learn as a result of sad experience that their approach to problems must be carried out methodically, systematically, and with painfully accurate attention to detail. Nor can they afford to be impatient if their first hypothesis proves to be inadequate. The majority of new developments come only as a result of attacking a problem over and over again.

In view of the high technical demands and the unusual complexity of the work, extensive academic training is naturally an important prerequisite. Whether the individuals work as chemists, chemical engineers, or mechanical engineers, they must have taken full advantage of their educational opportunities and acquired a tremendous body of knowledge and skills before they arrive on the industrial scene. Ordinarily, then, our top research and development people will have obtained high academic grades in college and in graduate school. And many of them will have earned a Ph.D. in their chosen field.

PRODUCTION SUPERVISION

The people who oversee the manufacture of the final product include supervisors, general supervisors, and plant superintendents. Hence, job requirements will vary with respect to the level of responsibility. The differences between supervisors on the one hand and plant superintendents on the other are those of degree rather than kind, however. We expect plant superintendents to have a higher degree of the essential qualifications than those possessed by general supervisors. Presumably, this was the reason they were promoted to their jobs. In turn, general supervisors rose from the supervisors rank because they had a little more of what it takes. Experience has shown that the following qualifications are generally basic for production supervision:

Good mental ability
Good verbal ability
Good numerical ability
Good mechanical comprehension
Ability to see the overall picture
Ability to plan and organize
Strong practical interests
Production-mindedness
Ability to improvise
Aggressiveness
Tough-mindedness
Self-confidence
Tact
Social sensitivity

Production supervisors are a special breed. They are the people who devote most of their attention to putting out day-to-day fires, eliminating production bottlenecks. It is their prime function to get the final product "out the door." Consequently, they must have exceedingly strong practical interests and must be unusually production-minded. Supervisors, general supervisors, or plant superintendents who are not highly motivated to get things done in a hurry are not worth their salt. Since production bottlenecks may occur in the most unexpected places, production people must be good improvisors, individuals who can solve problems for which there has been little time to prepare. On the basis of their ingenuity and past experience, they must somehow make the thing work, even though a better solution to the problem may subsequently be found.

Anyone who is called upon to solve problems must, of course, have a fair amount of mental ability. Because the production supervisor's job is so much concerned with ability to communicate to others, verbal ability represents an important requisite. Numerical ability perhaps plays just as important a role as verbal ability in this type of work. A certain degree of number facility is involved in such job functions as scheduling, preparing time sheets, and analyzing statistical reports. Here, too, the ever-increasing introduction of robots into the manufacturing process places a premium on quantitative analysis. More often than not, the manufacturing process has to do with making "hardware," objects such as appliances, airplanes, automobiles, and furnishings. Such an activity, therefore, requires mechanical know-how and understanding.

Although production supervisors are first and foremost leaders, they must also have some traits of the administrator in their makeup. They are faced with the problem of planning and organizing their work, and must be able to see the broad picture. If they give an inordinate amount of attention to one specific aspect of the work, the manufacturing process as a whole will suffer.

This type of work places unusually heavy demands on the leadership function. Production supervisors must have those qualities that enable them to inspire their people, motivating them to get out the production in the shortest period of time. Confronted with the task of supervising some employees who may be hard to handle, the supervisors must be particularly tough-minded, aggressive, and self-confident. At the same time, they cannot afford to ride roughshod over their subordinates. A certain amount of tact and social sensitivity is important here not only in dealing with subordinates but in dealing with the union as well.

SALES

There is perhaps more variation in sales jobs than in any other single business function. They range all the way from high-pressure, foot-in-the-door selling to low-pressure, technical sales service. Hence, some of the traits listed below will loom more important in some sales jobs than in others. But all salespeople have two important functions in common: they are required to contact people, and they are called upon to persuade others to their point of view. These functions inevitably demand the following qualifications:

Good verbal ability
Good self-expression
Extroversion
Color
Infectious enthusiasm
Sense of humor
Persuasiveness
Practical interests
Strong desire to make money
Aggressiveness
Tough-mindedness
Self-confidence
Tact
Social sensitivity
Self-discipline
Perseverance

The best salespeople are normally those who need the stimulation that comes from dealing with people in order to find job satisfaction. Quite the opposite of the reflective individual, they tend to be extroverted, aggressive, colorful, and infectiously enthusiastic. They call upon these traits in their efforts to persuade others to buy their product. Competition being what it is, the sales job is not an easy one. The better people are highly articulate, possess good basic verbal ability, and know how to handle themselves adroitly in face-to-face situations. The latter ability, of course, involves tact and social sensitivity. Salespeople must know when to talk and when to keep still, and must be continually alert to the customer's reactions. This permits them to take a different tack if they note that their first approach is not getting across. A good sense of humor is indispensable in many types of sales jobs.

Salespeople's lot can be quite an arduous one. They often live out of suitcases and spend days at a time on the road away from their families. There must be some motivation, then, that attracts them to this field, in addition to the one of having a chance to deal with people. That motivation is usually compensation. Most salespeople are extremely practical and have a strong desire to make money. Because many salespeople are paid on a commission basis, the better ones find that they can make more money in sales than in any other type of work for which they might qualify. It is true that sales jobs as a whole pay better than many other types of work.

The task of getting a hearing demands certain traits of personality. Busy executives often feel that they do not have time to see the salesperson and instruct their secretaries accordingly. In order to gain a hearing, then, salespeople must be unobtrusively aggressive and self-confident. Too, they must be sufficiently tough-minded to take rebuffs in stride.

Many salespeople work largely on their own, with very little supervision from their immediate superiors. This calls for a good bit of self-discipline. The ones who go to the movies in the afternoon just because they have made a big sale during the morning seldom turn out to be top producers. They must be constantly aware of the law of averages, that the more calls they make the more sales they are likely to get. In going after big accounts, moreover, they cannot become discouraged. They must persevere, calling on that account again and again until they finally make the sale.

FINANCE

This category includes a series of jobs ranging from the accounting clerk to the company comptroller. Again, although there is a marked similarity in the traits required in all of these jobs, the degree of each trait required will vary in accordance with level of responsibility. The lower-level jobs, of course, do not make as much demand on the intellectual and administrative factors. In practically all financial jobs, however, the following traits and abilities play an important role:

- High-level mental ability
- High-level numerical ability
- Good verbal ability
- Good clerical aptitude
- Ability to think analytically and critically
- Ability to plan and organize
- Attention to detail
- Good judgment
- Ability to see the overall picture
- Carefulness
- Methodicalness
- Orderliness
- Introversion

Although employees in the financial field, of course, deal with people, they are principally concerned with figures and with things. Their work is likely to be rather confining, and the people who adjust most easily to this type of work are, therefore, inclined to be somewhat introverted. Since even the smallest error must be found before reports are submitted, financial people place great stress on accuracy and close attention to detail. As a group, they are very careful, methodical, and systematic.

High-level intelligence, combined with superior numerical facility, are prime requisites in financial jobs. Arithmetical computation is not in itself sufficient. Practically all of these jobs require a high degree of mathematical reasoning. Statistical data must be *interpreted* in the light of the facts and in the light of the company's needs. Clerical detail must be handled quickly and accurately. This is why the better people tend to have high clerical aptitude. At some point, financial statements and other reports have to be prepared for top management. Hence, a degree of verbal ability is necessary.

At the upper levels, finance people are required to supervise relatively large groups of workers. Since the majority of their subordinates are likely to be somewhat introverted, however, they are normally not required to exert dynamic, tough-minded leadership. Rather, their leadership is of an administrative character. Principal emphasis here is placed upon good judgment, ability to plan and organize, and ability to see the broad picture. Comptrollers must be able to watch all the company operations and must be able to assimilate and integrate their findings so that they can keep their fingers on the financial pulse of the entire enterprise. Above all, they must be analytical and critical. Comptrollers take nothing for granted; they are accountable to top management and therefore must not only be in possession of the facts but must be aware of the underlying reasons.

Modern industry is showing an increasing tendency to diversify and to develop multiple products. Multiplant operations make the financial job all the more complex. To qualify for top-level positions in this field, then, individuals should have sound academic training. Today, many of the better young candidates have a master's degree in business administration, with a major in finance.

EMPLOYEE RELATIONS

There was a time when little thought was given to the demands of employee relations work. For this reason, the personnel staff in many companies were not carefully selected or trained in their specialty. Nor were these people given the chance to develop the skills with which to do their job—at least to the same degree as personnel in other jobs.

It is good to be able to report, however, that the situation is gradually changing and that employee relations is finally emerging as a profession. This happy development is due primarily to two factors: the labor unions and management's final awakening to the need for stimulating the growth and development of all personnel. Because their tactics have been so effective, labor unions have literally forced management to staff its employee relations department with more competent people, men and women who can meet with labor leaders on an equal footing. After many years of neglecting the human element in an industry, management has at long last discovered that its work force represents its greatest single asset. Today, many progressive organizations sponsor comprehensive programs designed to help each individual realize his or her greatest potential. These programs include more effective selection and placement procedures, better-designed merit-rating procedures, and a wide variety of employee-training procedures. Such activities obviously require able people at the helm.

The employee relations function, as it now exists in the more progressive organization, may be divided into two categories: personnel services and labor relations. The former includes recruiting, selection, placement, wage and salary evaluation, employee benefits, and training. As might be expected in view of the differences between these two functions, the qualifications necessary for success in the personnel services end of the business vary somewhat from those required in labor relations work. There are many individuals capable of doing a bang-up job in personnel services who are completely incapable of bargaining with unions. The best qualified employee relations person, of course, will possess qualifications for both types of jobs. These are the people who have the best chance eventually of heading up the employee relations department. In order to clarify the difference between the two major employee relations functions, requisite traits are listed separately below:

Personnel Services	*Labor Relations*
Good mental ability	Good mental ability
Good verbal ability	Good verbal ability
Good self-expression	Good self-expression
Ability to think analytically and critically	Ability to think analytically and critically
Good judgment	Judgment
Ability to plan and organize	Shrewdness
Social drive (desire to help others)	Aggressiveness
Genuine liking for people	Tough-mindedness
Extroversion	Courage of one's convictions
Friendliness	Self-confidence
Warmth	Fortitude
Tact	Perseverance
Social sensitivity	Fair-mindedness
	Ability to improvise

Many people are initially attracted to personnel services because they have a genuine liking for people and are strongly motivated to help others. This is all to the good because these qualities play an important part in such activities as placement, training, and employee benefits. Individuals who carry out these duties are usually extroverted, friendly, and the kind of people to whom others like to take their problems. To help others with their problems, a personnel employee must be able to approach individuals and win their confidence. This obviously takes an abundance of tact and social sensitivity.

But people in personnel must not be so highly motivated to help others that they permit their hearts to run away with their heads. Many of their duties—particularly that of employment interviewing—call for mature, objective decisions. Because these decisions involve people rather than things or ideas, they should be nonetheless objective and impartial. Practically every personnel function involves the evaluation of people in one way or another. Hence, the job requires intelligence, judgment, and good powers of analysis. Personnel people work largely through the verbal medium, moreover, and should be able to communicate effectively.

Although people in the labor relations field need many of the traits and abilities required by people in personnel services, their job demands an additional constellation of personality characteristics. They have to deal with representatives of labor, many of whom are aggresive, hard-boiled, and able strategists. Thus, labor negotiators have to be exceedingly tough-minded, so that they will be able to take it when the going gets rough. They must be self-confident, aggressive, and have the courage of their convictions. Good labor negotiators are also shrewd individuals, people who have a little of the "Yankee horsetrader" in their makeup. At the same time, they must develop a reputation for being completely fair; otherwise they will never be able to win the confidence of labor representatives or develop a working relationship with them.

Bargaining sessions consume long, weary hours during which each side jockeys for position. Company representatives at the bargaining table must learn to meet fire with fire, match persistence with persistence, and maintain their position without getting discouraged. They also have to be good improvisers, in the sense that they can cope with unanticipated developments. All of this takes its toll of many individuals. As pointed out above, there are numerous people in personnel services who simply do not have the resilience and mental toughness to stand the gaff in labor relations.

MATCHING THE APPLICANT WITH THE JOB

We have discussed at length the need for acquiring a complete understanding of the jobs for which applicants are to be selected. Remember, though, that the worker specifications outlined above, while not all-inclusive, nevertheless represent the *ideal* worker. In the appraisal of candidates, it is unlikely to find any one individual who possesses all the favorable factors for any given job. All of us have our shortcomings, and it has already been pointed out that the interview that brings to light no unfavorable information is a poor interview. Almost every candidate will therefore lack some of the desirable factors. But the best of these people will have assets in such abundance that they compensate for their liabilities. The interviewer's job, then, is to find the applicant who has the most desirable qualifications for a specific job.

At this point, it is only fair to ask the question, "How do we go about determining whether or not an applicant actually possesses the appropriate qualifications?" Well, a few of these qualifications can be determined by means of aptitude tests. But tests are primarily useful in measuring *abilities alone.* It is necessary therefore to rely upon the interview as a means of appraising *personality, motivation, interests, character,* and the *nature of intellectual functioning.* Subsequent chapters of this book show how the various selection steps may be used to accomplish this task.

CHAPTER 5

Preliminary Selection Steps

No matter how well trained their interviewers are, companies should not select new employees on the basis of the interview alone. This is far too time-consuming as well as extremely inefficient. In this chapter, then, we will discuss the techniques that can be used to screen out the less qualified applicants.

Since the final interview is a time-consuming and hence relatively expensive procedure, it should be used only with those candidates who satisfy the minimum job requirements. The more progressive companies, therefore, utilize a series of screening techniques designed to eliminate rather quickly those applicants whose qualifications are inappropriate. Such devices, when properly used, are of value to the candidate as well as to the company. The overall hiring procedure normally consumes several hours, and candidates should not be asked to waste their time being processed for jobs which they have little chance of obtaining. An employment setup that does not allow for reasonably quick screening is not only inefficient but also unfair to the individual.

Unfortunately, however, many organizations still use a short (15-minute) interview as a sole basis for selecting entry-level people. This is not only ineffective—no interviewer, no matter how well trained, can make an appropriate employment decision in only 15 minutes—but needlessly overcrowds the employment office. In periods of peak employment, applicants may be required to wait several hours for their 15-minute interview.

The selection of higher-level people in many companies is almost equally ineffective. This usually consists of a series of interviews with department heads and other key people. Since most such people have not been trained in the techniques of developing information and interpreting it correctly, the results are often far from what they should be. In any panel of five individuals, there may be one or two keen observers of human nature, persons who *can* make a good employment decision. But their votes are frequently overridden by others in the panel who base their decisions on hunch alone. Panel interviewing represents a decided ordeal for higher-level applicants. They are subjected to a day-long experience during which they are usually asked the same questions over and over again. This is not only hard on the applicant but bad for the company image.

In companies where interviewers have been trained, there is only one evaluation interview. If the decision in that interview is negative, no further interviews are scheduled. Rather, the unsuccessful applicant is assigned to a person of lower rank who provides a tour of the company for public relations purposes. This is a great time saver for important people who would normally participate in a panel interview and can actually save thousands of dollars over a period of a year.

Some years ago, the author was asked to review selection procedures for hiring college graduates in a very large company. At the outset, he was told that this technically oriented company placed such high value in hiring the best qualified new people that each of five top managers spent at least 1 hour interviewing every single candidate. In that year, they had each interviewed 196 candidates and selected 27. By placing a dollar figure on the value of 1 hour's time for managers at the top level, multiplying that by 5 and again by 196, it was determined that the company was spending well over $100,000 per year on a selection program that produced less than thirty people—and not doing a very good job of it at that! This is a classic example of the extent to which an inefficient selection program can waste the valuable time of highly placed people. By training interviewers to do a much better job of preliminary selection on the college campuses, installing aptitude tests, and training personnel people to conduct the evaluation interview, only a fraction of the initial population of candidates were subsequently referred to the five top managers—all of whom expressed astonishment at the greatly improved calibre of the people they were now seeing.

As implied above, when the evaluation interviewer's decision is positive, applicants are then scheduled with other people in the organization whose purpose may be that of checking technical qualifications and selling the applicant on the company. Certainly, applicants have the right to meet and talk with the person for whom they will be working as well as other important individuals in the organization. This should help them make up their mind as to whether or not they wish to accept the employment offer.

Companies with well-organized personnel departments utilize a number of screening devices such as a preliminary interview, an application form, aptitude tests, and the reference check. As important as these steps are, however, at some point the all important hiring decision must be made and that normally occurs at the end of the final interview. Hence, the final interview represents the solid core of any good selection program.

The early selection steps, then, have two functions: (1) to eliminate those applicants whose qualifications can be determined as inappropriate at that stage, and (2) to provide information that will be helpful to the interviewer at the time of the final decision. In effect, these selection steps represent a series of screens through which the successful applicant must pass, each screen being constructed of finer mesh than the previous one so that only the most appropriately qualified candidates will survive. This means that the final interviewer sees only a fraction of the number of people who apply for jobs and is thus able to spend as much time as needed with each surviving candidate.

Despite the fact that this book is primarily concerned with interviewing techniques, some discussion of preliminary selection devices helps to place the interview in proper perspective.

RECRUITING

It is axiomatic that no hiring program can be effective unless the number of applicants for a given type of work is substantially greater than the number of jobs to be filled. The very word "selection" implies the choice, for any given task, of the one best qualified individual from among a number of available candidates. Wherever careful selection is applied, it is of paramount importance that there be a relatively large reservoir of candidates from which the final selectees are chosen. This is what is known as the *selection ratio*. Ordinarily this ratio should be at least five or six candidates for each person finally selected.

The law of supply and demand always operates in so far as the labor population is concerned, and the available pool of candidates for jobs requiring highly developed skills and long years of training is always limited. At the same time, it is important to choose the best people obtainable. In times of great industrial activity, many companies take a defeated attitude toward the recruiting problem. They give up too easily, without having tapped all possible sources of supply. Too often, they settle for a "warm body." More alert organizations, on the other hand, maintain an aggressive recruiting policy. This is especially important today in order to find and hire qualified minorities. Some companies pay a premium to any current employee who personally recruits people who are eventually hired. Other companies contact minority clubs and other organizations as a part of their recruiting program. And many organizations hire students for summer jobs at the end of their junior year. This not only provides a firsthand impression of the student's worth but also weighs heavily in that student's eventual employment decision once college has been completed.

Most recruiting for higher-level jobs is of course done on the college campuses. There the recruiter has approximately one-half hour to evaluate each interested student and prepare for the next one. Thus, the recruiter may see as many as fifteen or sixteen students in a given day and this turns out to be a very grueling day indeed. Suggestions for carrying out this interview are discussed subsequently in this chapter.

APPLICATION FORM

The application form represents such an important initial screening device that most companies would do well to examine critically their own application forms. Are they up-to-date in the sense that they do not ask for information which is currently illegal, such as an applicant's specific age, marital status, or number of dependents? Do they provide space for coded information concerning sex and age, as a means of monitoring the applicant flow and insuring the selection of a sufficient number of minorities and females? Do they provide space for an applicant's likes and dislikes on various jobs and best and least liked subjects in school?

Since as many as 50 percent of all applicants for lower-level jobs—and a high percentage of applicants for higher-level jobs as well—can be eliminated on the basis of application data alone, the application form should obviously contain as much information as possible. As noted earlier in this chapter, the elimination of a sizeable number of applicants at this first stage of selection means that final interviewers will be required to see fewer people and hence will be able to spend more time with the people that they do see. Obviously, too, the elimination of large numbers of applicants at the very beginning of the selection process saves the company a great deal of time and money.

Worker specifications represent the key to the proper elimination of applicants on the basis of the application form. Thus, if the specifications indicate a minimum number of years of specific experience or education, application forms can be quickly scanned to determine those individuals who satisfy those requirements as well as those who do not. The latter can of course be screened out at this time.

If, in the interest of hiring people with good job stability, a company has the requirement in writing that it will not hire individuals with more than two jobs during the past 5 years, additional candidates can be eliminated on that basis. Gaps in dates of employment—except in the case of full-time homemakers—raise further questions. If such gaps cannot be satisfactorily accounted for in the subsequent preliminary interview, some persons may be eliminated on that basis. Failure to move ahead or to achieve reasonable raises in pay over a period of time raise still further questions—questions that must be discussed in the preliminary interview.

When worker specifications prescribe a fair degree of mathematical facility, persons who least liked "number crunching" on previous jobs and least liked mathematics in high school or college would not seem to represent a good "fit" for the job in question. If all other aspects of a person's history seem suitable, though, such an individual might be passed on to the employment test stage for the purpose of determining just how much mathematical aptitude he or she possesses. Finally, if a job requires shift work and if an applicant indicates distaste for shift work or flat refusal to do it, elimination becomes automatic.

THE PRELIMINARY INTERVIEW

The preliminary interview has three primary functions: (1) to make certain that the applicant has answered all questions on the application form, (2) to *screen out* candidates who are obviously unqualified for the job or jobs in question, and (3) to provide information for the final interviewer on those applicants who have been *screened in.* Because important decisions must be made within a short period of time—usually 5 to 10 minutes—the preliminary interviewer should be well-trained and exceedingly perceptive.

Preliminary interviewers usually use the completed application as the basis for their brief discussion with applicants. If some previous job appears to have some relevance to the job for which the candidate is applying, the interviewer may ask for a more complete description of that experience. If an individual's education or background appears limited, the interviewer may ask about any additional schooling, such as evening courses, correspondent courses, or on-the-job training.

The decision to eliminate a given candidate from further consideration is normally based upon factors discussed in the previous section on the application form—inability to explain adequately gaps in employment, too many jobs during the past few years, unimpressive history in terms of job progress or educational attainment, or lack of the specific experience or training required for the job in question.

It is a matter of common sense, though, that only those candidates who are obviously unqualified should be screened out by means of the application and preliminary interview. Doubtful cases should be screened in, thus giving the individual an opportunity to take the employment test and perhaps to participate in the final interview. This is particularly true in the case of minorities and females, where affirmative action goals must be kept in mind. It is conceivable that final interviewers—with more time to explore an individual's history, may be able to discover some compensating asset for what appears to be a somewhat serious shortcoming. This is not to say that employment standards should vary with respect to sex or race. In the final analysis, employment standards should be the same for men and women and for minorities and nonminorities alike.

Perceptive preliminary interviewers can frequently uncover information that should be followed up in the final interview. Such information should, of course, be written down and passed along to whoever makes the final decision. For example, the preliminary interviewer may discover that a given individual left a certain job before obtaining the next position. Although this normally reflects poor judgment and some degree of immaturity, it would normally be insufficient to eliminate that person from further consideration. At the same time, it could represent valuable input for the final interviewer. Or, the preliminary interviewer may get the feeling that an applicant is not telling the truth, but because of lack of sufficient time may not be able to document this sufficiently, and, accordingly, passes on these impressions for further investigation by the final interviewer.

The Campus Interview

The campus interview obviously represents a preliminary interview since surviving candidates are normally invited to the plant location for further evaluation. It is not unusual for a campus interviewer to see some fifteen students on a given day and perhaps invite only three or four of these students to visit the company. Preliminary interviews carried out on the college campus are normally limited to one-half hour, during which the interviewer normally spends about 20 minutes interviewing the individual and the other 10 minutes talking about the company and preparing for the next interview. Since many company representatives who visit the college campus are not at all trained, their interviews are often haphazard, and hence provide them with little real information upon which to base a decision. When campus interviewers have been professionally trained, it is recommended that instead of trying to cover all aspects of the student's experience, they spend their 20 minutes in an in-depth discussion of the individual's education, both in high school and college. (See Chapter 9.) Grades, the amount of effort required to obtain the grades, and college board scores should provide reliable evidence of intelligence and aptitudes; the amount of effort the individual spends on academic work provides good clues to motivation; decisions involving the choice of college and choice of major study provide clues to judgment and maturity; probing for reasons behind subject preferences reveals clues to analytical power; and participation in extracurricular activities frequently reflects clues to leadership and ability to get along with people. The information gathering aspect of the campus interview should end with a discussion of career goals and specific job interests.

Students who do not impress the recruiter should be given the company's promotion material and told that they will be contacted if their overall qualifications turn out to be better than those of the other students who are interviewed. Since most recruiters select only three or four students for subsequent plant visitation from among the fifteen or sixteen people they see on a given day, this gives them a valuable few minutes at the end of the other eleven or twelve interviews to rest and prepare for the next candidate.

The selling function, of course, should be done at the end of the interview, by which time recruiters will have identified those few students to whom they wish to offer opportunities for plant visitation and further evaluation. Since, by the end of the interview, recruiters already know a great deal about the students that impress them, they are in a position to sell *specifically* rather than *generally*. For example, if they have identified a student "who wants to get ahead in a hurry" and has the qualifications for rapid upward mobility, the recruiter can call attention to young people in his or her company who have already made it to positions of considerable responsibility. Or, if the impressive candidate has married while in college and already has a child or two, the recruiter can stress the company benefit program. This type of selling is individually structured and far more effective than attempts to sell the entire company story.

Obtaining Candidates' Permission for Reference Checks

One important function of the preliminary interview is that of obtaining an applicant's permission to carry out reference checks on previous places of employment, *whether or not the company plans to make a check on every applicant.* It is now rather common knowledge that information provided on application forms frequently differs from information provided by previous employers. Some applicants tend to exaggerate and some others are guilty of failure to tell the truth. But if applicants have signed a statement authorizing a prospective employer to verify application information, they are more likely to tell the truth, particularly since such statements usually include a clause that any misrepresentation will be cause for elimination from employment consideration or for immediate discharge. When individuals sign such a statement, moreover, they are also more likely to provide a truthful account of their vocational and educational history in their final interview.

Preliminary interviewers should carefully observe applicants' behavior at the time they sign the authorization for release of information. If they seem at all reluctant or tentative, this observation should be recorded and passed along to the person who carries out the final interview.

Applicants who are screened *in* on the basis of their application forms and preliminary interviews should be told about the next step in the selection program. In companies with a more sophisticated personnel department, this step would normally be that of taking aptitude or dexterity tests. Under current EEO guidelines, however, employment tests can be included in the selection program only if they have been adequately validated, in the sense that they have been found to provide a positive indication of ability to perform on a given job. In those companies where tests are not a part of the selection program—and that includes most companies today—applicants who survive the preliminary interview will proceed directly to the final interviewer.

APTITUDE TESTS

As noted earlier, aptitude tests as an important preliminary selection step have largely disappeared from the industrial scene over the past few years. So many charges of discrimination have been leveled at these tests since the enactment of the Civil Rights Act that most companies now believe that it is illegal to use any kind of employment test. But this is not the case at all. A careful reading of the EEO Guidelines reveals that aptitude and dexterity tests may still be used *providing they have been statistically validated, in the sense that a positive relationship can be shown between the test scores and success on the jobs for which the tests are being used as a predictor.* The Civil Rights Act, then, does not state that tests cannot be used, the act simply requires that any test utilized in the selection program must have been appropriately *validated.* Since far too many companies were using aptitude tests without any knowledge as to whether or not such tests were making any positive contribution, the Civil Rights Act has had a positive effect. It is only unfortunate that so many companies have eliminated the use of tests entirely rather than to undertake validation studies. Actually, aptitude tests have a long history of reliability in measuring such factors as mental ability, verbal ability, numerical ability, mechanical aptitude, clerical aptitude, as well as manual and finger dexterity. Such tests can provide far more valid results than can be obtained by means of the interview, no matter how well-trained the interviewer may be. Every effort should therefore be made to restore tests to their rightful place in the selection program.

Unfortunately, most companies do not have the expertise to develop and validate their own tests. But there are many reputable consulting organizations who specialize in this function. Companies desiring to restore aptitude tests to their selection programs should retain the services of a knowledgeable consultant to help them with this phase of their program.

Validity Generalization

Validity generalization, or transportability, represents a relatively new concept that enables a much wider utilization of aptitude tests than is generally realized. The term simply means that if a test can be shown to be valid for a given job in one plant situation, that same test can be assumed to be valid *for that specific job* in other plant locations. In a class action suit (*Pagues v. Mississippi State Employment Service*) in the U.S. District Court for the Northern District of Mississippi, the court stated: "Allegation that validity is specific to a particular location, a particular set of tasks, and to a specific application population is not true." In support of this opinion it has further been stated (*Friend and Fuller, et al. v. Leidinger, Fulton, Thorton, and Fionegan*), in the U.S. Court of Appeals for the Fourth District: "To require local validation in every city, village, and hamlet would be ludicrous." The impact of these rulings is far reaching indeed. For one thing, they enable an organization to use tests *that have already been validated elsewhere* for certain specific jobs. And, if a corporation has developed and validated a test for a given job for one plant or office setup, the rulings enable it to use this same test in the selection of applicants for the same job in other plants and offices. Thus, if a test publisher in its manual for a given test can show positive validation and reliability for a test of clerical aptitude, for example, any organization can assume that this test will be valid in its own setting, providing it is used for the same job and for a similar population to the job and population upon which the test was originally standardized.

The State Employment Service

Many personnel people are not aware of the fact that the state employment service can be of tremendous assistance to their organizations. This agency will screen applicants to company specifications and even administer a variety of employment tests that have already been validated for a large assortment of jobs. We know of one large corporation, for example, that utilizes the state employment service to screen and test applicants for employment in sixteen different states. The utilization of this service represents tremendous assistance to any company, since it eliminates the necessity of conducting preliminary interviews and giving employment tests. Moreover, companies using the state employment service do not have to be concerned with the validity of the tests that this agency utilizes since they only give tests that have been developed and validated by the United States Employment Service (USES). Over a period of many years, the USES has developed and validated tests for an astonishingly large number of jobs, ranging from automobile assembler to arc welder. Most of these jobs are designed for entry-level plant and office jobs.

It is important to note, however, that the state employment service is available only to those companies that have appropriately developed affirmative action goals in writing and to companies who request a sufficient number of minorities and women to meet these goals. When state employment services are requested, this request must be put in writing. And it must be agreed in the request that actions taken by the state on behalf of an employer are the liability of the employer, not of the state. This means that the employer must know exactly what the state is doing so that it can, if necessary, defend this procedure. Any relatively large corporation would do well to take its request for assistance directly to the office of the state director.

REFERENCE CHECK

Ideally, it would be preferable to check references prior to the final interview so that discrepancies between application data and reference check could be discussed at the time. In most cases, however, this is impractical because the return of reference information usually takes several days or even weeks. As a consequence, it is more practical to complete the final interview and then run reference checks on only those who have survived that final stage of the selection process.

Personnel people know that reference checks have their limitations. Some previous employers fail to respond and those who do respond are often reluctant to report any negative information. Therefore, it is best to request only factual information such as dates of employment, positions held, reasons for leaving, and attendance record. Reference checks are usually run on only the last 5 years of employment; attendance records are usually limited to the past 2 years.

Reference checks, as indicated in an earlier chapter, should be made only by mail. In large corporations, it may not be possible to run a check on every single person to be hired. In that case, the company will check perhaps one out of three or one out of five, making certain that on a percentage basis it processes an equal percentage of white males, females, and minority applicants.

Discrepancies

In cases where there is a substantial discrepancy between application information and the reference check—or where information of a derogatory nature is returned to the company by a previous employer—applicants must be given an opportunity to present their side of the story. If the discrepancy is sufficiently serious and if the applicant fails to convince the interviewer of his or her honesty, the applicant is normally turned down for employment. If that person has already been employed, he or she will usually be terminated. In all fairness, though, such an applicant must be given a hearing.

PHYSICAL EXAMINATION

Physical examinations are expensive—ranging anywhere from $50 to $100 per person. Hence, only those applicants who survive the final interview should be referred to the medical department. The principal purpose of the physical examination is to determine if applicants can physically perform the work for which they are being hired (critically important in the case of the handicapped). This decision can only be made by a qualified physician and hence should never be made by anyone in the personnel department.

Documentation

As in the case of all the other selection steps, a record must be compiled as to why an individual was medically rejected or limited for employment. The notation may be brief, but it must be specific and to the point. All comments should be dated and signed for future verification.

PRELIMINARY SELECTION STEPS PROVIDE VALUABLE LEADS FOR THE FINAL INTERVIEW

As pointed out several times in this chapter, there should be open lines of communication between those who carry out the preliminary selection steps and the final interviewer. The preliminary interviewer frequently develops information which is inconclusive and should be passed on to the final interviewer. The person who administers the company's aptitude test can also make valuable observations. That person may notice that an applicant "jumps the gun," beginning the test before the starting signal has actually been given and continuing to work after the stopping signal has been indicated. Such behavior might represent a possible clue to dishonesty in certain situations or might indicate that the applicant has a strong need to be competitive. Forewarned, the final interviewer is therefore in a position to follow up in an area that might have otherwise escaped attention.

Having discussed the preliminary steps of the selection program, we are now ready to take up the final step—the final interview. This is discussed in two parts: Developing Relevant Information and Interpreting Information Developed.

PART TWO

Developing Relevant Information

CHAPTER 6

Nature of the Evaluation Interview

In the final analysis, interviewers are faced with only two broad objectives. They must be able to develop relevant information, and they must be able to interpret the information they bring to light. These objectives are sufficiently complex, however, that the remaining chapters of this book are directed to their acccomplishment. The next three chapters are concerned with helping interviewers obtain the necessary information. The final chapters of the book are devoted to interpretation.

In earlier chapters of this book we have referred to the final, or evaluation, interview as the most important selection procedure. This is the most critical aspect of the selection program since it is here that all information obtained from the preliminary interview, the application form, the aptitude tests, and the reference check is integrated with other factors of the individual's background and the final decision is made. Applicants who have survived to this point obviously have something to offer. They have passed the employment tests, they have demonstrated some stability in their employment history, and their previous work history and educational background reflect some degree of relevance in terms of the jobs for which they are being considered. But there are still very important questions about these individuals that have not yet been answered. Up to this point, we do not know how diligently they will be willing to work, whether they are likely to get along well with people, whether they can adapt to the environment of the plant or office, whether they can solve complex problems, or whether they have potential for leadership. It is to these important areas that we address ourselves in the final interview.

ESSENTIAL ASPECTS OF THE FINAL INTERVIEW

We have commented earlier that a vast majority of interviewers are "turned loose" in their jobs without any formal training at all. As a consequence, many interviewers do not interview in accordance with any plan and, hence, do not use their time effectively, many do far too much of the talking themselves, and many, perhaps unconsciously, base their final decision on surface impressions because they do not know how to probe for relevant, hard data.

In the kind of interview described here, we *do* operate according to plan (see the Interview Guide in the Appendix). We take applicants back to their earlier work experience and proceed chronologically through all their jobs up to their present position or last job. From there we discuss educational background, starting with high school and proceeding to college and graduate school. During all this discussion, we probe for clues to behavior in an effort to get a clear picture of their strengths and shortcomings.

This is the type of interview, moreover, where the applicant has center stage and is encouraged to do most of the talking. Using techniques which are discussed in a subsequent chapter, interviewers develop such a high degree of rapport that applicants talk spontaneously and, hence, usually provide a clear picture of who they are and what they are like deep down inside. In such an interview, interviewers usually find it necessary to talk only about 15 percent of the time. This gives them a first-rate opportunity to sit back and analyze clues to behavior as they are reflected in the applicant's spontaneous remarks.

Unlike interviewers who base their hiring decision on a hunch or surface impressions, we make every effort to *document* our findings with concrete data drawn from the applicant's history. Thus, a finding such as *willingness to work* should be based upon such evidence as early conditioning to work as a young person, long hours spent on certain jobs, "moonlighting" (working on two or more jobs at the same time), or carrying out a substantial (20 hours a week or more) part-time job while carrying a full academic load in school.

PHILOSOPHY OF THE INTERVIEW

Experience has shown that the best way to predict what a person will do in the future is on the basis of what he or she has done in the past. Although it is possible for individuals to grow and develop, and in that way to *modify* their behavior, few people are likely to overcome completely the effect that long years of behaving in a certain manner has produced in them. Hence, if a man has worked hard all his life from the time he was a teenager, he is very likely to work hard for his new employer. And if a woman has shown the ability to adapt to new and changing situations in her previous job experiences, she is more likely to be able to make whatever adjustments may be required in the new job for which she is being considered. Moreover, if she has been able to stay with most of her previous jobs for a reasonable period of time—3 to 5 years—she is quite likely to remain with her new employer for a like period. Finally, if candidates have demonstrated the *ability to get along with people* on previous jobs, in extracurricular activities in school, or in activities outside of work or school, they are very likely to get along well with people in their new plant or office situation.

FUNCTIONS OF THE INTERVIEW

In addition to the integration of all information obtained from previous selection steps, it becomes the function of the interviewer to (1) determine the relevance of an applicant's experience and training in terms of the demands of a specific job, (2) appraise his or her personality, motivation, and character, and (3), in the absence of aptitude tests, evaluate mental ability.

The third factor—mental ability—is of particular importance in selecting people for higher-level jobs. Most companies prefer to hire individuals with potential for advancement, and here intelligence plays an important part. Other factors being reasonably equal, the extent to which an individual is capable of promotion to more complex and demanding jobs is frequently determined by the amount of mental ability he or she possesses. Suggestions for making these determinations appear in later chapters of this book.

Once all these factors have been assessed, the interviewer is in a position to make the final hiring decision. This is of necessity a subjective decision, a decision based upon the interviewer's experience, judgment, and training. But, in this type of interview, the decision should be based on factual evidence rather than the unsupported hunch. In the final analysis, interviewers not only evaluate a candidate's assets and liabilities in terms of the demands of a given job, they must also judge the extent to which the assets *outweigh* the liabilities, or vice versa. Only in this way can they rate applicants as excellent, above average, average, below average, or poor.

Since most applicants approach the interview with the objective of putting their best foot forward, the interviewer must be motivated from the very beginning to search for unfavorable information. Otherwise, the interviewer is likely to be taken in by surface appearances and behavior. Interviewers are human and thus, despite their efforts to maintain objectivity, they react more favorably to some persons than they do to others. When the initial reaction is favorable, the interviewer has a natural tendency to look only for those clues that will confirm the original impression. It must be remembered, though, that no one of us is perfect; we all have shortcomings. *The interview that results in no unfavorable information is inescapably a poor interview.*

Actually, this interview is an exercise in indirection. By means of adroit suggestions, comments, and questions, we try to elicit spontaneous information without having to ask direct or pointed questions. Obviously, if we are unable to get the desired information by means of indirection, our questions must become gradually more direct. Even so, we try to soften such questions by the use of appropriately worded introductory phrases and qualifying adjectives. Specific techniques for accomplishing this objective will be found in a later chapter.

CHAPTER 7

Developing Rapport and Helping the Applicant to Talk Spontaneously

In an effort to help applicants "open up" and tell their entire story, a number of techniques are utilized which have been clinically tested over the years. If this is done successfully, applicants gradually develop confidence in the interviewer, and realize that it is to their advantage to disclose not only assets but also those areas which need further improvement. Only in this way can optimal placement be made. They thus become partners in the interview, assume center stage, and spontaneously discuss their life story.

In far too many interviews, the so-called *question and answer technique* prevails. In such an interview, the interviewer asks the questions; the applicant answers the questions and waits for the next one. This type of interview not only is stilted and mechanical but, more seriously, also gives applicants an opportunity to *screen their replies.* Thus, they're inclined to provide responses which they think will put them in the best light, rather than tell the story as it actually is. Moreover, interviewers do almost half the talking, leaving applicants with that much less of an opportunity to discuss all the relevant aspects of their background.

The question and answer approach to interviewing also tends to take on the aspects of an inquisition. Applicants feel that they are being *grilled* and hence are uncomfortable. As a consequence, they often provide as little information about themselves as possible *and almost never discuss any of their shortcomings.*

In this chapter we will discuss a completely different kind of interview. Instead of putting applicants on the spot, the interviewer should try to develop a harmonious relationship, one in which applicants not only feel comfortable but also develop so much confidence in the interviewer that they begin to talk spontaneously. Instead of waiting for the next question, therefore, they tend to discuss their background with appropriate elaboration, to the extent that their discourse becomes spontaneous. When people talk spontaneously, information seems to well up and bubble out in such a way that there is no need or, indeed, opportunity to screen their replies. Hence, spontaneous information is much more likely to reflect an individual's true feelings, needs, or anxieties, and more often than not, spontaneous information contains clues to shortcomings. Remember, interviewers must become aware of applicants' shortcomings as well as their assets. Otherwise, not only is it impossible to make appropriate job placements but individuals may be hired for job situations in which they would be incompetent and conceivably quite miserable.

Techniques for developing rapport discussed in this chapter work so well that some applicants tend to talk too much—to the point that the problem becomes one of *controlling* their discourse rather than getting them to open up. Interviewers who take the time to adopt these techniques will discover that they have a completely new tool at their disposal, a tool that will not only help them in the interview but also come to their assistance in many other aspects of their lives. People who have learned how to develop rapport become better supervisors, do a better job of feeding back appraisal information, and even become more popular at parties.

SMALL TALK

In any conversation between two people, it is only natural to begin with some pleasantry rather than to delve directly into the purpose of the meeting. As far as the interviewer is concerned, in fact, this becomes an important aspect of establishing initial rapport. This is the interviewer's first opportunity to get applicants to assume a major portion of the conversational load. If they can be helped to do most of the talking during this early phase of the interview, they naturally assume this to be their role throughout and often fall into this role without any difficulty at all. However, if the small talk revolves around a series of short, direct questions, such as "How was your trip?" it usualy leads to a question and answer approach where the interviewer does as much as half the talking. In that case, applicants have the right to assume that their role is one of simply answering any question that may be addressed to them rather than talking spontaneously.

The Importance of Beginning Small Talk with a General Question

Rather than pose questions that invite short yes or no responses, it is more desirable to use a general "pump-priming" question—one that cannot be answered without a fair amount of discussion. Such questions require preparation, however, and cannot be expected to be phrased on the spur of the moment. Prior to the interview, therefore, the interviewer should study the completed application, in an effort to come up with a topic on which the applicant might be expected to talk freely and perhaps enthusiastically. Such a topic might be concerned with a particular interest, some indicated achievement such as a scholarship, or perhaps differences encountered living in two different parts of the country. The interviewer should be armed with one or two such topics prior to the interview. Whatever the topic, the initial question should be broad enough in nature, so that the applicant will be required to talk 2 or 3 minutes in order to answer it. Several examples of such pump-priming questions are listed below.

1. "I notice from your application that you apparently like to ski. Tell me how you got involved in skiing and where you most enjoy it. What kind of satisfaction do you get out of it?"
2. "In looking over your application, I noticed that you were given an award at the Ford Motor Company for making a valuable suggestion concerning your work. Tell me what the award involved and what the suggestion accomplished."
3. "I notice from your application that you have worked in California as well as here in the midwest. How do the two areas of the country compare with respect to things like climate, cost of living, recreational opportunities, attitude of the people, that sort of thing?"

Questions such as those listed above are sufficiently complex that it usually requires at least 2 or 3 minutes to answer them. If the applicant stops after a sentence or two, simply wait, drawing upon the technique to be discussed later—the calculated pause. In posing any incidental question designed to promote small talk, interviewers should make an effort to be as pleasant as possible, treating the subject as what it actually is, an "ice breaker," rather than a more serious part of the interview.

As long as the applicant keeps talking, interviewers should not take any part in the discussion at all. They should simply smile, nod their heads, and engage in other nonverbal, supportive behavior discussed later on in this chapter. They should never break in with questions of their own, no matter how interested they may be in the topic under discussion. At this stage of the interview, it does not matter at all what applicants say, so long as they take over the conversation. Should their conversation come to a halt, interviewers can perhaps keep it going a little longer by repeating a part of the original broad question which has so far been unanswered. Small talk ranging from 2 to 4 minutes is usually sufficient to ease whatever nervousness an applicant may have initially experienced. The sound of one's own voice in a strange situation usually helps to develop confidence, ease initial tension, and build rapport. When applicants are not immediately put on the spot by being asked to tell about some more serious aspect of their background, they do not feel the need to sell themselves, and, thus, they have the chance to relax and to chat informally about matters which are of no great concern.

THE CALCULATED PAUSE

We have mentioned that interviewers should wait out applicants who stop talking without having answered all parts of a multifaceted question. This is called the *calculated pause,* and is used as a *conscious technique.* Interviewers without much experience tend to become uncomfortable whenever a slight pause in the conversation occurs and are therefore likely to break in prematurely with unnecessary comments or questions. But experienced interviewers purposely permit a pause to occur from time to time because they know that applicants will frequently elaborate on a previous point rather than allow the discussion to come to a standstill. The applicant often senses that the interviewer's silence calls for a fuller treatment of the topic under consideration.

In the conscious use of the pause, interviewers *must not break eye contact.* If they look down at their guide, applicants naturally assume that they are formulating another question and, hence, wait for that question to be articulated. However, if interviewers do not break eye contact and *look expectant* as the pause elongates, applicants feel a certain degree of pressure and usually search quickly for something else to say. Obviously, if applicants fail to respond within a few seconds, interviewers should relieve the pressure by asking another question. To do otherwise might risk a loss of rapport.

Under normal circumstances, the calculated pause is remarkably effective in drawing out spontaneous information. Equally important, interviewers have to do less talking when they use an occasional pause and, therefore, perfect the art of becoming a good listener.

Once perfected, the calculated pause is a powerful technique, particularly when not used too frequently. It also has wide application outside the interview situation. It is a useful tool for salespeople in determining a customer's needs, it is widely used in the legal profession, and it is a valuable technique for use in labor negotiations in determining what is on the other person's mind.

FACIAL EXPRESSIONS

We have just mentioned that interviewers should *look expectant* as a means of making the calculated pause effective, but looking expectant and being *facially responsive* are conscious techniques that should be utilized throughout the interview. Anyone can manage an expectant look by lifting the eyebrows a little and smiling slightly. This expression gives the interviewer the appearance of being *receptive* and serves as a powerful tool in getting the subject to open up. People who are facially responsive react facially as well as verbally to another individual's comment. When that individual smiles, the interviewer should smile; when the applicant talks about an unfortunate experience, the interviewer's face should show concern.

Facial expressions play a particularly important role when asking questions that border on the personal. The edge is taken off a delicate or personal question when it is posed with a half smile with the eyebrows raised. And, as we shall see later on, facial expressions are of paramount importance in probing for an individual's shortcomings. Finally, facial expressions help to give one the appearance of being understanding, sympathetic, and receptive. There are some individuals, in fact, who are so adroit with facial expressions that they are able to keep the subject talking almost by that means alone. It is a matter of fact that some people's countenances are naturally more animated than others. Thus, some people find it necessary to work at being facially responsive, while others find it very natural.

People being trained as interviewers sometimes raise the question, "Isn't it possible that I will look like a phony if I try too hard to become facially responsive?" The answer to this, of course, is a qualified "yes." Facial expressions, as in the case of all other conscious techniques, can be overdone and can give interviewers the appearance of being artificial and insincere. Experience has shown, however, that *most people do not use enough facial expression.* It is the rare person indeed who tends to overplay this aspect of interviewing technique.

When we stop to realize that there are only two means at

our disposal in getting through to people in social situations—facial expressions and voice—it certainly behooves all of us to make maximum utilization of whatever talents we have in these two important areas. One has only to look at television programs to note how effective people can be who have had specific training in vocal and facial expression. Although most of us cannot approach this professional level, we can do a lot more with our faces and with our voices than we are currently doing. Conscious effort along these lines can pay big dividends in improved interpersonal relationships.

VOICE

It has often been said that a series of lessons with an elocutionist will enhance anyone's career. This is because people judge us not only by what we say but also by how we say it. In fact, others may not hear what we say if we have not learned how to speak effectively. This is particularly true in the interview situation where we consciously use the voice as a rapport-building technique.

The art of persuasion obviously relies heavily upon the voice. In the interview, we use every means at our disposal to persuade applicants to reveal all their qualifications and characteristics—shortcomings as well as assets. In their attempts to improve vocal effectiveness, interviewers must keep two things in mind: (1) they must not talk too loudly, and (2) they should try to use all *ranges of the voice.* When interviewers talk too loudly, they tend to threaten applicants to some extent and to push them off center stage. Since applicants should do some 85 percent of the talking, they must be "front and center" during the entire interview. When interviewers talk too loudly, they tend to relegate the candidate to a minor role. Since interviewers do not want that to happen, they should try to keep their voices at a rather low conversational level, in that way encouraging the applicant to take over.

It is much easier to teach people to speak more softly than it is to teach them to use all ranges of their voices. In particular, interviewers should concentrate on greater utilization of the upper range of the voice. When applicants are asked questions or given compliments, for example, interviewers should try to use the upper range of the voice. This has the effect of sounding more interested in what the other person may have to say, and, in turn, that person becomes more highly motivated to give the answer sought after and does a more complete job of revealing innermost thoughts.

As in the case of facial expressions, vocal intonations should mirror the applicant's moods. When applicants discuss unfortunate or unhappy aspects of their background, the interviewer's voice should take on a sympathetic tone, and when applicants divulge something of a highly personal nature, the interviewer's voice should reflect an understanding quality. Complete responsiveness on the part of the interviewer has an unusually powerful effect upon the other person, making that individual not only willing but often actually anxious to talk about things that are uppermost in her or his mind.

Of course, vocal inflection can be overdone. This should be avoided at all costs because it gives the impression of insincerity and may have the effect of alienating individuals rather than attracting them. Again, though, it is the rare individual who falls into this trap. Most of us do not use sufficient vocal intonation and hence could profit from training in this area. For many years, the General Electric Company has sponsored a course called "Effective Presentation." This course has become one of the most popular courses in the GE training program, with some people finding it so helpful that they have taken it a second time.

Interviewers would be well-advised to take courses of this nature if such courses exist in their organization.

LUBRICATION, OR REINFORCEMENT

There is perhaps no more powerful tool in the interviewer's arsenal than that of commenting positively on an applicant's achievements. Some people in the field refer to this as "stroking," some call it "reinforcement," and others just refer to it as "giving an applicant a pat on the back." We like to think of it as "lubrication." Just as a drop of oil from time to time keeps a piece of machinery running, so do positive comments interspersed throughout the interview help to maintain rapport and keep applicants talking. For years, psychologists have experimented with some system of reward to train both animals in the laboratory and human beings. For example, reinforcement, or some system of reward, has proved effective in training retarded children to dress and feed themselves.

In the interview situation, lubrication, or reinforcement, can be both verbal and nonverbal. Comments such as "Very impressive!" or "You deserve a lot of credit for that!" or "Excellent!" give applicants the feeling that their achievements are being appropriately recognized, and they respond accordingly. Such achievements as (1) high grades in school (2) promotion on the job, (3) unusually long hours spent on a given job, (4) election to class office, or (5) being invited back for a second summer of part-time work merit favorable recognition on the part of the interviewer. When achievements of this kind are recognized by interviewers in the form of a compliment, applicants often visibly warm to the discussion and become increasingly expansive and spontaneous in their ensuing remarks. To be appreciated is a human need, and the job applicant is no exception in this respect.

Few people realize, however, that lubricating responses can be *nonverbal* as well as verbal. Frequent nodding of the head and sounds of affirmation such as "Uh huh" and "Hmmm" help applicants feel that interviewers are paying attention to their discourse and appreciate what they are saying. Actually, one-word interjections such as "Fine!", "Terrific!", or "Impressive!" can be worked into the discussion without interrupting the applicant at all. The frequency with which forms of lubrication are utilized during the interview depends largely on the applicant's makeup. If the person is a relatively sophisticated, secure individual, a considerable amount of lubrication would not be appropriate. In such a case, nonverbal reinforcement and a few verbalized comments would normally be sufficient. If an applicant is insecure and relatively unsophisticated, a great deal more lubrication would be in order.

As noted earlier, intonation plays an important part in supportive comments. When the voice is consciously placed in the upper register, rather than mumbled or "swallowed," the comment takes on greater significance. It has the effect of making the interviewer sound more impressed with the applicant's achievement. This has the long-range effect of building so much rapport that applicants become subsequently more willing to discuss some of their shortcomings. People do not mind talking about some of their problems if they are absolutely certain that the listener is completely aware of their successes.

PLAYING DOWN UNFAVORABLE INFORMATION

Just as applicants are complimented on their achievements, so are their problems or difficulties *played down.* This is done to make it easier for individuals to talk about negative aspects of their backgrounds, and since we are searching for shortcomings as well as assets, this becomes an important part of the interview technique. Playing down takes the form of some casual, understanding remark. If, for example, a woman talks about the "terrible time she had with mathematics in school," this can be played down by such a sympathetic remark as, "All of us have different aptitudes; the chances are that you may have been a lot stronger in the verbal area." Or, if a young man admits to lack of self-confidence, the interviewer might say, "Self-confidence is a trait that most people develop as a result of living a little longer and acquiring more experience."

When applicants discuss unfavorable information of a more serious nature, such as poor attendance on a previous job or a fiery temper, a casual, sympathetic remark on the part of the interviewer would *not* be appropriate. In such a case, it is better to compliment the individual for being able to recognize the problem and face up to it. An appropriate comment might be, "The fact that you are aware of this situation and have been able to face up to it means that you have already taken the first step toward doing something about it." Such a statement by no means makes light of the individual's problem but does acknowledge being able to face up to it, and this is usually enough to make a person feel better about having revealed the difficulty.

There is one further thing to keep in mind. Interviewers should *never tell applicants anything that is untrue.* If a person should admit to a lack of initiative, for example, one would never say, "Oh, that is something you should be able to overcome very easily." Since traits of this kind tend to become quite deeply imbedded in the personality structure, they are *not* easily overcome. Most applicants would be aware of this and hence would detect the ring of insincerity in an interviewer's comment.

We would like to emphasize once again, though, the

importance of playing down unfavorable information. The interviewer who gives the slightest indication that judgment is being adversely influenced by unfavorable information will get no further information of this kind. Once interviewers react negatively—either verbally or facially—they disqualify themeslves as sympathetic listeners. No one willingly and spontaneously talks about difficulties and failures in a climate where the listener does not give the appearance of being understanding. On the other hand, when such information is not only accepted without surprise or disapproval but also played down, the applicant is permitted to *save face* and hence usually finds it easy to discuss additional negative data if this should be part of his or her history.

COMPREHENSIVE INTRODUCTORY QUESTIONS

Although the first comprehensive introductory question is asked immediately after small talk, we are discussing this technique at the very end of this chapter in order to give it emphasis. The comprehensive introductory question represents *the single most important technique for getting applicants to do most of the talking.* This type of question is so comprehensive, in fact, that many applicants can talk several minutes and still not answer all aspects of the question.

Once the small talk has come to an end, interviewers bridge the gap between the small talk and the first introductory question with a comment such as, "Let me tell you a little bit about our discussion today." They then direct the conversation to the real purpose of the session by making an appropriate *opening remark.* This general opening remark should include a statement of the company's interest in placing new employees in jobs that make the best use of their ability. It should present an *overview* of the interview by pointing out that the discussion will include as much relevant information as possible about work history, education, and interests. A question such as the following will usually suffice: "*In this company, we believe that the more information we can obtain about people applying for work the better able we will be to place them in a job that makes best use of their abilities. I would therefore like to have you tell everything you can about your work experience, education and training, and present interests.*"

Having provided the applicant with the discussion of the purpose of the interview and having given an overview of the general topics to be considered, the interviewer launches immediately into a discussion of previous work experience, the first topic that appears on the Interview Guide (see Appendix). This is accomplished with the first comprehensive introductory question, for example, "*Suppose you begin by telling me about your previous jobs, starting with the first job and working up to the present. I would be interested in how you got each job, your duties and responsibilities, the level of earnings, your job likes and dislikes, and any special achievements along the way.*" The very comprehensiveness of this question provides applicants with a basis for a considerable amount of discussion and, as indicated above, represents the single most important factor in getting them to talk for as much as 85 percent of the interview time.

After the work experience has been completed, interviewers should launch into the second topic for discussion —education. A question such as the following will do the job here: "*Suppose you tell me now about your education, starting with high school and working up through college. I would be interested in the subjects you liked best, those you did not care so much for, the level of your grades, your extracurricular activities, and any special academic achievements. What subjects did you like best in high school?*

Applicants are not expected to remember every single item in the introductory question. They will often have to be reminded, for example, to discuss subject preferences or asked to talk at greater length about extracurricular activities. Such follow-up questions, though, are simply *reminders* of some of the things applicants have been initially asked to talk about. As such, they do not represent new questions and hence do not require quite so much concentration on the applicant's part.

The Importance of Memorization

Interviewers are advised to *memorize verbatim* the questions presented above. This will make their interviews a lot smoother, and because they do not have to concern themselves with formulating such questions, they are much more free to *listen* to what applicants have to say.

Assume Consent

In verbalizing introductory questions, interviewers should use every means at their disposal to *sell* candidates on the desirability of providing the necessary information. In particular, they should consciously use appropriate facial expressions and vocal intonations. And their very manner should *assume consent.* Just as an effective salesperson assumes that the customer wants to buy, so the expert interviewer assumes that applicants will be happy to respond to all of his or her questions. Questions are best phrased *positively,* in such a way that there is no alternative but to answer them. The phrase "suppose you tell me" is always more effective than the phrase "I wonder if you would be willing to tell me." The latter choice of words provides the alternative of not answering and thus fails to assume consent. Also, it gives the impression that the interviewer is not confident and thus may not be certain whether or not he or she should ask the question.

The techniques discussed in this chapter are almost foolproof in terms of getting spontaneous information and getting the applicant to do the major share of the talking. Interviewers, in fact, who study these techniques carefully and use them as described here will often be quite amazed how productive they can be.

EEO CONSIDERATIONS

1. Do not overdo rapport-getting techniques with minorities or women. This is not necessary, and they will be quick to discern the special treatment.
2. Do not assume a "holier than thou" attitude or "talk down" to the applicant. Interviewer and interviewee must be on the same wavelength.
3. Be careful about informal chitchat before beginning the interview proper. Interviewers have been known to make such statements as, "I have a daughter about your age, and I can't imagine her wanting to work in this industry."
4. Informal talk at the end of the interview can also create problems. There have been instances where interviewers began talking about sports but, without being aware of the impression they were making, ended up by taking a stand on racial issues. As soon as the interview has been completed, thank the applicant, say you will be in touch with him or her, and stand up as an indication that the discussion has been concluded.
5. Minorities and females who anticipate a negative hiring decision monitor the interviewer's facial expression very

closely. In such cases, therefore, interviewers should try all the harder to mask their true reactions. Facial expressions that reflect a negative reaction have been known to lead to charges of discrimination. In these cases applicants charge that the interviewer was biased —that they "never had a chance."

6. Never patronize members of a protected group (minorities, females, or the handicapped) by indicating in any way that they are being hired because the company has an EEO program. Such a statement may lead applicants to believe that they are not being hired on the basis of their qualifications, and people do not like to think that they have been accepted only because standards have been lowered or rules have been bent.

CHAPTER 8

Probing More Deeply for Clues to Behavior

Most interviews, in the hands of untrained interviewers, are little more than *surface* discussions—discussions that seldom reveal what a person is like deep down inside. This is why attempts to validate the interview as a selection device have seldom shown positive results. Most interviewers do not get a truly clear picture of such important factors as an applicant's motivation, level of maturity, or basic intelligence. The untrained interviewer simply does not possess the *tools* to probe for important factors of this kind.

In this chapter, therefore, we will make every attempt to supply these tools—in the form of probing questions that have been developed over a lifetime of interviewing. Some of these questions appear on the Interview Guide and should be used verbatim. It is suggested that interviewers make a lap for themselves by crossing their legs and placing the interview guide on the knee. This position makes it easy for them to refer to the guide constantly and read the questions off of the guide verbatim.

In the previous chapter we presented comprehensive introductory questions designed to launch the discussion in each area of the interview, but those questions, of course, will by no means do the entire job. Interviewers must use so-called *follow-up questions*—questions that follow the comprehensive introductory question—to keep applicants talking and to probe more deeply for clues to behavior. Actually, follow-up questions represent an extension of the comprehensive introductory question. They are used to prod applicants from time to time, in this way helping them to reveal their life story to the fullest extent and to become more definitive concerning its important aspects. Actually, interviewers' remarks should be interjected so artfully that the interviewers seldom, if ever, assume center stage. Rather, they dart in and out with such facility that applicants seldom become aware of the fact that their discourse is being directed.

INTERVIEWING AS CONVERSATION

Since interviewing also represents *conversation* between two people, comments are usually more natural than questions. Whenever a comment can be substituted for a question, in fact, conversation flows more smoothly and interviewers lessen the impression of being *investigative* in their approach. If they want more information on a given subject, they can frequently get such information by the simple comment, "That sounds very interesting." So encouraged, the applicant is quite likely to provide further elaboration without having been specifically asked to do so. We do not want to give the impression here that there is anything wrong with asking questions. Comments interspersed with questions, however, provide more variety and help the interview to seem more natural.

Keep Questions and Comments Open-Ended

There is a great tendency for interviewers to put words in the applicant's mouth by asking leading questions or making leading comments. By so doing, they unintentionally structure their remarks so that a favorable response is strongly suggested. A comment such as, "I suppose you found that job very boring," pushes the applicant to answer in the affirmative even though that may not have been the case at all.

A leading question such as, "Did you rank pretty high in your high school class?" makes it difficult for the applicant to give a negative response. Since the interviewer has asked a leading question, the applicant is greatly tempted to say "Yes." The applicant whose grades were poor, and who honestly admits it, may realize at once that this could create a negative impression and may become uncomfortable in the interview situation and unwilling to offer any more potentially negative information.

In order to avoid such leading comments or questions, the interviewer should keep remarks *open-ended.* An open-ended question is one that does not telegraph an anticipated response, leaving the applicant free to discuss favorable or unfavorable information. A question such as, "What about grades in high school," gives no clue at all as to the weight which the interviewer may place on grades. In such a question, applicants are free to structure the reply themselves, pointing out that their grades may have been average, above average, or even below average.

There is a wonderful phrase—"To what extent"—that makes any question open-ended. Instead of using a leading question such as, "Were you successful on that job?" the question can be open-ended by saying, *"To what extent* were you successful on that job?" Or, instead of saying,

"Did you *enjoy* that experience?" one might say, "*To what extent* did you find that experience satisfying?" in that way converting the question to an open-ended situation.

There is another remarkably effective way to ensure an open-ended response—the use of the question, "How did you *feel about* that situation?" When you say, "Did you *like* the people there?" you push the person to say "Yes." But, when you say, "How did you *feel about* the people there?" you can anticipate an objective response.

Talk the Applicant's Language

There is no quicker way to lose rapport than to use words which are outside the applicant's vocabulary. The applicant becomes quickly confused and is made to feel inferior. Interviewers who are good listeners can determine an applicant's range of vocabulary in a relatively short period of time and subsequently make every effort to use words which the applicant readily understands.

Questions and Comments Must be Work-Related

To stay within EEO guidelines, questions must be primarily concerned with the relevance of an applicant's work history and education to the job under consideration. The primary concern should be the extent to which applicants can handle a job and will make mature, stable employees. As mentioned in previous chapters, questions should no longer be asked about specific age, marital status, number of dependents or personal finances.

At the same time, interviewers do still have the right to determine *how well* applicants have performed on their previous jobs or in school. This is obviously work-related because it provides strong clues concerning an individual's ability to handle a job for which he or she is being considered. If there is a consistency of good performance on previous jobs, it can be assumed that good performance may be expected on a new job.

FUNCTION OF FOLLOW-UP QUESTIONS

As we have already seen, the function of follow-up remarks is essentially that of helping the applicants present a clear picture of their qualifications. By means of adroit questioning, interviewers must be able to draw out applicants so that they can present their real assets. Equally important, interviewers must be able to structure the discussion in such a way that they get a clear picture of candidates' shortcomings. Within this broad framework of objectives, however, follow-up remarks serve a number of specific functions.

Reminding Applicant of Omitted Parts of Comprehensive Introductory Questions

The questions that are used to introduce the discussion in each of the major interviewing areas are so comprehensive that candidates will often forget to discuss some of the items in response to the comprehensive introductory question alone. Usually they will have to be *reminded* to discuss such job factors as likes, dislikes, earnings, and accomplishments. And they may have to be reminded to discuss such things as subject preferences, grades, and extracurricular activities. Then, there are other items listed under each interviewing area on the Interview Guide that may have to be brought to the applicant's attention in follow-up questions. For example, if an applicant fails to tell why he or she left a certain job, the interviewer will have to bring this up in the form of a casual follow-up question.

Getting Further Work and Education Information Relevant to the Job

We have already noted that the interviewer must have a clear mental picture of job and worker specifications at the time an applicant's qualifications for a given job are discussed. As the interview progresses, the extent to which the applicant's work history and education measure up to these job and worker specifications should be mentally checked by the interviewer. The applicant will not know which aspects of his or her background to emphasize, in terms of establishing the relevance of past performance to future work responsibilities, since the applicant has not been acquainted with these specifications. The interviewer must therefore be helpful in this regard.

To use an example, let us assume that technically trained people are being interviewed for a job that involves a considerable amount of report writing. In this case, the interviewer would use follow-up questions in an effort to determine the amount of report writing a given candidate has done in previous jobs and the degree of writing facility acquired. The interviewer would, of course, try to mask the intent of the questions with appropriate phrasing and casual, offhand presentation. It could be phrased, "In connection with your research and development work with that company, was there more emphasis placed on the actual technical experimentation or on the writing up of results?" After the discussion the interviewer might add, "How did you feel about your accomplishments there? Did you feel that you were relatively more effective in the actual experimentation or in the report writing?" Even though the applicant may feel that he or she made the greatest contribution in laboratory experimental work, information concerning report-writing ability will usually be volunteered in response to such a question. And he or she will often place a relatively objective value judgment on writing ability, particularly since it will not be clear how important this may be for the job in question.

Clarify True Meaning of Applicant's Casual Remarks

Clues to the applicant's behavior will not always be clear-cut. In response to a question concerning job dislikes, for example a candidate may say that detail work was less satisfying. Now, the interviewer cannot assume from such a remark that the applicant cannot do detail work. The interviewer must try to pin down this clue by fixing the *degree* of dislike. In this case, a response to the original remark could be, "Many people find detail work much less interesting than other aspects of their job." This kind of a sympathetic response often encourages the applicant to elaborate. In so doing, an *intense dislike* of detail may be revealed in the form of an open acknowledgement that he or she is not very proficient in the type of work that requires close attention to detail. Or the applicant may indicate that, while not enjoying detail, he or she nevertheless finds it relatively easy to carry out when it is an important part of the job. Obviously, the interpretation of these two responses would be quite different. The first response, if supported by other clues pointing in the same direction, would lead the interviewer to the possible conclusion that the applicant was not a good detail person. The second response, on the other hand, would lead to no such conclusion.

Searching for Support of Early Established Hypotheses

Highly skilled interviewers often pick up little clues to the applicant's possible behavior relatively early in the discussion, and these clues help them to establish a *hypothesis* with respect to the possible existence of certain assets or liabilities. They know, however, that such hypotheses must be supported by more tangible evidence; otherwise they must be rejected entirely. Interviewers therefore use exploratory questions to probe for clues that might support their hypothesis. If none is found, they must, of course, discard that hypothesis and search for new ones.

For purposes of illustration, we will assume that the interviewer has obtained some initial impressions of the applicant that point in the direction of superficiality, lack of depth, and limited powers of analysis. As he leads the applicant from area to area, he will, of course, be on the lookout for supporting evidence or for the lack of it. From time to time, he will interject so-called "depth questions" —questions that require a fair amount of analysis. For example, he may ask the applicant what a job has to have in order to give her satisfaction. Or he may ask what gains in terms of personality development accrued as a result of military experience. If the candidate's responses to a series of such questions reveal little ability to dig beneath the surface, the interviewer may rightly conclude that the individual is indeed superficial and without much ability to analyze.

Let us take another example. In this next case, we will assume that an interviewer has formed an early hypothesis that an applicant may be somewhat lazy. Let us say that she has arrived at this tentative judgement because of a man's professed unwillingness to work overtime hours. In order to check and support this initial hypothesis, the interviewer will use follow-up questions to probe specifically for such factors as (1) how much effort the applicant may have expended on other jobs, (2) how hard he studied in school, and (3) any demonstrated willingness to carry out constructive tasks either at home on in the community after putting in a regular work day. If she finds that the candidate (1) took the easy way out to avoid tackling difficult problems, (2) studied just hard enough to get by, or (3) decided against graduate work because it would have meant going to school at night—if she is able to get consistent information of this kind—she is able to *document* her views concerning the candidate's lack of motivation. The point to remember here, though, is that this kind of information probably would not have been brought to light had it not been for the fact that the interviewer probed for the appropriate clues by means of follow-up questions.

Quantifying Information

In the effort to *document* the findings with respect to the applicant's behavior, it is important to get as *definitive* responses as possible. When successes, failures, or even reactions are spoken about in general terms therefore, the interviewer must get more specific answers. For example, if he simply indicates that his grades in college were "above average," a good follow-up question would be: "Does that mean that your grades ranked you in the top ten percent of your class, the upper quarter, the upper third, or perhaps the upper half?" Or, if a candidate merely indicates that she was given a raise in salary after her first six months on the job, the interviewer must follow through with: "What did that amount to in terms of dollars?" Again, if a candidate indicates being "out of work for a while," it is important to establish how long the unemployment actually lasted.

Controlling the Interview Conversation

As we shall see in Chapter 9, follow-up remarks are used also to *control* the interview conversation, so that applicants are not permitted to wander off the track and the interview does not get out of hand. Since an entire chapter is devoted to this important aspect of interviewing skill, we will not concern ourselves at this point with the specific ways in which follow-up questions are used to control the interview. At the same time, we can point out here that follow-up questions and comments are used to (1) push the applicants along when they go into too much irrelevant detail, (2) ensure intensive coverage of each interviewing area, and (3) direct applicants' attention to those aspects of their background which give the greatest promise of providing evaluative information concerning behavior.

KINDS OF PROBING QUESTIONS

We mentioned previously that many interviewers fail to probe beneath the surface because they do not have the tools to do the job. The material that follows provides such tools in the form of three kinds of extremely important questions.

The Laundry List Question

Applicants almost invariably find some areas more difficult to discuss than others. Confronted with a question that requires considerable analysis, they frequently "block" and find it somewhat difficult to come up with an immediate response. In such a situation, the interviewer comes to the applicant's assistance with a *laundry list* question. As the name implies, this kind of question suggests a variety of possible responses and permits subjects to take their choice. If candidates block on the question, "What are some of the things that a job has to have to give you satisfaction?" the interviewer may stimulate thinking by such a laundry-list comment as, "Well, you know some people are more interested in money, some want security, some look for the satisfaction of working with their hands, others enjoy working as a member of a team, and others like a job that takes them out of doors a good bit of the time. What's important to you?" Given a variety of possible responses, applicants are normally able to get their thoughts together and supply a considerable amount of information.

The laundry-list question can also be used as a means of confirming clues to behavior that the interviewer has obtained from some previous aspects of the discussion. Let us assume, for example, that an applicant has dropped some hints that seem to indicate a dislike for detail. The interviewer can often follow up on such clues by including a reference to detail in the laundry-list question at the end of the discussion of work history. For example, the interviewer may say, "What are some of the things that a job has to have in order to give you satisfaction? Some people want to manage whereas others are more interested in an opportunity to come up with new ideas; some like to work regular hours whereas others do not mind spending additional hours on a job—hours that might interfere with family life; some like to work with details while others do not; some are quite happy working at a desk while others prefer to move around a good bit—what's important to you?"

If, in response to the above question, the candidate said, "Well, I certainly do not want anything that involves a lot of detail; actually, I'm not at all good at that type of work," the interviewer would certainly have obtained further confirmation of the subject's reaction to detail. The very fact that the individual selected this item for discussion reflects the importance she attaches to it. If the applicant were being considered for a job where attention to detail figured importantly in the worker specifications, her response could be interpreted as revealing a relatively serious shortcoming.

Besides taking a candidate "off the hook" alleviating the tendency to "block," the laundry-list question has the further function of spelling out to the applicant what the interviewer specifically has in mind. By the very nature of the items used in the series of possible responses, the interviewer encourages the applicant to respond specifically rather than generally, and makes certain that the responses will be helpful in the evaluation of the individual. Toward the end of the candidate's discussion of work history, for example, the interviewer asks him what he has learned about his *strengths* as a result of working on various jobs. In order to tell the applicant what the interviewer specifically has in mind, he uses such a laundry list as: "Did you find that you worked a little harder than the average individual, got along better with people, organized things better, gave better attention to detail—just what?" Such a laundry-list question helps to "tie down" individuals' responses, so that they talk in terms of *traits of personality, motivation, or character.*

"Why" Questions

Experienced interviewers know that *why* an individual took some course of action is frequently more revealing than *what* he or she did. This is true because why people do things tells us a great deal about their judgment, their motivation, and other factors of their personality structure. Probing for why an applicant left a given job, for example, may provide clues to such factors as inability to relate to authority (problems with the boss), inability to do the work, dissatisfaction with close supervision, or the kind of restlessness that motivates a person to move on to something new. When applicants leave a job before obtaining another one, a why question may reveal a tendency to rationalize, to try to explain away one's failure. A reply such as, "I couldn't very well look for a new job while working 8 hours a day on the present job," taken even at face value indicates poor judgment and immaturity. But it also may be a cover for precipitative action based on a quick temper or even for having been fired.

It is not only important to find out what applicants liked or disliked about their job but perhaps more important still to learn the why of their likes or dislikes. This is what is meant by probing more deeply. If a woman indicates that she liked working with computers, a why question such as, "What is there about working with computers that appeals to you?" would be in order. Such a question may reveal that she has a flair for mathematics, that she enjoys problem solving, that she appreciates the accuracy and thoroughness that are a part of such detailed work, or that she enjoys an opportunity to work on her own without close supervision. When a man indicates a dislike of mathematics in school, a question such as, "What was there about math that turned you off?" would be in order. A reply such as, "I never could understand what I was supposed to do," could conceivably provide a clue to mental ability.

When a woman, for example, indicates that she has an *ability to get along with people*, the interviewer should dig deeper by saying, "What traits do you have that make it possible for you to get along with people as well as you do?" The reply to that question may reveal such valuable traits as tact, empathy, or sensitivity to the needs of others.

It is suggested that why questions be used sparingly throughout the interview. For one thing, there is not sufficient time to probe for the why of everything the applicant says. Also, too frequent use of this technique puts too much pressure on the applicant and results in the feeling that he or she is being grilled. Hence, the technique must be reserved for probing in the most fruitful areas. These areas obviously differ from person to person, but with practice and experience interviewers will learn how to recognize fruitful areas for further probing when they occur.

Double-Edged Questions

Double-edged questioning is used to make it easy for applicants to admit their shortcomings and to help them achieve greater self-insight. The questions are double-edged in the sense that they make it possible for the subject to choose between two possible responses. Moreover, the first alternative is usually phrased in such a way that the subject would not choose that alternative without feeling possessed of the ability or personality trait in question to a fairly high degree. The second alternative is phrased so that it is easy for the applicant to choose that alternative, even though it is the more undesirable of the two possible responses. Hence, this type of question is used only to probe for shortcomings.

Having asked applicants to reveal their strengths, one can logically follow up with a question about their shortcomings. A question about shortcomings can be presented as a laundry-list question, with the double-edged question used as a follow-up. Thus, an interviewer might say, "What are some of the things about yourself that you would like to improve? Would you like to develop more self-confidence, acquire more tact, learn to control your temper better, improve your attendance record—just what?" If the applicant finds it difficult to answer this question, the interviewer may probe more specifically with a *double-edged* question such as, *"What about tact; do you have as much of that as you would like to have, or is this something you could improve a little bit?"* Given something specific to talk about, most applicants tend to respond quite spontaneously and often reveal a good bit about their shortcomings.

In interviewing people for office jobs, interviewers often find a double-edged question such as, "What about your ability to spell; do you have that ability to the extent that you would like, or is that something you could improve a little bit?" quite revealing. How confident the individual may be in her or his ability to spell is often revealed in tone of voice or facial expressions. If there is any hesitancy in the reply or if the person frowns, this may be indicative of a problem area. The point here, though, is that the double-edged question was used to launch this discussion. Most people find it much easier to discuss things that they could *improve* rather than qualities that they *lack*. Thus phrased, the double-edged question represents an adroit way to introduce the subject of shortcomings.

How to Soften Direct Questions

In their efforts to probe more deeply for clues to behavior, some interviewers tend to be too blunt and direct in their questioning. Since this risks a possible loss of rapport, many such questions can be softened by the use of appropriate *introductory phrases* and *qualifying words*. Such introductory phrases as the following will help to soften almost any direct question:

Is it possible that . . . ?
How did you happen to . . . ?
Has there been any opportunity to . . . ?
To what do you attribute . . . ?

Qualifying words and phrases such as "might," "perhaps," "to some extent," "somewhat," and "a little bit" are also effective in softening direct questions.

A study of the two types of questions listed below will reveal the extent to which the direct question has been softened by means of introductory phrases and qualifying words. The questions on the left are obviously too direct; those on the right are more appropriate.

Too Direct	*More Appropriate*
1. Why did you leave that job?	1. *How did you happen to* leave that job?
2. Why do you think you had trouble with your boss?	2. *To what do you attribute the minor* difficulties you experienced with your supervisor?
3. How much money did you save that summer?	3. *Was there any opportunity* to save *any* money that summer?
4. Why did you decide to take a cut in pay in order to get transferred to that other job?	4. *What prompted your decision* to take a cut in pay in order to get transferred to that other job?
5. Do you lack self-confidence?	5. Is self-confidence *perhaps* a trait that you might improve *to some extent?*
6. Are you overly sensitive?	6. *Is it possible* that you *may* be *somewhat* over sensitive to criticism?

NOTE-TAKING

Discussion of the techniques of the interview would not be complete without some reference to the taking of notes. This subject, incidentally, has stirred a considerable amount of controversy over the years, some authorities claiming that note-taking results in a loss of rapport and others indicating that the interviewer should feel free to take as many notes as he or she desires.

We take the view that the decision as to whether or not to take notes should be made on the basis of the *experience and training of the interviewer.* This is another way of saying that the untrained, inexperienced interviewer should *not* take notes, while the well-trained interviewer should be able to carry out this activity without any loss of rapport.

At the time trainees are learning to use the recommended information-getting techniques, they are of course rather unsure of themselves, and a bit awkward in almost everything they do. They have their hands full establishing rapport, without attempting anything in addition. And it is true that the taking of notes does tend to diminish rapport if this is not done adroitly and unobtrusively. Moreover, interviewers will normally have little difficulty remembering the salient aspects of the candidate's background, provided they write up the case immediately after the discussion has been concluded.

On the other hand, one who has achieved genuine skill in the use of such techniques as facial and vocal expression, pats on the back, playing down of unfavorable information, and adroit questioning should be able to take notes in such a way that the applicant becomes almost unaware of this activity. The candidates usually become so absorbed in the discussion that they take little notice of the skilled interviewer's note-taking.

As indicated above, however, any writing done by interviewers should be carried out as unobtrusively as possible. Thus, they should keep a pad of paper on their knee throughout the discussion and should keep a pencil in their hands at all times. The simple movement of placing the pencil on the desk and picking it up at frequent intervals can often be distracting.

Notes should only be made when candidates relate objective data concerning their background or when they tell about their past achievements. Whenever they impart information of a highly personal or derogatory nature, interviewers should obviously refrain from any writing. Rather, interviewers should wait until applicants volunteer the next bit of favorable information and, at that time, record both the favorable information and the unfavorable data previously obtained.

Finally, skilled interviewers learn to record their findings without diverting their attention from the candidate or breaking eye contact for more than a few seconds at a time. This places the note-taking function in its proper perspective, as a seemingly minor aspect of the interview.

EEO CONSIDERATIONS

1. Keep questions job-related.
2. Do not ask questions of minorities or females that you would not ask of nonminorities or males.
3. Never ask questions out of curiosity alone. All questions should have a valid purpose.
4. Never ask a single female about her plans for marriage.
5. Never ask a female if she has someone to care for her children while she works or what her plans are for having children.
6. Do not ask an older worker how many more years he or she plans to work. This could be construed as age discrimination.
7. If the job involves travel, working long hours, or potential transfer, attitudes toward such conditions cannot be asked of females alone. If this question is to be used, it must be used with *all* applicants—males and females alike.

CHAPTER 9

Techniques of Control

In the two previous chapters devoted to the techniques of the interview, emphasis has been placed primarily on ways and means of getting the applicant to talk freely. This of course represents a first objective. The interviewer can learn little unless the applicant talks spontaneously.

Spontaneous discourse in itself, however, is not sufficient. Discussion must be guided and channeled in such a way that applicants tell what the interviewer needs to learn rather than simply what they themselves want to relate. Indeed, it is quite possible for an applicant to talk as long as 3 hours in an uncontrolled situation without giving as much salient and evaluative information as could have been provided in 1½ hours of guided conversation.

Teaching interviewers how to exercise optimum control represents one of the most difficult tasks in the entire training procedure. During the early stages of their training, interviewers invariably exercise too little control. In their desire to get spontaneous information, they are inclined to let applicants go on and on, just as long as they talk freely. At that stage of their training, they are often afraid to direct the conversation for fear that such direction might inhibit the flow of conversation. As a result of this completely permissive approach, applicants often are allowed to ramble excessively in discussing their backgrounds and to go into too much detail on topics that may not be particularly relevant. As a consequence, the interview suffers from lack of intensive coverage in the important areas and from lack of balance—too much emphasis on one area of the applicant's background and too little on other areas. In addition, such an interview takes far too much time.

With proper training, though, interviewers gradually learn to use just the right amount of guidance and control, and they learn to do this tactfully and unobtrusively. In the very early stages of the interview, they permit applicants to talk quite freely, even though some of the resulting information may not be particularly relevant. They do this in order to *set the pattern* of letting candidates do most of the talking. Once this pattern has been established, though, they do not hesitate to interject comments and questions at critical points, in order to ensure intensive coverage and sufficient penetration in each area of the applicant's background.

WHY CONTROL IS NECESSARY

As noted above, measures of control are designed to (1) ensure adequate coverage of each area of the applicant's background, (2) secure appropriate penetration into the truly salient aspects of the candidate's previous experiences, and (3) utilize the interviewer's time efficiently and economically.

Appropriate Coverage

Some applicants build up such a head of steam that they tend to *take over the interview* and run away with it. In so doing, they may skip over some important areas too quickly and leave out other factors entirely. They tend to discuss only what they want to tell rather than what the interviewer needs to know.

When applicants begin to take charge and to race over their history too rapidly, the interviewer should step in and control the situation, tactfully reminding such a person to discuss likes and dislikes on each job, reason for leaving, and the like. Otherwise the individual could conceivably cover an entire area such as work experience in as few as 10 minutes, without providing any real clues to behavior or any substantial information about accumulated skills.

The real challenge of interviewing is to get maximum coverage in the shortest period of time. In order to do this, interviewers direct the discussion with the image of the job and worker specifications uppermost in mind. Since they have by far the better knowledge of the job requirements, they are responsible for leading the discussion into the most fruitful areas. If interviewers know, for example, that a given job requires a fair amount of mathematical facility, they will make sure that applicants cover such factors as math grades, amount of study time required to obtain those grades, and how applicants evaluate their own ability in the mathematical area.

Balance

During the early stages of their training, interviewers frequently fail to apportion interviewing time appropriately. They permit the candidate to spend far too much time on one area of his or her background and far too little on some of the other areas. Such interviews lack balance.

Problems concerned with balance usually occur as a result of allowing the applicant to provide too much irrelevant detail about previous work experience. In an insufficiently controlled interview, some applicants find it quite easy to spend as much as 1½ hours discussing their previous jobs. In so doing, they naturally include a lot of unnecessary and irrelevant information. When this occurs, the interviewers suddenly realize that too much time has been spent on the work area. Then, in order to complete the discussion within a reasonable period of time, they push the applicant through the other background areas too rapidly. The ensuing lack of interview balance precludes comprehensive evaluation of the individual's qualifications. In fact, lack of interview balance can frequently lead interviewers to completely erroneous conclusions concerning the candidate's suitability. In spending too much time on the work history, they may, for example, skip over educational background so fast that they fail to bring to light highly critical information—information that could have provided the real key to understanding the individual's behavior.

Now, it is not reasonable to expect all information supplied by applicants to be relevant. Of necessity, much of the discussion provides little more than a framework that is used by interviewers as a basis for probing into more fruitful areas. At the same time, interviewers must continually guard against excessive and irrelevant detail. They must continually ask themselves, "Am I learning anything about the applicant's behavior or anything about the extent to which he or she meets the job specifications, as a result of this particular segment of the discussion?" If the answer is "No," the candidate must be tactfully pushed along to another topic.

In order to achieve proper balance, interviewers should

place a clock on the table. And they should casually refer to the clock at rather frequent intervals. Time spent in the various interview areas with applicants for higher-level jobs should be apportioned roughly as indicated below. (These time limits can be appreciably shortened in interviews with candidates for lower-level positions—usually 40 to 45 minutes.)

Work history—55 to 65 minutes
Education—15 to 20 minutes
Present social adjustment—5 to 10 minutes

The above timetable permits a minimum of 1 hour and 15 minutes and a maximum of 1 hour and 35 minutes. It must be emphasized, though, that these time allowances are to be used only as a rough *guide*. Since there are such marked differences between individuals, it will obviously take longer to interview one person than another. Factors that influence interviewing time requirements are primarily those of *age* and *psychological complexity of the individual*. Older applicants normally require more time because they have more experiences to be discussed and evaluated. Regardless of age, the individual who is complex psychologically requires greater time because there are more facets of the personality to be considered.

There are cases, too, where the suggested timetable may have to be modified with respect to the amount of time required for a given interview area. If the applicant is fresh out of college, for example, and has had few summer or other part-time jobs, it will obviously be unnecessary to spend as much as 55 minutes on the work history area. In evaluating such an individual, proportionately more time should be spent on education and on the other areas of the background.

The suggested timetable is therefore a very flexible one. But if interviewers spend more than the indicated time on a given area, they should at least be aware of it and should have a good reason for so doing. As indicated above, the timetable serves as a guide or check. If, for example, interviewers suddenly discover that they have spent 30 minutes on work history without touching upon any of the jobs held by the applicant during the past 10 years, they know that they will have to move the individual along more rapidly if they are to have sufficient time to explore the remaining areas of the individual's background.

Penetration

In general, applicants supply two types of information: *descriptive* information and *evaluative* information. If the interview is not sufficiently controlled, almost all of the information may be of a descriptive nature. Applicants may describe the companies for which they have previously worked, go into elaborate details concerning job duties, and talk a lot about the fun they had in college. Now, some of this descriptive information serves a purpose, but it does not tell us much about the individual makeup.

Hence, interviewers must control the discussion to get evaluative information—information that can be used as a basis for determining the applicant's personality, character, and motivation. By artful and tactful questioning, they must *penetrate* to the candidate's basic reactions to key situations, with a view to determining the possible effects of those situations on the individual's growth and development. For example, to learn that a man spent 5 years in the army, attended a variety of schools, fought in the tank corps overseas, and was awarded a Bronze Star is not sufficient. We want to know, in addition, how he got along with his superior officers, how well he adjusted to military life, and how much he developed and matured as a result of the overall experience. Normally, the average applicant will not supply answers to these questions unless his or her discussion is *channeled*. In other words, the interviewer must find a way to cut off descriptive information and probe more deeply for evaluative data.

Economy of the Interviewer's Time

Good interviewers are always jealous of their time. Although they must not in any way convey this fact to the applicant, they nevertheless use control in order to complete interviews in the shortest possible time and still get the best possible picture of the candidate's qualifications. The interview that runs for 2½ to 3 hours is ordinarily an inefficient one. Such an interview not only consumes more time than is necessary but results in so much irrelevant detail that interpretation becomes more difficult. In other words, the interviewer has difficulty separating the wheat from the chaff primarily because there is so much chaff.

If interviewers are to assume a normal case load of two to three comprehensive interviews per day, they cannot afford to spend much more than 1½ hours per interview and still have time to write up their notes. Moreover, interviewing is a very fatiguing experience because of the attention factor. If interviewers spend too much time on one interview, they will not have sufficient energy to give other applicants the attention they deserve.

The indicated case load of two to three evaluation interviews per day may strike some as a surprisingly low number. It is true, of course, that employment interviewers can conduct a relatively large number of *preliminary interviews* in a single day. And they can carry out as many as six or seven final interviews on applicants for lower-level plant or office assignments. But it is unreasonable to expect them to do more than three comprehensive interviews per day in the case of persons being considered for higher-level positions. Since the evaluating of key applicants represents such a critical function, it is much better to hire and train additional interviewers than to overload the interviewing staff.

TECHNIQUES OF CONTROL

It is one thing to talk about the needs for control and quite another to discuss how it can be accomplished. Fortunately, though, we have two effective techniques to draw upon for this purpose: (1) the Interview Guide and (2) interruption.

Interview Guide

Many inexperienced interviewers approach the interview with no plan at all. They simply pick out some item of the application and go on from there. Such interviews usually suffer from inefficiency and ineffectiveness. Applicants tend to ramble in their discussion and fail to cover some of the more important aspects of their backgrounds.

The Interview Guide, found in the Appendix of this book, provides a "track to run on" and hence represents a very important aspect of control. This guide can bring order, system, and intensive coverage to a discussion that might otherwise have been inconclusive. The Interview Guide not only specifies the sequence of the discussion but also includes important factors to be taken up in each major area. The guide is so important that interviewers are advised to keep this form on their laps and refer to it every 2 or 3 minutes throughout the interview. This permits the interviewer to use questions on the form verbatim and ensures against omission of important items.

After they have used the guide for awhile, some interviewers feel that they no longer need it. However, as soon as they put it out of sight, they invariably leave out some important aspect of the candidate's background. No matter how much experience interviewers may have, therefore, they should always operate with the guide before them.

Some interviewers also feel self-conscious about reading questions off the form and hence try to paraphrase these questions, using their own words. This is a mistake in two respects. In the first place, experience has shown that reading questions from the Interview Guide does not disturb applicants in the least. In the second place, most interviewers find it very difficult to formulate questions on the spur of the moment that are as effective as the questions printed on the guide.

Interruption

When an applicant begins to talk too much—particularly in terms of irrelevant detail and descriptive information—the interview must be controlled by means of *interruption.* Interruption represents a very effective means of control, but this technique must be employed so subtly that applicants do not realize that they are being interrupted. In order to accomplish this, two additional techniques are utilized: *timing* and *lubrication.* It is of course impolite to interrupt people in the middle of a sentence, and, yet, if we wait until the end of a sentence, they will already have launched into the next sentence by the time we get around to interrupting them. Hence, the interruption must be *timed* to occur before they have actually completed the sentence. Interviewers therefore learn to interrupt as soon as applicants have completed a thought but *before they have had a chance to complete the sentence.* Moreover, an interruption is always accompanied by a lubricating comment such as, "That's very interesting," or "That must have been very satisfying." The lubricating comment represents the introduction to the comment that will redirect the discussion and move applicants along to another topic. If, for example, an applicant tells too much about his or her likes on a given job, the interviewer may say, "You must have found that very satisfying. Tell me about some of the things you did not like quite so well."

As will be noted from the above, timing means *anticipating the end of a thought* and lubrication in this sense means *making a positive or favorable comment.* Utilization of these two techniques tends to soften the interruption in such a way that applicants may not even realize that they are being interrupted. Because interviewers have commented favorably on a given topic under discussion, applicants are willing to relinquish that topic and permit themselves to be redirected to a new subject.

Interviewers should not be too hasty in interrupting applicants when they wander off the track or go into a bit too much detail, because hasty interruption risks the loss of rapport. Give individuals a minute or two to get the uninteresting or irrelevant topic "off their chests" before shutting them off and redirecting their conversation.

Let us assume that a male applicant, for example, races lightly over his first two or three jobs, apparently thinking that they are not germane to the discussion. Since this would normally occur at the very beginning of the interview and since a pattern should be established of having an applicant carry the conversational ball, he would be allowed to talk for 3 or 4 minutes, then, just as he was about to put a period at the end of a sentence, the interviewer would inject a positive comment and redirect him to a more thorough treatment of his first job. The interviewer might say in this instance, "You have certainly had some interesting early experiences—so interesting in fact that I would like to know more about them. Suppose you tell me more about your likes, dislikes, and earnings on that first job."

Let us take another example, where an applicant, a woman, perhaps, conceivably wanders off the track and launches prematurely into another interview area. In response to the question, "What did you like best on that job," she might reply, "I enjoyed the calculations. You know, I am very good in math. I won the math prize in high school and did exceptionally well in calculus. Our high school had two very fine math teachers, and I learned a lot in their classes." If this woman was not interrupted, she might very easily go on to further discussion of her high school experience and forget all about the discussion of her various jobs. After she has been given a minute of two to discuss her mathematical proficiencies, therefore, the interviewer interrupts by anticipating the end of one of her thoughts with a comment such as, "I think it's great that you have such an interest and aptitude in math—particularly since you want to become a systems analyst. Tell me about some of the other things you liked on that job with Carter Steel." Because this woman has not been interrupted in the *middle* of a thought and because she has received a favorable comment about her mathematical proficiency, she would normally be quite willing to be redirected back to her work experience.

The Importance of Interviewing Manner

Despite the fact that interviewers only do about 15 percent of the talking, they nevertheless guide the discussion by their very manner and by the way they carry out their role.

Although they are friendly, disarming, and permissive, there is a point beyond which they cannot be pushed. By means of vocal and facial expressions, they assume consent. This means that they ask their questions and make their comments in such a way that the applicant is expected to answer. This inner firmness creates an atmosphere of "remote control." Thus, interviewers take active control only when they have to, but they are always ready to step in when the occasion demands. Since interviewers are already in the power position—it is the applicant who is seeking the job—they can usually maintain control in a very unobtrusive fashion.

Upon occasion, one meets an applicant who is inclined to be facetious. Such a person may make light of some of the interviewer's questions or may even challenge their relevancy. Such a situation obviously requires firmer control. When a question is challenged or treated facetiously, interviewers should simply restate the question, giving their reasons for asking it. By their general manner rather than by anything they say, interviewers underscore their seriousness of purpose. This approach almost invariably prevails, the applicant becoming very cooperative thereafter. Some applicants like to test the interviewer, just to see how far they can go. Once they determine the point beyond which they cannot go, they usually become very cooperative.

OTHER FACTORS OF CONTROL

Applicants obviously vary widely with respect to their interview behavior. It is therefore impossible to discuss all situations where control may be necessary, but there are some general rules that may be applied in almost every case.

Develop Information Chronologically and Systematically

Applicants, of course, are given considerable freedom in their choice of subject matter, but they should nevertheless be encouraged to supply information chronologically and systematically. In discussing their work experience, for example, they should be asked to start with the very first job and work up to their most recent experience. This not only gives a sense of order to this segment of the interview but also makes it easier for the interviewer to ascertain the applicant's vocational achievements over the years. In the educational area, it is always best to start with the first years of high school and go on to the subsequent years or even to college if that level of education has been attained. This gives interviewers an opportunity to see how applicants fare as they progress to more difficult academic subject matter and have to compete with more able individuals. (Many of the less gifted people drop out of high school after a year or two.) The interview guide, of course, spells out the indicated chronology.

Exhaust Each Interview Area Before Going on to the Next One

Constant reference to the Interview Guide helps interviewers to get all important information in one area before going on to the next. One might find, for example, after completing the work history that he or she has neglected to determine an applicant's earnings. The interviewer should go back and get this information before launching into education.

When an applicant is permitted to crisscross between areas, it becomes very difficult for interviewers to evaluate total achievement in one area. Moreover, after the applicant has left the room, they invariably find that they have forgotten to get some important bit of information.

When omissions do occur and when interviewers do not become aware of this until they are midway in the next area, they should complete the discussion in the current area before going back to get the desired information. To interrupt in the middle of a discussion of education in order to get job earnings breaks the applicant's train of thought and makes it more difficult later for him or her to resume the discussion of education at the point at which it was interrupted.

With Older Applicants, Emphasize Recent Positions

With applicants 35 years old or older, there is little point in developing elaborate information on very early jobs. Unless an early part-time job had some unusual feature, there is little need to probe for likes, dislikes, and earnings. Rather, confine that discussion to such simple facts as duration of employment, number of hours worked, and reason for leaving.

With an older applicant who has a long job history, there is not sufficient time to obtain complete information on every experience. Moreover, older applicants probably haven't changed much in the last 10 years, but may be quite different from the way they were 15 or 20 years ago. This means that we move through early jobs quite rapidly and then give more exhaustive attention to recent experiences.

With Recent High School Graduates, Explore Summer Jobs Thoroughly

Many young applicants tend to skip over summer jobs too quickly, feeling that they are not relevant to the job for which they are applying. Summer jobs may not be entirely relevant, but they do tell us a great deal about applicants—the *initiative* they may have demonstrated in getting these jobs, the capacity to *adapt to and stay with boring or routine assignments, the ability to get along with people* from diverse backgrounds. Hence, when applicants tend to race over summer experiences, interviewers must use control with a comment such as, "I would like to know a lot more about that first summer job—how you got it, what you did, your likes, dislikes, and so forth."

EFFECTIVE CONTROL REQUIRES JUDICIOUS PACING

Here we return to a subject discussed at the beginning of this chapter. If spontaneity of response is to be maintained, control must be exercised tactfully, unobtrusively, and *at appropriate intervals.* This means that the interviewer must never ask a series of questions one after the other. This gives the appearance of grilling applicants and puts them on the spot. Thus, after asking a penetrating question, the interviewer must find other ways to encourage discussion before asking a second penetrating question. These other ways consist of facial expressions, verbal pats on the back, vocal intonations, and consciously designed pauses.

In a sense, the interviewer is not unlike the coachman of yesteryear. In guiding his six-horse team, the coachman learned to pace his horses so that they would cover the necessary miles without becoming too fatigued. In so doing, he would let them gallop for a while and would then pull them up to a walk. So it is with interviewing. Interviewers encourage applicants to talk spontaneously, but every once in a while, they stop them to keep them on the track or to probe more deeply for salient information.

Then they immediately give them their head, encouraging them to carry on. In short, they consciously *pace* the interview in such a way that they get all the necessary information without *pressing* the applicant and without losing rapport.

EEO CONSIDERATIONS

1. With those minorities or women where rapport seems more difficult to establish—and with such nonminorities as well—do not control quite as strictly. Permit such candidates to talk freely, even if the discourse tends to ramble and to be descriptive in nature. Although this will result in "more chaff along with the wheat" and will take more time, it will nevertheless provide more clues to behavior than would have come to light in an interview that was more strictly controlled.
2. With applicants who are particularly sensitive about the possibility that they may not be hired, interviewers should be especially adroit in the manner in which they interrupt such applicants for purposes of control. The timing and lubrication that are a part of interruption must be handled with great care. A sensitive person who feels that he or she has been cut off may interpret the cause of the interruption as a function of race, sex, or a handicap rather than as a function of completing the interview on time.

PART THREE

Interpreting Information Developed

CHAPTER 10

Interpretation, An Introduction

Since securing information has such a direct bearing on the evaluation of the applicant's overall qualifications, discussion in previous chapters has already touched upon certain factors of interpretation. When, as in the case of securing and interpreting interview information, activities are performed simultaneously, it is somewhat difficult to discuss one activity without considering the other. In the remaining chapters of this book, emphasis swings from securing information to interpretation of findings. Because of the interdependence of the two, however, no effort will be made to confine the discussion to interpretation alone. In fact, subsequent chapters will be concerned with the *specifics* of exploring and interpreting each major area of the interview. Chapter 11, devoted to interpretation of work-history information, will also include further suggestions for carrying out the work-history discussion. In like manner, succeeding chapters will deal with education, present and social adjustment.

Prior to any discussion of information obtained from the

various interview areas, some consideration must be given to the interpretation process itself. In this present chapter we shall therefore discuss some general factors of interpretation. This material represents background information concerning the process of evaluation as a whole. These general factors must be kept in mind in evaluating all interview findings, regardless of the interview area from which such findings emerge.

COMPLEXITIES OF INTERPRETATION

Evaluation of interview data represents an involved mental process. In the first place, interview data are not made up of hard, cold facts that can be reduced to any precise mathematical formula. For the most part, they are composed of clues that alert the interviewer to the possible existence of certain traits of personality and motivation. In the second place, the interview produces a large mass of information *only part of which is relevant in terms of interpretation.* As the discussion progresses, the interviewer must constantly separate the wheat from the chaff. In the third place, a given applicant's qualifications comprise a relatively large number of individual traits and abilities. Interview data must therefore be obtained and organized in such a way that there is sufficient supporting information for evaluating each of the requisite characteristics. It is not enough to know that the applicant has had sufficient technical training and experience; the interviewer must also decide the extent to which that applicant possesses such characteristics as honesty, willingness to work, ability to get along with others, emotional stability, self-confidence, and ability to plan and organize.

In general, it is far easier for novices to learn how to secure the necessary information than to learn how to interpret the findings they obtain. This is because most people respond quite readily to the information-getting techniques discussed in previous chapters. Within two or three days novices can learn to apply these techniques so effectively that they usually experience little or no difficulty in getting the candidate to "open up." But learning to interpret is another matter. People in general do not fall into any set pattern of traits and abilities. There are wide individual differences. In briefing a trainee for a given interview, therefore, one cannot predict the kind of information he or she is likely to encounter. Of course, certain broad predictions can be made on the basis of the application blank, test, and reference data, but such data usually tell relatively little about the applicant as a unique human being.

It is also difficult to teach interviewers to be objective. Unless there is an opportunity to subject the trainees to an extended period of supervised interviewing practice, they frequently drift into such pitfalls as interpretation by "gut feeling" rather than hard interview data. In evaluating an applicant's overall qualifications, moreover, interviewer-trainees tend to arrive at hiring decisions that place too much weight on certain factors and too little on others.

Despite the complexities of evaluation, experience has nevertheless shown that appropriately qualified individuals *can* be trained to interpret interview findings with a relatively high degree of accuracy. Such training requires extended periods of supervised practice and exposure to a variety of applicants, as discussed in Chapter 15.

FIRST CONSIDERATIONS

Since there is no point in interpreting information which we do not believe or cannot take at face value, we must first try to determine whether or not an applicant is telling the truth and whether or not the individual's standards are unrealistically high or low. Although answers to these two questions may not be obtained until the interview is perhaps half over, it seems logical to treat these two factors here before getting involved with interpretation per se.

How to Determine if an Applicant Is Telling the Truth

There are at least three valid means of determining the extent to which an applicant may be telling the truth: (1) *internal consistency, (2) the amount of unfavorable information an applicant provides,* and *(3) an obvious tendency to exaggerate accomplishments.*

By "internal consistency," we mean consistency of information between the two major areas of the interview, work history and education. Hence, if an individual is immature, evidence of this should appear in *both* of these major areas. It would be most unlikely, for example, that an applicant would reflect a high degree of maturity as a part of her or his work history but a low degree of maturity with respect to education. If such a situation should occur, the interviewer should immediately suspect that the person might not be telling the truth. To be more specific, a male applicant, for example, might reflect immaturity by mentioning unsound reasons for leaving jobs, poorly thought-out vocational goals, or aspirations way out of line with his abilities. In order for the discussion of education to be internally consistent, this same applicant might be expected to reveal such clues to immaturity as (1) studying hard on only those courses which he liked, (2) rationalizing failures by blaming teachers or the school system, or (3) selecting a major course of study with no thought at all as to how that major might be used after getting out of school. It is when the data become *inconsistent* that the interviewer should begin to question the applicant's story. Thus, if the applicant cited above claimed that he (1) did his homework every single evening, (2) studied a lot harder on the courses that he did not like in order to get good grades, or (3) never cut any classes, the interviewer might begin to feel that he was telling us what he thought we wanted to hear rather than what actually happened.

When applicants appear to be on the level and provide a fair amount of unfavorable information along with the more favorable data, this can be regarded as firm evidence that they are telling the truth. If, for example, a female applicant admits that she was fired from a given job, that her attendance was not all that good, or that her typing speed is only 30 words a minute, the interviewer gets the feeling that she is telling us her life story just as it actually occurred. With such an applicant, therefore, considerable credence can be placed on statements about achievements.

Some applicants have a rather strong tendency to exaggerate their achievements, and this is quite easily picked up on. In discussing outside interests, for example, a woman might claim that she reads four or five books a week. If that same woman had indicated a dislike of verbal subjects such as English, foreign languages, and history, her claim of reading four or five books a week would be internally inconsistent and probably an exaggeration. Likewise, a man who claims never to have spoken a word in anger strikes us as too good to be true and is probably exaggerating.

As we shall see later on in this chapter, however, applicants' characteristics should not be judged on single clues. Rather, the interviewer should try to develop a *series of clues* before making a judgment on a characteristic as important as, say, honesty. How to develop this kind of documentation is the subject of the three chapters on interpretation.

It may seem to some that no applicant would be likely to provide some of the negative information indicated above, but that is simply not true. When interviewers are successful in developing rapport and getting spontaneous information, they find themselves regularly obtaining information of a negative character that is even surprising to them.

Unrealistic Personal Standards

Even when the interviewer believes that applicants are telling the truth, not all their comments are taken at face value when it has been determined that their personal standards are unrealistically high or low. When asked to tell about his shortcomings, a male applicant, for example, might indicate that he "probably should work a little harder." This might seem completely inconsistent if the interviewer has already developed a considerable amount of hard data supporting a willingness to work very hard. The interviewer may then suspect that the applicant's professed shortcoming stems from his tendency to be a perfectionist and hence to feel that he never does anything as well as he should. In such cases, interviewers rely upon accumulated hard data (clues to willingness to work hard picked up through the discussion of work history and education) rather than upon applicants' statements regarding their shortcomings. Personal standards may also indicate seeming inconsistencies at the other end of the spectrum. When asked to indicate her strengths, a woman, for example, may claim to be a hard worker when all the hard data indicate that just the opposite may be the case. But the inconsistency here may be based upon *low per-*

sonal standards rather than upon dishonesty. Some people's standards are so low that it does not take much to satisfy them. Hence, they may think of themselves as hard workers when this is actually not the case at all.

Fortunately, the hard data (clues to behavior) usually turn out to be consistent with an applicant's own assessment of his or her abilities. It is easy to believe an applicant's claim to being a hard worker when the interviewer has already noted such factors as spending long hours on a variety of jobs, carrying out as many as two or three jobs simultaneously, or putting in a full summer of extremely hard manual work such as unloading boxcars. Inconsistencies that are due to unrealistically high or low personal standards will not be frequent, but they should be identified as such when they do occur.

PROCESS OF INTERPRETATION

As one might expect, it is easier to train interviewers to secure the necessary information than it is to train them to interpret the findings. Since interpretation obviously involves a mental process, it requires a fair amount of analytical ability—ability not only to recognize clues to behavior but to catalog such clues in terms of assets and shortcomings. A good interview produces a large mass of information *only part of which is relevant in terms of interpretation.* As the discussion progresses, the interviewer must constantly separate the wheat from the chaff, searching for clues to such characteristics as willingness to work, ability to get along with others, emotional maturity, and leadership potential.

Interpretation as an Ongoing Process

Interviewers who wait until the end of the interview to decide what they think of an applicant are hopelessly lost. The interpretation process, in fact, begins as soon as applicants enter the room and continues until they leave. Clues to behavior build throughout the interview so that an applicant's overall qualifications normally become quite evident by the time the interview has been concluded. Interviewers who do a good *ongoing* job of interpretation should know whether or not they want to hire the individual by the time that person leaves the room. This may not necessarily be possible during the early part of an interviewer's training, but as the trainee interviews more and more people, he or she will find it increasingly easy to catalog clues to behavior and to arrive at employment decisions earlier. In interviewing more and more people, moreover, interviewers build up a *frame of reference* which enables them to compare the qualifications of a given applicant with those of all the other people they have recently seen.

Interviewers Learn to Mask Their Reactions

As the applicant's story unfolds, interviewers mentally scrutinize each bit of information for possible clues to behavior. Yet they carry out this evaluation process in such a way that they completely mask their true reaction and hence do not give the applicant the slightest inkling of how they are interpreting a remark. To do otherwise might risk loss of rapport. An interviewer who registers surprise or disapproval as a result of uncovering unfavorable information frequently turns applicants off to the point where the interviewer never succeeds in getting them to open up again.

Cataloging Clues

As soon as an applicant enters the room, interviewers should begin to get impressions of that individual in terms of possible effectiveness in the job for which he or she is being considered. It may be noted, for example, that a candidate presents a nice appearance and has an appreciable amount of poise and presence—clues that may be cataloged mentally as factors in the person's possible effectiveness with people. As the interview progresses, the interviewer may become impressed with the complete candor with which the applicant discusses strengths and shortcomings and may catalog that as an indication of sincerity and maturity. (Individuals who know themselves in terms of their strengths and limitations are often more mature than their chronological age group.) Later on, the candidate may indicate that he or she often stays on after quitting time in order to get a job done or even comes in on a Saturday. The interviewer catalogs this, naturally, as a clue to conscientiousness and willingness to work. And so it goes throughout the interview. Each statement the applicant makes is carefully examined in terms of its implied as well as its obvious meaning. Resulting clues to behavior are then mentally cataloged as possible indications of such traits as willingness to work hard, emotional maturity, adaptability, ability to get along with people, and leadership potential.

Relevance of Applicant's Work History and Education

Interviewers look not only for clues to behavior but also for the extent to which an applicant's previous experience and training have provided adequate preparation for the position in question. If the job in question, for example, involves excessive detail, interviewers would be quick to note any previous detail-oriented experience and how the individual reacted to this. They know full well that individuals who have already experienced this kind of work know what they are getting into and adapt to it much more readily than someone without such experience. This is not to say that applicants without this kind of experience would necessarily be rejected. It simply means that those who have had this experience, other things being equal, would receive more favorable consideration.

Mentally Organize a List of Assets and Liabilities

As the discussion progresses, interviewers mentally compile a list of the applicant's strengths and shortcomings with respect to the job under consideration. Although their outward manner is permissive and disarming, they nevertheless evaluate analytically and critically everything an applicant has to say. As the interview progresses from work history to education and finally to outside interests, a general pattern of behavior normally begins to make itself evident. Thus, interviewers may get clue after clue attesting to a candidate's forcefulness, willingness to accept responsibility, and strong drive to get things done quickly. At the same time, since a high degree of strength in certain areas may be accompanied by concomitant shortcomings in other areas, interviewers may also pick up a series of clues indicating lack of tact, inflexibility, or even ruthlessness. As they catalog such clues, they find it increasingly possible to build a list of assets and liabilities. In fact, such a list of assets and liabilities should be so well documented by the end of the discussion that interviewers can write them out immediately after the applicant leaves the room. At that point, interviewers make the hiring decision on the basis of the extent to which the assets outweigh the liabilities or vice versa.

Searching for Clues to Mental Capacity

In addition to the search for personality traits and relevance of previous experience and training, interviewers also look for the *level of the applicant's basic abilities.* As noted in Chapter 5, aptitude tests can be of tremendous help in establishing the level of a candidate's mental, verbal, and numerical ability, clerical aptitude, and mechanical comprehension. However, such test results are not always available, and in such cases interviewers must do the best they can to establish ability levels on the basis of interviewer findings. Specific suggestions for accomplishing this task will be found in subsequent chapters. Suffice it to say here, though, that some of the best clues to mental ability will be found in such factors as (1) level of grades in terms of effort required to get those grades, (2) college board scores, and (3) an applicant's ability to respond to the more difficult depth questions.

WHAT TO INTERPRET

As indicated earlier, every interview results in *relevant* and *irrelevant* information. Actually, much of what the applicant may have to say is likely to be *descriptive,* providing little in the way of clues to behavior. Interviewers, of course, try to keep such information to a minimum, controlling the discussion so that applicants concentrate on evaluative data. Even so, a certain amount of descriptive information is certain to ensue. Interviewers naturally pay as little attention as possible to such irrelevant data, constantly identifying the important information and making their interpretations accordingly.

In general, the more relevant information is likely to be found in applicants' *attitudes* and *reactions*. Thus, interviewers learn much more about people as a result of their attitudes and reactions toward a given job than from a description of the job duties. Such attitudes and reactions often provide specific clues to such important factors as emotional maturity, willingness to work hard, tact, and self-confidence.

Since interviewers are also looking for the relevance of applicants' work experience and education in terms of the job for which they are being considered, interviewers must carry a mental picture of the job and worker specifications into the discussion with them. When listening to the description of previous jobs, for example, the interviewer must be quick to notice any similarity between those jobs and the job for which the applicant is being considered. It must also be decided whether candidates are capable of performing the job in question with minimum orientation or whether a protracted training period will be necessary to bring them to a productive level. In like manner, the interviewer must evaluate candidates' education, deciding whether or not they have the kind and quality of technical training that will enable them to perform effectively.

HOW TO INTERPRET

We have talked above about the importance of determining the *relevance* of an applicant's work history and education. This is a relatively simple task since one has only to compare what candidates have done in the past with what they may be expected to do on the job for which they are being considered. All that is required is an ability to get information and a clear picture of the demands of the job in question. Understanding and utilizing the process described below—the concept of *contrast*—will help immeasurably in carrying out this interpretative function.

Concept of Contrast

This process involves the continual contrasting of each aspect of an applicant's job and school history with the specifications of the job under consideration. In those areas where little or no contrast is involved—or where the difference is in a positive direction—no real adjustment problem exists. This of course represents a favorable finding. On the other hand, where the contrast is appreciable, candidates might be expected to experience a very real adjustment problem in acclimating to the new job situation. Although the difference may be insufficient to exclude applicants from further consideration, such a difference nevertheless represents an unfavorable factor.

Let us assume, for example, that a given job calls for work of a highly confining nature. Applicants who have done confining work as a part of their previous experience —and who have apparently been able to accept it quite readily as part of the job—might be expected to be able to adjust to the new job much more easily than applicants without such experience. With the former group the contrast would not appear to be very great, while with the latter group the contrast would in all likelihood be significant.

Another such unfavorable contrast would be found in applicants who are already earning more money on their present job than what they would be paid as a starting salary on the new job. They might express a willingness to take the new job at a lower salary because it may offer greater long-range opportunity. Once they have been on the job for a while, however, a certain amount of dissatisfaction is likely to develop. This dissatisfaction may be stimulated further by a spouse who finds it necessary to make ends meet on a smaller budget. Many such individuals decide that they can't wait for future salary increases and begin looking for another job. If, on the other hand, applicants are to be paid a starting salary in excess of their present earnings, they can be expected to be more satisfied with their new lot, other things being equal. This of course represents a difference, or contrast, in the positive direction and is evaluated by the interviewer as a *favorable factor.*

The kind of close supervision involved in previous jobs and in a proposed new assignment may also provide an unfavorable contrast. A secretary who has had previous experience running an office and taking care of much of the correspondence might become quickly dissatisfied in a new job where every single piece of correspondence was dictated and where everything was very closely supervised. When such individuals take new positions involving much closer supervision and much less opportunity to exercise their own initiative, they normally find adjustment somewhat difficult. The alert interviewer recognizes the potentially unfavorable contrast and adds this to the list of negative factors.

Interpretation by Direct Observation

One can make *some* valid judgments about people simply by observing them directly. Thus, interviewers find it quite easy to evaluate such obvious characteristics as appearance, poise, presence, grooming, and self-expression. They simply observe an applicant's outward behavior during the discussion and make their judgments on these characteristics accordingly.

It is even possible to learn something about personal forcefulness and tact by means of direct observation. For example, the interviewer might note that a given candidate's personality has considerable impact and that the individual is exceedingly forceful and dynamic in conversation. Since personal forcefulness represents an element of leadership, the interviewer would be quick to note that as a favorable factor. However, that same individual may frequently interrupt an interviewer in the middle of a sentence or may talk disparagingly about certain minority groups. This kind of behavior obviously represents a lack of tact and social sensitivity.

It must be pointed out again, though, that interpretation by direct observation is limited to the more obvious or easy-to-evaluate characteristics. It is of very little use in determining the more important factors such as willingness to work, emotional maturity, intelligence, and perseverance. Yet, interpretation by direct observations is the only means available to most untrained interviewers. This is why the interview has often fared so poorly when subjected to validation studies.

Interpretation by Inference

Since interpretation by direct observation represents a relatively limited device, what method do we use to evaluate the more important characteristics? We use a time-tested method called *interpretation by inference.* By definition, this means that we *infer* from a *series of clues* the extent to which an individual possesses a given trait or ability. The phrase "series of clues" in this definition is extremely important since it would be most unfair and inaccurate to base an evaluation on a single unfavorable situation. Even if a person admits to having been fired from a given job, that, in itself, would not represent an adequate basis for assuming the person was a troublemaker or a poor worker. It is conceivable, in fact, that the supervisor may have been at fault. But, if there are problems on other jobs, if the person talks disparagingly about coworkers, and if there were disciplinary problems in school, we can determine with some assurance that this individual is not able to get along with people very well. This assurance stems from the fact that we have developed a *series* of clues rather than based our evaluation on a single happenstance. And, because these clues have spanned two areas of the interview—work history and education—we have established a pattern of internal consistency. When an individual has any given trait in some abundance, clues to such a trait will not be limited to a single area of the interview. Rather, such clues will surface in both the work history and education.

In the effort to document a trait such as immaturity, clues to this important shortcoming might surface in the work history as poor judgment in leaving certain jobs and unwillingness to make current sacrifices for future gains, or as aspirations which are quite out of line with the individual's abilities. Clues to this same shortcoming could conceivably come to light in the educational area in the form of rationalizing failures—blaming poor grades on the teachers or schools. Clues of a similar nature might be identified in a failure to study for subjects which the person did not like or in poor judgment in selecting a major course study.

In evaluating older individuals, persons in their early forties for example, the interviewer must be very careful not to evaluate them in terms of *what they were like 15 or 20 years ago.* A young man, for example, in his early twenties may have been quite footloose and fancy-free, hopping from one job to another without any sense of direction at all, but that same individual may have settled down to the point that his history over the past 10 years or so may have been very stable. Hence, the evaluation is based on clues to behavior grounded in the person's more recent history.

We have indicated earlier that clues must be interpreted as soon as they become evident. This provides interviewers with a beginning or starting point on which they can build later on. Using such a clue as a *temporary* supposition, they mentally catalog it as a possible indication of a given trait. With this supposition as a foundation, they subsequently probe at appropriate intervals throughout the discussion for additional specific clues to support the supposition. In the case cited above, an interviewer would have obtained an early clue to immaturity, thus providing a temporary supposition; however, since clues to immaturity were not evident in the man's history for the 10 most recent years, the interviewer would have had to throw out the initial hypothesis. On the other hand, some people never seem to grow up. Evidence may show that job-hopping, chronic dissatisfaction with practically every job, and poor judgment are still deeply rooted in an individual's behavior. In such a case, there is ample evidence—in the form of many clues pointing in the same direction—to eliminate the candidate from further consideration.

For purposes of further illustration, let us assume that an applicant has expressed a strong dislike for detail in connection with a prior clerical job. The interviewer catalogs this appropriately and wisely decides to wait, listen, and not *prejudge*, at the same time, actively probing for further evidence, particularly in those areas which would be most likely to provide clues to a dislike of detail. Thus, when the applicant discusses a subsequent job as a computer programmer, the interviewer, knowing that this type of work involves a great amount of detail, will try to get further evidence of this trait by stimulating in the applicant a spontaneous recital of likes and dislikes in that job. If the individual does not mention attention to detail as either a like or a dislike, the interviewer may ask a question specifically about the applicant's feelings concerning the detail involved. Later on, the interviewer may probe in like manner for the candidate's reaction to a detail-oriented subject in school such as mechanical drawing and toward the end of the discussion may try to get further confirmation of a possible dislike of and inability to carry out detailed work by bringing this up under self-evaluation as a possible shortcoming. Utilizing the *double-edged question*, the interviewer might say, "What about attention to detail? Do you have as much of this as you would like to have, or is this something that you could improve a little bit?" If, at that point, the applicant candidly admits to not handling detail well, the interviewer will have brought to light a serious shortcoming, *providing that the worker specifications indicate attention to detail as an important requisite.*

We therefore see that interpretation by inference goes on throughout the interview, the interviewer making tentative hypotheses and probing specifically for confirming evidence. Remember, too, that interviewers are charged with the responsibility of developing clues to a *variety* of characteristics. They are therefore confronted with a mentally demanding assignment. This is the primary reason why they must be so skilled in the mechanics of the interview that these become almost second nature. Once this level has been achieved in the sense that interviewers do not have to concern themselves about mechanics anymore, they automatically become better *listeners* and can devote the major portion of their attention to the process of evaluation.

Hypotheses Based on Leads from Previous Selection Steps

Since the final interview is preceded by such employment steps as the application form, the preliminary interview, and the aptitude tests, it represents an ideal opportunity to follow up on some of the *leads* which may have emerged from some of those early steps. Such leads often give the interviewer a tremendous head start as far as the interpretive process is concerned. Even before the interview begins, for example, the interviewer may have a lead to possible lack of motivation. Let us assume that the tests of mental ability reflect a high level of intelligence. The interviewer will expect to see this reflected in above-average grades in school. If such does not turn out to be the case, the interviewer will immediately probe for reasons why, suspecting low-level application or disorganized study habits. Or, in another example, the preliminary interviewer may have noted a slight tendency to be evasive. With that lead in mind, the final interviewer will be immediately alerted for any signs of dishonesty. Thus, by studying information available to them before the interview, interviewers can frequently develop usable hypotheses which they carry into the discussion and seek to support or reject on the basis of the evidence presented. It should be emphasized, though, that a lead is just that and nothing more. If it cannot be supported by hard data, it must be discarded.

TRAIT CONSTELLATIONS

Experience has shown that certain traits tend to be related to each other and hence *may* be found in a single grouping or constellation within one individual. Thus, if it is possible to identify the *key trait* of a given constellation, it is more than possible that certain related traits may also be found in the individual's makeup.

In three of the four trait constellations discussed below, the key trait frequently becomes evident within the first 5 or 10 minutes of the interview. A knowledge of the constellation permits the interviewer to probe specifically for the possible existence of related traits as soon as the key trait has been identified. This, again, gives the interviewer an initial advantage in terms of diagnosing traits of personality and motivation. In other words, the interviewer can form hypotheses more quickly and can specifically direct the probing in a more meaningful manner.

Familiarity with trait constellations may represent a real danger in the hands of inexperienced interviewers. Such people may be tempted to assume too much and may even attempt to type individuals. Nothing could be further from our purpose. Just because interviewers identify a key trait, they *cannot automatically assume* that the individual possesses the related assets and liabilities. In fact, it would be the unusual individual indeed who possessed all the suggested related traits. Moreover, some individuals possess the assets related to the key trait but have few if any of the liabilities. Once the key trait has been identified, interviewers simply look for the *possible existence* of the related characteristics. True, they probe specifically for the possible existence of these traits, but they discard the hypothesis if they are not able to come up with substantial supporting evidence.

Interviewers should familiarize themselves thoroughly with the trait constellations outlined below. A knowledge of these possible relationships can be of tremendous help in probing for clues to behavior. Whenever interviewers are able to identify the *key trait* of a given constellation, they *may—but not invariably—* find subsequently that the applicant possesses some of the related assets and liabilities that go with that key trait.

Once again, it must be emphasized that the knowledge of possible trait constellations should be used solely as a means of developing initial hypotheses. If the hypothesis cannot be supported by subsequent documentary evidence, it must be discarded completely.

Key Trait: Strongly extroverted

Assets	*Shortcomings*
Warmth	Impatience
Friendliness	Impulsiveness
Enthusiasm	Tendency to make snap decisions
Aggressiveness	Inability to think analytically
Self-confidence	Little organizing and planning ability
Persuasiveness	Carelessness
Seldom worries	Lack of thoroughness
Ability to improvise	Disregard of detail

Rationale

As indicated above, strongly extroverted individuals are frequently good improvisers in the sense that they are able to think quickly on their feet and can normally rise to the occasion by acceptably handling situations for which they have had no opportunity to prepare. This particular ability, by the way, is often found in top-flight salespeople who are continually called upon to handle customer objections that cannot be anticipated. Now, ability to improvise represents an obvious asset but, at the same time, this ability often leads to the development of certain shortcomings. Strongly extroverted individuals, for example, sometimes depend too much upon the ability to improvise. As a result, they become a "seat of the pants" operator, confident of their ability to handle any situation that may arise. By temperament, too, they like to get one thing out of the way quickly so that they can go on to the next. As a consequence of their proven ability to improvise, they are not inclined to let problems worry them, and they often do not take sufficient time to prepare for various assignments. Thus, they do not take time to think things through beforehand. This means, of course, that they do not cultivate the habit of analyzing a situation, or organizing and planning for it in advance. Hence, they tend to skim over the surface of matters and do not always dig deeply enough to investigate the heart of the problem. Because they operate so much on the spur of the moment, they frequently make snap decisions—decisions too often born of impatience and impulsiveness. Hence, they are often careless, lacking in thoroughness, and not inclined to give appropriate attention to detail.

Extroverts often compensate for their shortcomings through the development of a very effective approach to people. Thus they cultivate warmth, friendliness, enthusiasm, forcefulness, and persuasive ability. Incidentally, these traits are normally prominent among the assets of successful salespeople. They enable salespeople to win others to their point of view. At the same time, any sales manager will be quick to admit that some of the best salespeople turn in the poorest reports, because of their impatience and dislike for detail. In an attempt to reward their best salespeople, moreover, many companies elevate such individuals to sales management. And, if the promoted individuals have many of the shortcomings of the extrovert, they are not likely to be able to turn in a top performance as a manager. For as a manager they must be able to plan, organize, analyze, and give attention to detail. Many companies are discovering that their best salespeople do not necessarily make their best sales managers.

Of course, many extroverts succeed in modifying their behavior. Confronted with tasks that demand attention to detail, ability to analyze, and ability to plan and organize, they sometimes acquire a reasonable degree of facility in these areas. This is one reason why it is dangerous to assume that an extrovert necessarily possesses the shortcomings listed above.

After an interviewer has identified an applicant as an extrovert during the first few minutes of the discussion, he should probe specifically for the possible existence of the above-mentioned shortcomings. Out-and-out extroverts can of course be quickly identified by their outgoing manner, gregariousness, and warm, friendly affability. As soon as this identification is made, the interviewer should say to himself, "I wonder if this woman is impatient and impulsive? I wonder how analytical she is? I wonder to what extent she gives appropriate attention to detail? I wonder how well she plans and organizes?" Having raised these questions, he should then proceed to try to find the answers by probing specifically for the possible existence of these traits. As a matter of fact, it is good to go through these mental steps even in cases where the applicant may be only somewhat extroverted. It is quite possible that such a person may have one or two of these related shortcomings. Suggestions on how to probe for suspected shortcomings will be found in subsequent chapters.

Key Trait: Strongly introverted

Assets	*Shortcomings*
Reflectiveness	Shyness
Analytical thinking	Self-consciousness
Imagination	Lack of confidence
Good attention to detail	Undue sensitiveness
Carefulness	Tendency to worry
Meticulousness	Poor improvisation
Methodicalness	Lack of poise
Orderliness	Tendency to be inhibited
Patience	Lack of mental toughness
	Lack of aggressiveness

Rationale

At the outset, it must be pointed out that introversion does not necessarily represent a shortcoming. In fact, introversion is a decided asset in certain positions where a fair amount of confinement is involved—in such positions as drafting, design, and certain types of research work. Because strongly extroverted individuals find it very difficult to adjust to jobs of a confining nature, they are seldom found in the positions enumerated above. Hence, in selecting an applicant for a given job, appropriate attention must be given to the type of temperament which is likely to be most appropriate for the position in question.

Although introverts frequently possess many important assets, they are likely to be unsure of themselves in social situations. Unlike extroverts, therefore, they are inclined to take great pains in preparing for a given assignment. In so doing, they take plenty of time to reflect about the task at hand and usually analyze it from every conceivable angle. They are sometimes so concerned about measuring up that they document their thinking in great detail, being very careful that their approach is logically planned and systematically organized. Since they give a great amount of thought to their approach, they are often able to come up with a number of new and original ideas.

But the introvert's lack of confidence is often outwardly reflected in a series of concomitant shortcomings. Many of these shortcomings limit the facility for dealing with people effectively. Thus the introvert is often shy, self-conscious, inhibited, unaggressive, and lacking in poise and presence. Some introverts are so insecure, moreover, that they tend to worry unduly and become oversensitive to criticism.

As noted above, the assets of this particular trait constellation provide a rather good description of the qualifications of the successful research and development person. This perhaps represents one reason why so many good research and development people tend to be on the introverted side. It is equally true, moreover, that many research people have a problem selling their ideas and often find it difficult to assume responsibility for the direction of others.

Again, pronounced introverts may be quickly identified in the early part of the discussion by means of direct observation. Such people are often ill at ease in talking with a stranger, their shyness, self-consciousness, and inhibited nature becoming noticeably apparent within the first 5 or 10 minutes of conversation. As soon as identification of the introvert takes place, the interviewer should ask herself, "I wonder if this man lacks confidence? I wonder if he is oversensitive? I wonder if he has a tendency to worry unduly?" Having set up these tentative hypotheses, she then tries to document them by probing for tangible evidence.

In making use of trait constellations as a basis for further probing, it is well to remember the tentative aspect of the hypothesis. Certainly, all insecure people are not introverts. Moreover, many introverted individuals attain a high degree of emotional adjustment and establish very effective relationships with other people.

Key Trait: Assertiveness

Assets	*Shortcomings*
Strong impact	Lack of tact
Dynamism	Insensitivity to feelings of others
Tough-mindedness	Ruthlessness
Good organizing ability	Strong ego
Decisiveness	Intolerance
Supreme self-confidence	Strong likes and dislikes
Production-mindedness (desire to get things done quickly)	Inflexibility
	Tendency to be too blunt and direct

Rationale

Because of the impact of their personality upon others, forceful individuals frequently manage to win election or promotion to positions of leadership. Such positions of course require decisive action and an ability to get the job done. If individuals are to operate successfully as leaders, they have to learn to organize. To leaders, results are what count the most; and they are expected to obtain these results in the shortest possible period of time. Leaders therefore become more concerned with the effectiveness of the group than with the problems of any one member of that group. Thus they do not hesitate to make tough-minded decisions that may tread on the toes of the few, if such decisions are good for the many—the overall organization. Remember, too, that it takes a great amount of confidence to make decisions at a high level. Decisions of this kind may have a pronounced, long-range effect on the entire organization. These are the decisions, moreover, that the timid, cautious individual finds it very difficult to make.

In their desire to get the job done quickly, however, forceful individuals sometimes give too little thought to the people involved. Occasionally, such people become so result-oriented that they do not care how they treat their subordinates so long as their goals are accomplished. This means of course that they are likely to be blunt, direct, and tactless. They may even be so insensitive to the feelings of others that they become ruthless. Because the experience of making decisions at high levels requires great self-confidence, forceful people who attain an important leadership position may become somewhat egotistical. If this occurs, they may come to regard their judgment as infallible, in which case of course they develop strong likes and dislikes, and tend to be inflexible and opinionated.

The above discussion pretty much depicts the "bull of the woods" type of boss who was much more likely to be found in industry 20 or 30 years ago than today. Due in large part to pressure from the unions, such people find it necessary to modify their behavior if they are to maintain positions of leadership. Workers promoted to supervisors who throw their weight around without regard to the people who work for them run head on into a series of union grievances. When such grievances become serious and time-consuming, supervisors' superiors call them on the carpet, telling them to modify their behavior or risk demotion to the ranks. The best of such supervisors take stock of themselves and gradually come to the realization that they will have to learn to work with people amicably and adroitly if they are to survive. Happily, the vast majority of present-day managers have profited from hard knocks incurred on their way up. Obviously, too, management in general is much more enlightened today and recognizes the importance of the individual as a human being, regardless of union pressure.

It is easy to recognize the truly forceful applicant within the first 5 minutes of the interview because of the impact she has on the interviewer and because of her tendency to take the conversational ball and run with it. As soon as the interviewer realizes that he is dealing with a forceful person, he should immediately start probing for such possible shortcomings as tactlessness, inflexibility, and a tendency to be egotistical and opinionated. When he finds evidence of such traits, he must decide how serious and deep-seated they are. In other words, is the candidate only somewhat egotistical or lacking in tact, or does she have these liabilities to such a serious degree that they would be likely to preclude the establishment of successful relationships with others?

Again, it must be remembered that many forceful people do not become leaders. And many forceful individuals may acquire very few of the assets or liabilities listed above.

Key Trait: Strong social drive (Strong desire to help others—a do-gooder)

Assets	*Shortcomings*
Genuine love of people	Lack of mental toughness
Selflessness	Impracticality
Tendency to be unassuming	Not sufficiently suspicious of others' motives
Missionarylike zeal	Tendency to take people at face value
Enthusiasm	Tendency to see only the best in people
Strong desire to encourage others' development	Gullibility/naiveté
	Lack of critical thinking

Rationale

Applicants who reflect this trait constellation derive their greatest satisfaction from doing things for others. They are not primarily motivated by money, power, or prestige. For the most part, they tend to be selfless and unassuming. The YMCA director and the social worker, to cite members of two occupations that fit into this category, are certainly not motivated by the desire for financial gain. Their greatest satisfaction comes from helping other people to fight their own battles. And they approach their work with as much or more enthusiasm than might have been the case were they primarily motivated by personal gain. The social worker will plunge into settlement house activity with the same kind of zeal shown by salespeople in their quest for new business.

Because of their strong desire to help others, socially motivated individuals are not always practical and tough-minded. Inclined to be overly sanguine, they are likely to believe that other people are guided by the same high principles that guide them. Since they are primarily concerned with helping others to better themselves, they tend to think only of their strengths, without giving proper consideration to their weaknesses. These people, moreover, often are considered a "soft touch." They willingly loan money without much concern as to whether or not it will be repaid. Helping another person in time of need is the primary consideration. Consequently, they tend to be naive, easily taken in, and not very critical in their thinking.

A reasonable degree of social drive represents an asset in many types of jobs. For example, a woman does not become a great teacher unless she is strongly motivated to help students learn—to stimulate their thinking and broaden their horizons. Effective supervisors in industry should also have a certain amount of social drive. They should be interested in bringing subordinates along so that they can grow and develop. Again, as in the case of the other trait constellations, social drive presents problems only when it becomes inordinately strong. The individual whose social drive becomes so strong that it overshadows everything else frequently develops many of the shortcomings described above.

The interviewer will normally be unable to identify social drive in the early part of the discussion. In fact, she may not get her first clue until she approaches the end of the work-history discussion. Then, in response to the interviewer's questions concerning factors of job satisfaction, the applicant may say, "In order to give me satisfaction, a job must provide an opportunity to make some contribution to the welfare of humanity." Later on, in discussing outside interests, the applicant may further reflect his social drive by the nature of his community activities. He may be entirely wrapped up in such affairs as scout work, YMCA work, hospital work, and community drives. The interviewer would then be prompted to probe for the *why* of such activities. If strong social drive seems to be indicated, she would of course probe for the possible existence of the shortcomings described above.

Precautions

Knowledge of possible trait relationships can provide interviewers with a powerful tool in terms of probing for clues to behavior. They must remember, however, that this knowledge only *suggests the possibility* of related traits, once the key trait has been identified. Moreover, only a fraction of the applicants will fall clearly into any one of the four trait constellations. And some applicants may reflect some of the strengths and shortcomings of two or three constellations. This knowledge must therefore be used cautiously and judiciously.

TRAIT DESCRIPTION

If we are to rate a given applicant on a series of traits, our understanding of the meaning of these traits must be as clear as possible. Unfortunately, psychologists themselves find it difficult to agree specifically on the definition of many traits of personality, motivation, and character. Hence, it is expected that many people will quarrel with the definitions listed below. At the same time, these definitions do provide a functional description of the trait and should therefore be of assistance to the employment interviewer.

Emotional maturity: the ability to behave as an adult, to take the bitter with the sweet, to face up to failure without rationalizing or passing the buck, to acquire self-insight, to establish reasonable vocational goals, and to exercise self-control.

Assertiveness: aggressiveness in social situations; impact of one's personality upon other people—not to be confused with drive to get a job done.

Tough-mindedness: willingness to make difficult decisions involving people for the good of the organization, to stand up for what one thinks is right and not to shrink from confrontations with others when necessary.

Social sensitivity: awareness of the reactions of others; judgment in social situations.

Conscientiousness: willingness to put in additional time and effort on a given task in order to complete it in accordance with one's personal standards.

Self-discipline: ability to carry out the less pleasant tasks without undue procrastination.

Initiative: self-starter; willingness to try new methods, provide one's own motivation without undue prompting from superiors.

Analytical capacity: ability to break down a given problem into its component parts in a logical, systematic manner.

Ability to plan and organize: ability to lay out a given task in logical sequence, approaching first things first in a systematic manner, planning future steps in such a way as to accomplish the whole task efficiently and thoroughly.

Critical thinking: ability to dig down deeply in order to get to the bottom of problems, to probe beneath the surface in order to test the findings in terms of one's own experience, hence not to take things at face value.

Self-confidence: willingness to take action based upon a realistic assessment of one's own abilities.

Emotional adjustment: ability to stand up under pressure, to take a reasonably cheerful outlook on life, to be at peace with oneself.

Team worker: willingness to do one's share of the work, ability to get along with other members of the team, willingness to subordinate one's ego to the extent that one does not try to become the "star" of the team or to claim too much credit for the joint accomplishment.

CHAPTER 11

Interpreting Work History

In the previous chapter, we talked about general factors of interpretation—what the process involves and how to go about putting it into operation. In this chapter, we get down to *specifics*; we consider what the discussion of work history may reveal about an applicant's personality, motivation, and abilities. In addition to establishing the relevance of applicants' previous work experience in terms of the job for which they are being considered, we need to look specifically for clues to such factors as mental capacity (if tests are not available), honesty, adaptability, and other work-related personality traits.

We have mentioned earlier that this kind of interview differs from most interviews in the sense that an attempt should be made to *document* the findings with hard data. Instead of coming away from an interview with a hunch that a given individual may be a hard worker, data to support such a finding should be sought, in the form of such factors as long hours spent on a given job without complaint, substantial numbers of hours a week working on a part-time job while carrying a full academic load, or perseverance on a summer job involving hard manual work for the entire summer. In the attempts to get hard data, moreover, every effort should be made to *quantify* information—to get numbers. When a person works on a part-time job while attending school, for example, the number of hours worked per week should be established. It might be as few as 6 or 8 or as many as 25 to 30. By the same token, it is not enough for people to say that their attendance record was "good." Employees' ideas of good attendance can vary greatly. Quantification should be established by asking the number of days absent during the year.

Applicants' work history ordinarily represents a major portion of their life's experience and, as such, not only provides an indication of their ability to do a certain job in question but also supplies many clues as to *how* they will do it. The manner in which a person works is often the best single source of information concerning personality strengths and weaknesses. It is fitting, then, that applicants be encouraged to give a rather exhaustive account of their work background, particularly as it pertains to items listed under work experience on the Interview Guide.

In this chapter, we will offer suggestions for structuring discussion of the work history. This will be followed by an item-by-item discussion of factors listed under work experience on the Interview Guide.

HOW TO STRUCTURE DISCUSSION OF WORK HISTORY

The reader will recall that, in the effort to get applicants talking spontaneously, the discussion of all major areas of the interview begins with a comprehensive lead question. In launching the work history discussion, interviewers may use such a comprehensive question as, "Suppose you start by telling me about your work experience, beginning with the first job and working up to the present. I would like to know how you got each job, what you did, your likes, dislikes, earnings, and so forth. Where do we start? Did you have any jobs while attending high school?" In talking about various jobs, applicants will normally provide spontaneous information concerning many of the factors listed under work history on the Interview Guide. When they fail to provide such information—or if they do not discuss important factors in sufficient detail—interviewers should prompt them by adroitly worded follow-up questions and comments.

Remember, too, that the work history should be kept pure, in the sense that the interviewer encourages applicants to concentrate on *jobs*, without supplying much information about other interview areas. When applicants begin to ramble or to provide too much descriptive information, the interviewer tries to control the situation by adroitly interrupting them with a carefully timed compliment and bringing them back to the subject under discussion.

Military service should be discussed at the point at which it occurs chronologically in the individual's work history and should be treated just like any other important job. Thus, in the case of a man who went into the army after completing high school, we would discuss the jobs he had while in high school and then launch into a thorough discussion of his army experience. This would be followed by a discussion of jobs he may have had after getting out of the army. In order to avoid spending too much time on the military experience, take individuals quickly through their various assignments. Then ask about their overall likes and dislikes about the military experience as a whole, rather than getting reactions to every assignment. Look for relationships with superiors and associates, any leadership experience, and specific skills (and/or training) which may be relevant to the job for which they are being considered. Since the military experience often represents a period of appreciable individual growth and development, it is usually beneficial to ask a question such as, "In what ways do you think your military experience changed you? What specific traits or abilities do you think you developed during that time?"

A discussion of each of the factors listed under work history on the Interview Guide follows in this chapter. Each factor is treated in some detail, in terms of both how to get the information and how to interpret the resulting data.

RELEVANCE OF PRIOR JOBS

Other things being equal, job relevance plays an important part in deciding the extent to which applicants may be qualified for a given job. The fewer *adjustments and adaptations* individuals have to make in moving from previous jobs to a new job, the more likely they are to find the new job satisfying, and the more quickly they should be able to make a meaningful contribution. If, in undertaking a new assignment, individuals are asked to perform operations under environmental conditions they have grown used to on previous jobs, they usually find it possible to adapt to the new job quite comfortably and quickly. On the other hand, if everything is completely new to them, they often suffer a certain amount of "culture shock," in the sense that they find so many new things to learn and to get used to that they initially have great difficulty getting organized and concentrating on what is expected of them.

As an applicant relates her or his job history, the interviewer mentally checks this experience against worker specifications of the job under consideration. If the applicant has indicated no job choice, the interviewer makes a mental comparison of the general similarity of the individual's work experience to the worker specifications which that experience most closely approximates. Before the interview is terminated, both interviewer and interviewee must have agreed on the specific job for which the applicant seems best qualified.

Essentially, evaluation of work experience involves an investigation of three simple questions:

1. What did the applicant do?
2. How did he or she do it?
3. What did he or she do it with?

Items listed on the Interview Guide will provide appreciable help in securing answers to these basic questions. These items are discussed here in the same order in which they appear on the Interview Guide.

DUTIES

As indicated previously, applicants should not be permitted to devote too much time to a description of job duties, particularly in the case of the initial jobs. When they get to their more important experiences, however, they should be encouraged to talk in some detail about what they actually did on these jobs. For the most part, interviewers do not expect applicants to have performed duties that are exactly the same as those they will be responsible for in a new job. Rather, they evaluate the general nature of candidates' experience, assuming that they should be able to carry out new duties that are generally similar to what they have done in the past. In hiring an engineer for the design of automatic-control systems for jet engines, it may not be absolutely necessary to find someone whose previous experience has been devoted to jet engines. If the candidate has successfully designed automatic-control systems for other highly technical power plants, such as those concerned with guided missiles or torpedoes, he or she should be able to assume design responsibilities on jet-engine control systems without too much orientation.

Information concerning the duties of the candidate's more important jobs also tells the interviewer about the degree of responsibility the candidate has assumed. Such responsibility may have been highly technical or it may have involved the supervision of other people. In either case, the interviewer needs to know the degree of responsibility assumed—the exact nature of the technical duties or the number of persons supervised. To get this information, the interviewer may have to interrupt the applicant's story from time to time, to get more specific information. As the candidate goes from one job to another, the interviewer has an opportunity to note the progress in assuming responsibility. Such progress—or the lack of it—may provide clues to the individual's general ability. Where considerable progress has been made, the interviewer will probe for the *why*—those specific traits and abilities that have been responsible for the individual's success. Where lack of progress is evident, the interviewer will be equally interested in trying to find the underlying reasons. In the latter case, particular note will be taken of any attempt on an applicant's part to rationalize failures, as a possible clue to immaturity.

In evaluating the degree of responsibility assumed in the course of military experience, the interviewer will be guided by the understanding that promotions frequently take place because the particular individual happened to be at the right place at the right time. In other military situations, the individual may have had little opportunity for promotion because she happened to find herself in a group where many of her associates had more experience and training in the particular specialty. At the same time, rapid promotion in the military establishment is normally based on ability and leadership qualifications. In such instances, the interviewer will naturally attempt to identify the particular factors responsible for the individual's success.

When interviewers encounter people who have made unusual progress, they should use the following question: What traits do you think you demonstrated that caused your supervisors to move you ahead so rapidly? This usually results in responses such as, "I worked very hard" or "I was very reliable; I never missed a day" or "I got along very well with people."

LIKES

Since attitudes and reactions to a particular job experience normally tell us much more about people than a recitation of job duties, a great deal of attention should be devoted to likes and dislikes. If candidates omit this from their discussion, they should be reminded by such a follow-up question as, "What were some of the things you liked best on that job?" Moreover, interviewers should not be satisfied with a single response. They should probe for additional likes.

Ideally, the most favorable situation develops when the applicants' likes on previous jobs correspond with important elements of the job for which they are being considered. If they have previously shown a liking for report writing, for example, they should find little difficulty adjusting to the report writing function on the job for which they are being evaluated. Or if they have shown a decided preference for jobs involving a considerable amount of contact with people, they should be able to adjust to the contact aspect of the new job with no great difficulty.

Likes on previous jobs can of course supply many clues to abilities, personality traits, and motivation. Someone who has shown a liking for responsibility—particularly where people are concerned—*may* have a certain degree of initiative and leadership ability. Someone who derives particular satisfaction from contacts with workers in the shop may possess a considerable amount of common touch. Since likes and abilities tend to be fairly highly correlated —in the sense that we tend to do best on those tasks we enjoy most—a liking for mathematics may indicate that the individual has a fair amount of aptitude for mathematically oriented work. And the individual may be accurate, precise, and temperamentally suited for work of a confining nature.

But likes are equally valuable in providing clues to possible shortcomings. The woman who liked a job because of its regular hours, frequent vacations, and lack of overtime work, may be the kind of person who does not like to extend herself by putting in extra effort on a job. If this can be supported by subsequent clues pointing in the same direction, the interviewer will have come up with an important finding concerning the woman's motivation. Or when a man says that he enjoyed a job because he was able to deal with high-level people from the best families, the implication may be that he is prestige-oriented. Of course, such a clue in itself provides only the slightest evidence. The interviewer mentally catalogues it, however, and subsequently looks for additional specific clues that may confirm it. If such confirmation is eventually forthcoming, he or she will have identified an important shortcoming in terms of the individual's ability to get along with people. As indicated above, likes may provide clues to both assets and shortcomings. Someone who enjoyed a given job because she had a good deal of freedom may be saying that she is the kind of person who, on the one hand, likes responsibility but, on the other hand, tends to be overly independent. In response to such a finding, then, the interviewer would do some two-step probing in an effort to find out what there was about having a completely free hand that gave the individual so much satisfaction.

THINGS FOUND LESS SATISFYING

Having had a chance to discuss likes in considerable detail, the candidate is normally quite willing to talk about dislikes, particularly if good rapport has been established. At the same time, the interviewer should approach this subject adroitly by softening the follow-up question. Instead of asking about a person's dislikes, he should pose such a question as, "What were some of the things you found less satisfying on that job?" It is possible that an applicant may not have any actual job dislikes in a particular situation, but considered relatively there are always some aspects of a job that are less satisfying than others. In the event that the candidate is able to come up with very little in the way of things that were less appealing to her, the interviewer should stimulate the discussion by means of a laundry-list question. He can say, "What were some of the other things that were less appealing on that job—were they concerned with the earnings, the type of supervision you received, the amount of detail involved, or perhaps the lack of opportunity to use your own initiative?"

If the interviewer has previously formed an initial hypothesis about certain possible shortcomings, he will include pertinent items in the laundry-list question. Thus if he suspects laziness, he might include such an item as "and an overly demanding supervisor" in the laundry-list question as one of the possible job factors the individual may have found less satisfying. Remember, too, that probing for job dislikes often results in spontaneous information as to why the person eventually left the job. If such information can be obtained indirectly and spontaneously, the real truth of the matter is more likely to be elicited. The candidate may say, for example, "I just couldn't see eye to eye with my supervisor, and quite frankly that was why I left." In such a situation, the interviewer would naturally probe deeper by saying, "Some bosses are certainly very hard to get along with. What was your boss's particular problem?" Once he has obtained the full story, the interviewer would of course *play down* the resulting information, in that way reassuring the applicant.

Information concerning job dissatisfactions can provide a wide variety of clues to the individual's possible shortcomings. He may admit, for example, that the mathematical-calculations aspect of his job represented a factor of dissatisfaction, and he may further disclose the fact that he does not consider himself particularly qualified in this area. The interviewer would then have a strong clue to lack of mathematical aptitude. If test scores are available and if they show below-average numerical ability, the interview finding in this case would confirm the results of the test. Another applicant may volunteer the information that she disliked being left on her own so much of the time without much direction from above. This might provide a clue to lack of confidence and a tendency to be dependent upon others. In another job situation, the candidate may reveal that the assignment was not sufficiently well structured. This may indicate a clue to the inability to plan and organize, as well as a possible lack of initiative. Still another may complain about the fact that he was required to juggle too many balls in the air at one time. Such a comment might point to the possible lack of flexibility and adaptability. Lack of general mental ability might be another possible interpretation. In any event, the interviewer carefully catalogues such clues and looks subsequently for supporting data.

Discussion of job dislikes can also reveal clues to assets. In fact, the very willingness to talk about dislikes frequently provides clues to honesty, sincerity, and self-confidence. In supplying negative information, the individual in a sense says, "This is the way I am constituted; if you don't have a place for me here, I am confident of my ability to locate something somewhere else." When an applicant discusses negative information candidly and objectively, the interviewer soon comes to the conclusion that she is getting the complete story, and she gives the person credit for being honest and sincere.

CONDITIONED TO WORK?

People who have become conditioned to hard work and long hours in the past can be expected to apply themselves with like diligence in the future. Particularly when they have found it necessary to extend themselves by working 60 or 70 hours a week or by going to school at night while carrying on a full-time job during the day, they normally develop a greater capacity for constructive effort than might otherwise have been the case. In contrast, when they are subsequently confronted with an 8-hour day, they find it quite possible to apply themselves vigorously throughout the 8-hour period without feeling unduly weary. A boy brought up on a farm often gets up at five o'clock, milks the cows before school, and does the chores at night after having studied all day. Having become accustomed to long hours, he normally finds it very easy to work hard in the shop for a normal 8-hour period, provided he can adjust to the confinement of indoor work.

A young woman who works after school and during summers while going to high school and college normally develops work habits that stand her in good stead later on. On the other hand, the college graduate who has never worked at all may be expected to find adjustment to the first postcollege job somewhat difficult. Of course, such individuals should not be excluded from further consideration because of lack of any kind of work experience, but this should nevertheless be included in the overall evaluation as a possibly unfavorable factor.

As the applicant talks about working conditions on previous jobs, the interviewer should mentally compare such conditions with specifications of the job for which he is being evaluated. If the job requires working under pressure, for example, the interviewer will look specifically for any previous jobs carried out by the applicant where pressure was an important factor. In addition, she will try to get the subject's reaction to such pressure. If an individual found it hard to work under pressure and even includes this as a reason for leaving a particular job, his qualifications for the new job would be viewed with some question. Or, if the new job is fast-moving and requires quick changes of reference, the interviewer would look specifically for previous exposure of the applicant to situations of this kind. If he has enjoyed and been stimulated by such working conditions in the past, this would obviously represent a definite asset. On the other hand, expressed dissatisfaction with conditions of this kind would represent a negative factor.

In an earlier chapter of this book, we discussed the value of not tipping one's hand—getting the information from the applicant before giving information about the job. This is especially true with respect to working conditions. If the individual really wants the proposed assignment, she will hardly be inclined to express dissatisfaction about certain job factors that she knows exist in the position for which she is applying.

Working conditions also include the degree of supervision to which individuals have become accustomed. Here again, using the job specifications as a base, the interviewer should try to determine the extent to which the type of supervision may be expected to represent an adjustment factor, in terms of the contrast between the degree of supervision to which applicants have become accustomed and the supervision they would encounter on the proposed assignment. As we have already pointed out in another chapter, people who have grown accustomed to relatively little supervision on past jobs—where they have ordered their own lives, laid out their own work, and made many of their own decisions—will ordinarily chafe under close supervision in a subsequent job situation. Obviously, they are not excluded from further consideration on this basis alone, but it nevertheless represents a negative factor. The type of supervision under which people worked in the past may provide clues to possible abilities and personality characteristics. If they have operated successfully without close supervision, for example, they may be the type of people who have a good bit of initiative and who have so much ability that their supervisors trust them to carry out day-to-day tasks without checking up on them very frequently. Moreover, natural leaders are normally people who like to work without close supervision. They enjoy the degree of responsibility that such a situation permits. And they derive satisfaction from an opportunity to exercise their own initiative.

LEVEL OF EARNINGS

Since information about earnings may represent a somewhat delicate subject in the case of some applicants, this question should be approached with considerable adroitness. In the first place, as noted earlier, interviewers should get candidates in the habit of talking about earnings by asking them to give this information on early jobs. Since few people object to talking about the salary they made on jobs some years ago, they willingly supply these facts. If, moreover, they are encouraged to give salary information on each job, they provide salary figures on their most recent experience pretty much as a matter of course. On the other hand, if interviewers wait for the most recent job experience before asking about earnings, applicants may try to fence with them. A question such as, "What happened to your earnings on that job?" usually proves quite efficient, since individuals normally discuss both starting and termination pay.

Pattern of earnings over the years represents one important criterion of the individual's job progress to date. In cases where the applicant's earnings have gone up rather quickly, it can usually be assumed that she is a person of some ability. In cases like this, the interviewer will want to probe for the reasons why the individual has done so well, since such probing may provide clues to her major assets. Again, the question, "What traits were you able to demonstrate that caused your supervisor to raise your salary so handsomely?" will often result in valuable information. On the other hand, earnings are not always a true reflection of ability. A man may have been in the right place at the right time, may have been given special treatment because his father was a partial owner of the company, or may have been successful in impressing his superiors on the basis of his persuasive personality rather than because of his real ability.

Just as a rapid rise in earnings normally points to the existence of assets, so does lack of salary progress frequently reflect a series of significant shortcomings. A woman in her middle thirties who has shown relatively little salary progress in the last 10 years is usually lacking in either ability, effectiveness of personality, or motivation. In probing for the reasons, however, the interviewer may find that the applicant has been confronted with circumstances somewhat beyond her control. He may find that the individual has been working in a relatively low-paying industry such as the utilities industry or that she has been reluctant to give up the security of that particular job because of the serious illness of a family member. In probing for the real reasons, the interviewer should obviously avoid such a direct question as, "How do you account for your failure to earn more money over the years?" Rather, he should approach this situation more indirectly, bringing up the question under the discussion of job dislikes. If the applicant does not mention salary as a factor of dissatisfaction, the interviewer can say, "How do you feel about your salary? Are you relatively satisfied with what you are making or do you think that your job merits somewhat more?" The subsequent response may indicate a number of interesting clues to behavior, including lack of salary aspirations, bitterness over lack of salary progress, rationalization of the situation, or general recognition of shortcomings and willingness to accept her lot in life.

In evaluating salary progress, one should keep the level of the individual's basic abilities in mind. If a person is bright mentally and has good general abilities, lack of salary aspirations may point to inadequate motivation. In the case of an individual who is somewhat limited intellectually but has nevertheless been moved along rapidly, subsequent frustration will almost certainly occur. Such a person has become accustomed to rapid promotion and hence expects this pattern to be maintained. The time will undoubtedly come, however, when mental limitations will preclude further promotion, at which time the person will probably become a most unhappy individual. On the other hand, a mentally limited individual who has learned to accept such limitations and not to expect too much has usually attained an admirable degree of emotional maturity.

In selecting an individual for a new job, consideration should be given to the relationship between the applicant's earnings on his last job and the starting salary on the job for which he is being considered. If he has already earned appreciably more than he can be expected to start at on the new job, serious dissatisfaction is likely to develop later on. At the time of the interview, he may profess a willingness to take the new job because of its greater opportunities. Once on that job, however, he will normally become relatively unhappy—at least until such time as his salary equals his previous earnings. On the other hand, the individual whose previous earnings have been substantially less than those of the job for which she is being considered represents a different kind of a problem. The interviewer naturally wonders why her earnings have failed to keep pace with her years of experience and probes for the underlying reasons.

REASONS FOR CHANGING JOBS

This is one of the most delicate aspects of the interview, since many applicants are sensitive about their reasons for having left certain jobs. Therefore, we try to get this information spontaneously and indirectly by probing for job dislikes. If this fails, however, we have to approach the situation more dircctly with a softened follow-up question such as, "How did you happen to leave that job?" In posing this question, the interviewer should of course give particular attention to her facial expressions and vocal intonations, in order to give the appearance of seeming as disarming and permissive as possible. Even so, some applicants may not give the real reason why they left a certain job. Hence the interviewer must be alert for any indication of rationalization, since this type of response usually means that the individual is trying to hide the real reason by attempting to explain away the situation. If an interviewer is not convinced that a person is telling the truth, she certainly should not challenge him at this point. To do so would be to risk loss of rapport and subsequent lack of spontaneous discussion throughout the remainder of the interview. Rather, she should wait until the interview is nearly concluded—when there is little or nothing to lose. If she is still interested in the candidate's qualifications, she can reintroduce the subject by asking him more directly to elaborate upon his reasons for the job change in question.

When a candidate leaves a number of jobs to make a little more money on subsequent ones, she may represent the kind of person who has too strong an economic drive. Now strong desire to make money is a definite asset on some jobs—particularly those involving selling on a commission basis. The salesperson who wants to make a lot of money is usually one who will work harder to get it. At the same time, when the economic drive becomes too strong, the individual often develops into something of an opportunist. In other words, she will immediately jump into any new situation that pays her a little more. Such a person seldom develops strong loyalties. The interviewer has a right to say to himself, "Since this person has a habit of leaving each job whenever she gets a chance to make a little more money, I wonder how long we would be able to keep her happy here?"

When an applicant leaves a series of jobs because of dissatisfaction with job duties or working conditions, he may be the type of person who lacks perseverance and follow-through. Perhaps unable to take the bitter with the sweet, he "pulls up stakes" whenever he is confronted with anything really difficult or not to his liking. If such proves to be the case, a clear indication of immaturity will be apparent. When dissatisfaction appears to be chronic from job to job, the individual concerned may be poorly adjusted emotionally, in the sense that he may be somewhat bitter toward life and may take a negative attitude toward things in general.

If reactions to a series of jobs indicate friction with supervisors or coworkers, interviewers should look specifically for indications of quick temper, inflexibility, intolerance, oversensitivity, and immaturity. When they suspect the possible existence of some of these traits, they should use such a question as, "How did you feel about your relationships with your superiors and associates on that job? Were you completely satisfied with these relationships or, in retrospect, do you think that they could have been improved to some extent?"

Discussion of reasons for leaving jobs may provide clues to assets as well as liabilities. In talking about a previous job from which he had been fired, for example, an applicant may assume some of the blame, indicating that he was "just off base" in that situation. Such candor often reflects objectivity, honesty, and maturity.

In leaving certain job situations, moreover, the individual may demonstrate such positive factors as initiative and desire for further growth and development. If she has been in a dead-end situation with little opportunity for promotion, she certainly cannot be blamed for leaving it. If she is a person of considerable ability and leaves a given job to obtain broader experience and responsibility, this is again something that one should expect in any competent individual.

In discussing job changes, it is often helpful to explore how such changes came about. Did the candidate take the initiative herself? Did the suggestion come from her superiors? Or was she recruited for a better job by another company? The latter, incidentally, may tell something about her general reputation in her field.

LEADERSHIP EXPERIENCE

Throughout the discussion of the work experience, interviewers should carefully note the frequency with which applicants have been promoted to supervisory responsibility, together with their reactions to such responsibility. If individuals have derived considerable satisfaction from this kind of experience, and if they have been asked frequently to take over the direction of others, they are quite probably people of some leadership ability. Certainly, a number of their previous superiors have thought so. Moreover, people who have led successfully in any situation have acquired skills in handling others that nothing but experience of this sort will provide.

In evaluating the possible effectiveness of an individual as a supervisor, look specifically for demonstrated ability to communicate, to plan and organize, to delegate important responsibilities to others, to be contagiously enthusiastic, to be fair, and to be sensitive to the feelings of others. It is equally important to find out whether the individual has shown a tendency to dictate to others or whether the candidate has been able to motivate other people to work because they like and respect him or her.

NUMBER OF PREVIOUS JOBS

In evaluating the applicant's work experience, interviewers should note among other things the frequency of job changes. Since many students in school do not get very much in the way of vocational guidance, it sometimes takes them a little while to find the right type of job once they have graduated. Hence, frequency of job change is not particularly unusual during late adolescence or in the early twenties. But if this pattern extends through the late twenties and thereafter, it can be assumed that such individuals may have some rather deep-seated problems. If they fail to stay with any of their jobs at least 3 years, they may very well be the kind of person who has not yet found him or herself, thus demonstrating immaturity. Many "job jumpers" lack self-discipline, perseverance, and follow-through. Some of them are opportunists and still others are not very stable emotionally. At the very least, frequent job changes should alert interviewers to the possible existence of serious shortcomings. In every case, however, they will want to probe specifically for the underlying reasons.

A certain number of job changes over a period of some years is of course to be expected. Many people have good reasons for leaving one job to go to another—to increase their earnings, enhance their opportunities for promotion, and broaden their experience. In some occupations, such as advertising, moreover, rather frequent job change is considered something of a matter of course. An advertising agency may obtain a large account and hire as many as thirty or forty additional people to handle this additional business. At the end of the year, the agency may lose the account and be forced to terminate a considerable number of its employees. Even so, such an organization can usually find a place for a new employee who has turned in an outstanding job performance.

ACHIEVEMENTS

Once interviewers have discussed the applicants' complete job history—from the first position to the most recent assignment—they should try to help individuals summarize *achievements*, in terms of abilities and personality traits, that have been brought to light as a result of their experience on various jobs. This is done by formally introducing the technique of *self-evaluation* for the first time in the interview. In order to accomplish this, the question which appears on the Interview Guide is utilized: "What did you learn about your strengths as a result of working on those jobs? Did you find, for example, that you worked harder than the average person, got along better with people, organized things better, gave more attention to detail—just what?" It will be noted that the technique of self-evaluation is introduced by means of a laundry-list question. This is because most individuals will not have taken the time to analyze their strengths in terms of the abilities and personality traits interviewers are seeking to identify. Hence, applicants need the assistance of the laundry-list question.

Helping Candidates Discuss Their Assets

Interviewers should ask individuals to discuss assets candidly, pointing out that they should do this objectively without any feeling that they are bragging. Immediately after each asset has been presented, moreover, interviewers should *lubricate the situation* by giving candidates a verbal pat on the back. If an individual indicates that he is a hard worker, for example, and if the interviewer has already seen abundant evidence of this trait, she might say, "I'm sure you are a very hard worker, and that's a wonderful asset to have!" On the other hand, if she has a question about the individual's motivation, she will simply nod her head, ask the applicant to indicate some of his other assets, and resolve to reintroduce the subject of hard work later on when talking about the individual's shortcomings.

Some candidates may find it difficult to list their real assets. In this case, interviewers should stimulate the discussion by pointing out one or two strengths he has already observed. Thus, he might say, "Well, I have observed that you seem to get along unusually well with people, and this of course is a tremendous asset in any job situation." After "priming the pump" with one or two such observations, the interviewer should pass the conversational ball back to the candidate, asking her to tell about some of her other strong points. If she seems to be unable to come up with any additional assets on her own, make use of the *calculated pause*, in this way giving her an opportunity to organize her thoughts. If, after 10 or 12 seconds, she is still unable to come up with anything, the interviewer should "take her off the hook" by introducing another asset which he has observed during the interview. In some cases, a considerable amount of "pump priming" may be necessary before the candidate begins to talk about some of her own strengths, but the interviewer should wait her out, using as much patience as he can muster.

The interviewer should not leave this important subject until he has developed a significant list of genuine assets, even if he has to interject a number of these himself. Once the applicant has been encouraged to think critically about her own strengths, she frequently warms to the task and generates a considerable amount of very useful information here. She may reveal, for example, that she gets along particularly well with people. And she may be able to document this by telling about the closeness of her relationships with certain individuals, pointing to correspondence and other contacts that she has had with those individuals since leaving the company, or by the fact that her friends surprised her with a dinner in her honor at the time she left. Or, she may list creative ability as an asset. In probing more deeply for evidence of such ability, the interviewer may find that the applicant has several patents to her credit and has published a series of articles in the technical journals. When such evidence is presented, the interviewer will of course want to know whether these patents and articles came as a result of the individual's single-handed achievement or whether other people were also involved. Since applicants are naturally interested in selling themselves, their stated achievements cannot always be taken at face value. This is why they should be encouraged to supply documentary evidence.

It is extremely important that the interviewer help the applicant develop a sizable list of assets, since this paves the way for a subsequent discussion of shortcomings. In other words, one cannot expect a person to discuss shortcomings at length if the applicant is not certain that the interviewer is well-acquainted with his or her strengths. More important still, in successfully developing a list of the candidate's achievements, the interviewer will have planted the seed of self-evaluation at this relatively early stage of the interview. And, as a consequence, the applicant may spontaneously volunteer further self-evaluative material during discussion of subsequent areas of the interview—education, and present social adjustment. It is for this reason that the technique of self-evaluation is introduced at this point of the interview.

DEVELOPMENT NEEDS

Having had an opportunity to discuss his or her strengths at some length, an applicant normally finds it relatively easy to talk about some of the areas that need further development. However, since this represents the first real confrontation in terms of asking specifically about shortcomings, appropriate rationale must be provided. This subject can be introduced by the question that appears in the Interview Guide: "Did you get any clues to your development needs as a result of working on those jobs? You know, we all have some shortcomings and, the person who can recognize them, can do something about them. Was there a need to acquire more self-confidence, more tact, more self-discipline—to become firmer with people—just what?" This question and the one pertaining to achievement appearing on the Interview Guide should be committed to memory verbatim, in that way helping interviewers develop more facility during the interview.

Helping Applicants Discuss Their Shortcomings

In discussing an applicant's developmental needs, always use the word "shortcomings" rather than "weaknesses," "faults," or "liabilities." The latter three words carry the connotation that the trait may be so serious that very little can be done about it. The word "shortcomings," on the other hand, implies that the trait is just a little short of what it might desirably be and that hence the person may be able to improve upon it or eliminate it. In talking about shortcomings, moreover, refer frequently to the phrase "ways in which you can improve yourself." Thus, instead of saying, "What are some other shortcomings?" it is better to say, "What are some other ways in which you might improve yourself?"

Immediately after each shortcoming has been presented, the interviewer should "play it down," in much the same way that any other piece of unfavorable information is played down throughout the interview. When an individual admits, for example, the need to develop more self-confidence, the interviewer might say, "Well, confidence is a trait that a lot of people need to develop further. I'm sure your self-confidence will improve with more experience." When a person admits a shortcoming, such as lack of mental toughness, the interviewer should play this down by complimenting the individual for having recognized it and for facing up to it. Thus, the interviewer may say, "You deserve credit for being able to recognize this. And, because you have recognized it, you probably have already taken certain steps toward eliminating it."

When the applicant finds it difficult or seems reluctant to present any shortcomings, the interviewer may stimulate the discussion by the use of *double-edged questions*. If an interviewer has already noted that the applicant is quite lacking in self-discipline, for example, she may say, "What about self-discipline? Do you think you have as much of this as you would like to have, or does this represent an area in which you could improve to some extent?" Such a question makes it easy for a person to admit shortcomings. Again, if the interviewer has noticed a general tendency to be lazy, she might say, "What about work habits? Do you think that you usually work as hard as you should, or is this something that you could improve a little bit?"

For the most part, indicated shortcomings can be taken pretty much at face value. Seldom will one draw attention to shortcomings that do not really exist. At the same time, there is the occasional individual—one who is exceedingly insecure and tends to underestimate his or her abilities—who will bring up something as a shortcoming that is not a deficiency.

The interviewer's role in the self-evaluation discussion is a pivotal one. If he tries to stimulate the discussion by introducing assets or shortcomings that are not part of the applicant's makeup, the latter quickly loses respect for him. On the other hand, if he is able to introduce traits that go to the very heart of the individual's personality and motivational pattern, the latter gains appreciable respect for him.

The Value of the Self-evaluation Technique

As noted above, this technique can be of considerable value to both applicants and the interviewers. Applicants gain by getting a clearer picture of their strengths and developmental needs, thus acquiring greater insight. And interviewers gain because they are frequently able to get more documentary evidence concerning a given candidate's overall qualifications.

When interviewers are able to get applicants to agree with them on the presence or absence of certain traits, this obviously provides strong support for the original diagnosis. When, for example, an interviewer has seen several clues to insecurity throughout the interview, she waits expectantly for some indication of this in the candidate's self-evaluation. If lack of self-confidence is spontaneously admitted, or admitted as a result of probing with a double-edged question, the interviewer has of course developed further confirmation of her original hypothesis. And since the person is aware of this developmental need, he may be able to do something about improving himself in this respect.

Occasionally the applicant will mention a trait that may not have consciously crystallized in the interviewer's mind but for which he sees abundant evidence as soon as it is verbalized. In other words, he may have been only vaguely aware of the trait but, when the applicant mentions it specifically, he can immediately think of a number of clues that actually pointed in that direction. If the applicant had not mentioned this trait, the interviewer might not have factored it into his overall decision.

When the candidate mentions an asset or shortcoming for which the interviewer has seen no support, it is well to ask the individual to elaborate. Subsequent remarks may convince the interviewer that the applicant actually possesses the trait in question, thus bringing to light valuable information that might otherwise have been missed. To illustrate this point, let us assume that the individual mentions mental toughness as an asset. If the interviewer has seen little or no evidence of this, she might say, "What are some of the things you have done in the past that helped you reach this conclusion?" In the ensuing discussion, the candidate may point to a series of confrontations that had not previously come up in the conversation. After getting this additional information, the interviewer may be quite convinced that the individual really is tough-minded. In this instance, the self-evaluation technique operated as insurance against leaving out something that was really important. In trying to justify tough-mindedness as an asset, on the other hand, the individual's supporting reasons may be altogether superficial. In that case, of course, the interviewer would simply nod her head and ask for additional strong points, still not convinced that the person is in fact tough-minded.

In dealing with young applicants who have had limited work experience, do not confine the discussion of strengths and shortcomings to the work situation alone. Broaden the laundry-list question as follows: "*What did you learn about your strengths as a result of working on those jobs or as a result of any of your other life experiences?*"

FACTORS OF JOB SATISFACTION

At this point, the interviewer has not only discussed the applicant's jobs but has tried to plant the seed of self-evaluation by asking for a summary of strengths and development needs of which the applicant has become aware while working on these various jobs. Hence, we can now give our attention to a very fruitful area—factors of job satisfaction. This subject can be well introduced with the laundry-list question on the Interview Guide: "What does a job have to have to give you satisfaction? Some people look for money, some look for security, some want to manage, some want to create—what is important to you?" Again, the applicant's response to such a depth question may provide clues to analytical ability and intellectual depth. One individual may say, "Oh, I just want a job where I can be happy and make an honest living." Another person may reflect a great deal more discernment and intellectual depth by such a remark as: "In looking for a new job, I have given this subject a great deal of thought. I am looking primarily for an opportunity to grow and develop—to find the type of job that will provide the greatest challenge and do the most to bring out the best that is in me. Money is of course important, but I consider that secondary. Security probably ranks at the bottom of my list, since I feel that I can always make a living somewhere." A response such as this tells the interviewer a good bit about the individual's drives and aspirations, as well as about the quality of his or her thinking. The applicant's lack of emphasis on security, moreover, may provide a clue to his or her self-confidence.

If a candidate "blocks" at this point, give him a chance to organize his thinking by making use of the *calculated pause*. If he still seems to have a problem, repeat part of your laundry-list question or select one of the items and ask him rather directly how he feels about it. The interviewer may say, "Well, how do you feel about security, for example? Is this important to you or perhaps not so much so?"

Actually, discussion of job-satisfaction factors presents the interviewer with an excellent opportunity to obtain further confirmation of clues that have come to her attention earlier in the work discussion. For example, if she has noted some dislike for detail, she can include the phrase,

"Some like detail while others do not," in her laundry-list question. If the applicant seizes upon this with the statement, "Well, for one thing, I certainly do not want to be involved with such detail; I prefer to delegate this to others," the interviewer is presented with additional confirmation of her original hypothesis. If the interviewer has a suspicion that the candidate may be lazy, she can include in her laundry-list question the phrase, "Some people want regular hours while others do not mind spending extra time on a job—time that may interfere with family life." Again, the applicant might say, "I believe that 7 or 8 hours a day on a job is enough for anybody. My family certainly comes first and I don't intend to let my job interfere." Such a statement may indicate that an individual is unwilling to make present sacrifices for future gains, and this also may provide an additional clue to lack of motivation.

When applicants appear to have answered the question on job satisfaction to the best of their ability, probe further, using some of the items in parenthesis at the end of this question on the Interview Guide. Say, for example: "What else should a job have to give you satisfaction? Should it be structured or unstructured?" Once that has been answered, say: "Should it be more theoretical or more practical?" After that response, say: "If you had a choice, would you prefer a job that had a fair amount of detail or one that did not have so much?" Responses to these questions can throw further light on factors that may enhance optimal placement.

Factors of job satisfaction represent a very fruitful area for discussion: hence, at least 4 or 5 minutes should be devoted to this subject. The interviewer should then mentally compare the applicant's expressed desires with the specifications of the position in question. If a woman is looking for a job that provides a great deal of mental challenge, for example, it would be a mistake to assign her to a job situation that made few mental demands. Or, if a man seems to be greatly interested in money, this factor should be considered in terms of the salary opportunities in the position for which he is being considered. Of course, many young people just out of school may not be able to come up with very much in the way of job-satisfaction factors. This obviously should not be held against them, since they have not been exposed to enough job situations to enable them to form any real conclusions as to the factors that give them greatest satisfaction.

TYPE OF JOB DESIRED

The work-history discussions should be concluded with a question concerning the kind of job for which the candidate is looking. In the case of older people with some years of specific experience in a given area, this question may be unnecessary, since they may be applying for a definite type of work. This may also be true in the case of people who were referred to the company as a result of a newspaper advertisement. On the other hand, many younger people have no specific job situation in mind. In fact, many such individuals are looking for some kind of guidance in this respect. If they do mention the kind of a job they think they would like to have, it is good to say, "What is there about that type of job that you think might interest you?" The ensuing discussion may reveal that the individual has some good and valid reasons for his or her choice and, in the case of a younger person, this would provide a definite clue to emotional maturity.

When a candidate says she really does not know what she wants, however, the interviewer should attempt to narrow the field for her to some extent. In the case of a recently graduated engineer, for example, he could say, "Well, do you think you might prefer basic research, development work, production, or technical service work?" The interviewer would then try to get the individual's reaction to these fields of work and compare these reactions with what he has already learned about the person as a result of the previous discussion. The individual frequently does a little self-evaluation at this point. She may say, for example: "Well, I certainly know that I don't want research or development work. I learned in school that I am no whiz on a purely technical assignment." If, on the basis of available test results and previous work-history discussion, the interviewer concurs with the candidate, he may then explore the individual's possible interest in production or technical service. Or, he may decide to postpone this particular discussion until the end of the interview—until he has learned more about the individual and thus has a better basis for helping her with her placement decision.

As the work-history discussion draws to a close, the interviewer mentally reflects on the candidate's total job accomplishment. Has the individual made normal progress in terms of salary? Has he acquired a solid background of experience in his specialty? Has he shown an ability to assume gradually increased responsibility? If the answer to any of these important questions is negative, the interviewer may begin to have a real reservation concerning the candidate's overall qualifications. In some cases, in fact, the situation may be so clear-cut that the interviewer can decide then and there not to hire the applicant. In such a situation, she would talk very briefly about the individual's educational background and then terminate the discussion. Not only is it unfair to waste the applicant's time but the interviewer also has to be economical with her own time.

EEO CONSIDERATIONS

1. Many members of minority groups need no special consideration with regard to the interpretation of work history. Their achievement speaks for itself.
2. There are other minority men and women whose work history does not appear very impressive because they have not yet been given an opportunity to demonstrate what they really can do. Since interviewers must try to *screen in* as many minorities as possible, it becomes their job to identify those individuals who have *potential* for greater achievement than their work history would seem to indicate. Some of the following areas may give evidence of such potential:
   - **a.** Probe especially for how each job was obtained, as a possible indication of initiative.
   - **b.** Look for any increased responsibility within a job, even though the job may have been rather routine. For example, the individual may have been promoted to lower levels of supervision such as crew leader, straw boss, or chief clerk.
   - **c.** Give special attention to indications of hard work, such as extremely long hours or physically demanding job duties. A good question here: "To what extent was that job demanding physically?"
   - **d.** Be quick to note significant progress from job to job in terms of more responsibility or higher pay, even though many of the jobs have been routine.
3. Do not be critical of job changes when the new jobs represent increasingly better situations. We cannot expect a person to stay with a low-level, uninteresting job for any great length of time if advancement is possible elsewhere. In probing for reasons for changing jobs, then, try to determine whether or not the new job

really did represent a measurable improvement over the previous one or whether the hopping from job to job is because the person finds it difficult to stay put.

4. In discussing *factors of job satisfaction*, give favorable consideration to the man or woman who seems to have a genuine desire to make something better of himself or herself, even though the individual may not yet have been given much of an opportunity. People who have not given up hope deserve more consideration than those who have become cynical or pessimistic.
5. With all applicants, the discussion of *strengths* and *shortcomings* at the end of the work history will be difficult. Interviewers must therefore exercise great patience in developing this information. They will have to do more "pump priming" in terms of introducing strengths and shortcomings that they have observed during the interview. But, once applicants have acquired a definite understanding of what they are expected to do, they can often come up with very valuable information about themselves.
6. In thinking back over the entire work experience, try to determine whether the person was consistently overqualified for many of the jobs held, in the sense that the person could have handled more responsibility if given an opportunity. This situation would seem to indicate that, with special training, the applicant could take over the job under consideration even though his or her work experience may not have been relevant to the job in question.

CHAPTER 12

Interpreting Education and Present Social Adjustment

Applicants for most higher-level jobs will usually be college graduates, and many will have gone to graduate school. These years represent a large segment of the individual's life, during which time he or she has had ample opportunity to display a considerable number of assets or shortcomings, as the case may be. Interpretation of the educational history, then, is not only concerned with whether or not the individual has acquired sufficient training to carry out the job in question; it is also concerned with the evaluation of abilities, personality traits, and motivation.

In the case of younger applicants, in particular, the educational experience may represent the most important period of the individual's life and, as such, may provide the greatest source of clues to behavior. Although education does not represent quite such a dominant factor in the case of older applicants, it is nevertheless exceedingly important. The traits that individuals develop while in school often remain with them throughout life. Moreover, the discussion of educational history frequently provides additional confirming evidence of traits that had been tentatively identified during the discussion of work experience. Thus, applicants who tend to be lazy on the job can be better understood if it can also be determined that they did not apply themselves in school. In other words, such people have never been conditioned to hard work and hence, have never developed strong motivation.

In this chapter, we shall discuss the items appearing under education and training in chronological order as they are listed in the Interview Guide. Each item will be discussed not only in terms of its contribution to the individual's educational attainment, but also in terms of possible reflection of clues to abilities, personality, and motivation.

STRUCTURING THE DISCUSSION OF EDUCATION

Having completed the discussion of work history, the interviewer uses a comprehensive introductory question to launch the subject of education. In so doing, she tries to make the transition from the first interview area to the second in such a way that the discussion appears to be a *continuing conversation*, rather than a segmented one. Thus, the interviewer may preface her comprehensive introductory question by saying, "That gives me a very good picture of your work experience; now tell me something about your education and training." In the comprehensive introductory question the interviewer should point point out that she would like to have the applicant talk about such factors as subject preferences, grades, and extracurricular activities. She should also indicate that she would like to have the individual start with a discussion of high school experience and go on from there to college. A comprehensive question such as the following should suffice: "*I would be interested in the subjects you liked best, those you did not like so well, the level of your grades, and your extracurricular activities. Start with high school and go on to college. What were your favorite subjects in high school?"*

Chronology is just as important here as it is in work history. The interviewer should get the full story of the candidate's high school experience before permitting her to talk very much about college. If the candidate jumps ahead by beginning to talk about college before she has given a complete picture of her activities in high school, the interviewer should control the situation by making a positive comment and redirecting her to the high school area. He might say, for example, "Being able to play on the college basketball team must have given you a great deal of satisfaction. By the way, were there any other extracurricular activities in high school?" In getting the high school story first, the interviewer can trace the candidate's progress through school. He may note, for example, that an individual did quite well with high school studies but experienced more difficulty as the subject matter became more difficult in college. Or he may observe that the candidate was a "big frog in a little puddle," while in high school but, up against sterner competition in college, was not able to compete successfully. Findings such as these represent probable indications of some limitations and help the interviewer to establish the level of the candidate's vocational ceiling.

In response to an adroitly worded comprehensive introductory question, the candidate will normally discuss much of her school experiences spontaneously. If she leaves out important items or does not discuss certain topics in sufficient detail, the interviewer will use appropriate follow-up questions in an effort to get the complete story. He will also use such questions to probe more deeply for the underlying implication of certain of the applicant's remarks. After the individual completes the discussion of her high school experience, the interviewer may wish to repeat part of his comprehensive introductory question by saying, "Suppose you tell me a little about college now—your subject preferences, grades, extracurricular activities, and the like."

BEST AND POOREST SUBJECTS

If the candidate forgets to include subject preferences in his discussion, the interviewer should approach this by asking about his subject interests, particularly since interests tend to correlate with abilities. She can say very simply, "What were some of the subjects you enjoyed most in high school?" Preference for such highly verbal subjects as English, history, and languages normally reflects a certain amount of *verbal ability*, particularly when grades in such subjects have been relatively high. If verbal ability represents one of the job requirements, the interviewer will have identified strong clues to an important asset. Another applicant may reflect strong scientific interests through preferences for chemistry, biology, and physics. When such preferences are combined with interest and ability in mathematics, considerable aptitude for work of a technical nature would normally be indicated.

In discussing subject preferences in college, it is good to ask the individual whether she most enjoyed the more practical subjects or the more highly theoretical courses. In the case of an engineer, for example, the interviewer might say, "Did you enjoy the more practical courses such as unit operations and your laboratory work, or did you derive more satisfaction from the more highly theoretical courses such as thermodynamics?" Lack of interest and ability in the more theoretical courses may sometimes indicate certain mental limitations—inability to deal with things in the abstract. This interpretation of course becomes all the more valid if test results reflect mediocre mental equipment. Other things being equal, the more practically oriented engineers usually derive greatest satisfaction from assignments in production, applications engineering, or technical service. The more theoretically inclined technical people usually get more satisfaction from research and development.

Subject dislikes, introduced by such a question as, "What were some of the subjects you found less satisfying?" can provide important clues to shortcomings. When an applicant dislikes a subject, it may mean that he had either little aptitude for that subject or failed to study hard enough to awaken an interest in it. When a person does poorly in a subject that represents an important factor in the specifications of the job for which he is being considered, an important shortcoming will have been identified. And this is particularly true when poor performance in school is supported by low aptitude-test scores. Some knowledge of course content in various fields is also helpful to the interviewer. If a given individual has relatively poor mathematical ability, the interviewer can understand the candidate's difficulty with physical chemistry, since this course has a rather high mathematical content.

It is not enough to know that an applicant liked or disliked a certain subject. The interviewer should be interested in finding out *why.* She does this by using a typical "why" question, "What was there about physics that seemed to trouble you?" In response the applicant might say, "Oh, I was completely over my head in that subject. Even though I studied hard, I never could quite seem to understand the theoretical aspects." Or in response to a question as to why he did not like quantitative chemistry, an applicant might say, "That subject requires a good memory, and memory has never been one of my attributes." As indicated in an earlier chapter, probing for the *why* of subject preferences often provides clues to analytical ability and intellectual depth. Some people may be unable to give other than superficial reasons whereas others can provide detailed, analytical statements. In any case, the information that flows from this particular discussion should be carefully checked with the requirements of the worker specifications.

GRADES

If the candidate does not specifically mention grades, the interviewer may say, "What about grades? Were they average, above average, or perhaps a little below average?" Note that such a question makes it relatively easier for the individual to admit grades that were below average. Where grades are indicated as above average, an attempt should be made to determine the applicant's actual ranking in the class. Was it upper half, upper third, upper quarter, or upper tenth? When a person provides a ranking, such as ninth in the class, he or she should be asked about the number in the class. It is conceivable that the entire class may have had no more than eleven or twelve students. On the other hand, a standing of ninth in a class of four hundred would represent a real achievement.

School achievement as reflected in grades may provide clues to *ability* and *motivation*. They also may reflect the academic standards of the school. In any case, the interviewer should make a real effort to identify the major factors responsible for grade level, whether such level is high or low.

If test scores are available, the interviewer's interpretation of grade level is greatly facilitated. A high score on a mental test means, among other things, that the individual has the ability to learn rapidly, absorbing new information quickly. Hence, such a person is expected to get good grades in school. When an individual with a high mental-test score indicates having made poor grades in school, the interviewer should be alerted to the possibility that the applicant did not work very hard. Further probing may indicate lack of perseverance, procrastination, or disorganized study habits. Moreover, many gifted people find it possible to get along in school without "cracking a book." Such people not only fail to make the best use of their abilities but may develop habits of superficiality, never learning to dig down to the bottom of things. If this habit persists through life, these individual are seldom able to realize their full potential.

In the case of an applicant with a mediocre mental-test score and top grades in school, the interviewer is faced with at least three interpretive possibilities. First, there is the possibility that the person may not be telling the truth. Secondly, the academic standards of the school may have been relatively low. Or in the third place, the individual may have studied so hard that high grades were obtained despite somewhat limited mentality. If the latter proves to be the case, the individual is almost certainly hard-working, persevering, and highly motivated to succeed.

High grades in a school of established high academic standards normally provide clues to both intellect and motivation. This is particularly true, of course, where the applicant has selected a difficult major course of study. In the best schools, a student has to have a reasonable degree of mental ability and has to study reasonably hard in order to achieve a good academic record.

THE OVERACHIEVER

People whose grades are better than might have been expected of them in the light of the level of their mental ability are known as overachievers. Many such people make high grades on the basis of sheer hard work rather than high native ability. Many naive interviewers assume that high grades reflect high intelligence but such an assumption cannot be made without knowing something about the academic standards of the schools attended and the effort involved in getting the grades.

Many overachievers end up with emotional problems. Some become victims of "burn-out." Others do very well so long as the demands of their jobs are such that they are able to compensate by means of hard work for what they lack in mental capacity. But, as they progress through various levels of management, the time will surely come when hard work alone will not be enough. Since they have never encountered this situation before, some of them become very frustrated and even "fall apart" emotionally. Hence, companies should make every effort to identify their overachievers and be very careful not to promote them beyond the level of their abilities.

COLLEGE BOARDS

The majority of people today under the age of 25 or 26 will have taken SATs (Scholastic Aptitude Tests) during their senior year of high school, and most of these people will have been told their specific scores on these tests. Scores on these tests give us a good "fix" on the applicant's mental ability, verbal ability, and quantitative or numerical ability. High school seniors take two specific tests prepared by Educational Testing Service in Princeton, New Jersey— one test on verbal ability and another test on quantitative or numerical ability. A perfect score on each of these two tests is 800. The table below represents the distribution of scores on each of the two tests made by the high school senior population.

Test Score	*Interpretation*
700–800	Excellent
575–700	Above average
425–575	Average
300–425	Below average
Below 300	Poor

However, the above distribution includes a great many people who never made it to college. Hence, the distribution for college graduates—the population we are dealing with here as candidates for high-level jobs—is appreciably higher than that shown above.

In fact, today the colleges with the highest academic standards look for a combined score on these two tests of 1300 to 1350. This means that a boy might be taken into a good engineering school with a verbal score of 575 and a numerical score of 725, since the engineering course content places greater demand on mathematical aptitude. Or, a girl with a score of 750 on verbal ability might be accepted into a top school of journalism even though her math score was no more than 550.

Even the less-prestigious schools look for a minimum combined score on the SATs of at least 1000. Hence, a score of less than 500 on either the verbal or the math test reflects a relatively low aptitude for a person who has graduated from college. And, of course, the higher the score, the better the aptitude.

As noted above, most young people will have been told their college board scores and will remember them because of their importance in getting into the college of their choice. Yet, some of them may be reluctant to disclose their scores, particularly if they are not especially good. As a result, they may simply say they have forgotten the scores. Failure to reveal SAT scores should not be regarded as a clue to dishonesty. An individual has a right to withhold this information if he or she so desires.

In approaching this question, the interviewer *assumes consent* with such a direct question as, "What were your college board scores?" Note that she does not say, "Do you remember your college board scores?" or "Did you take the college board examinations?" Applicants are much more likely to respond to a direct, definitive question here since the interviewer does not make it easy for them to "get off the hook." If they profess not to remember their scores, the interviewer can say, "Well, were they in the 500s, 600s, or 700s?" Or she may say, "Did you do better on the verbal or the mathematical test?"

It has been the author's experience that most younger people will respond to the question on college board scores, particularly if good rapport has been established and maintained. The resulting information—providing you feel that you can believe the individual—can be unusually helpful, particularly if it is consistent with clues to intelligence and aptitudes which have come to light previously. Of course, some applicants may not remember their SAT scores correctly or may even lie about them. Hence, if the reported scores do not seem consistent with other clues to aptitudes, they should be disregarded.

The test are normally taken in the junior year of high school for practice and taken again in the senior year. The latter represents the official score and is often appreciably better than the score achieved during the junior year. Hence, the interviewer must make certain that the scores the person provides resulted from tests taken during the senior year.

Since these tests are taken during the high school experience, the subject of college boards should be introduced during the discussion of high school, immediately after getting the individual's high school grades and class standing.

EXTRACURRICULAR ACTIVITIES

The degree to which individuals have participated in extracurricular affairs may provide many important clues to personality traits. If little or no participation has taken place, individuals may have a tendency to be shy, self-conscious, inhibited, and introverted. In fact, they may freely admit that they tended to be "backward" and retiring at that stage of their lives. Of course, such people may have changed materially over the years, but the chances are very good that certain vestiges of these shortcomings may remain today. On the other hand, people may say that they did not participate in student activities because they did not care very much for the type of classmates with whom they were associated. Such a remark should prompt the interviewer to get further elaboration as a possible indication of snobbishness, intolerance, or a "sour grapes" attitude. The latter in particular may indicate some lack of emotional adjustment. Obviously, still other people fail to participate in student activities because of lack of motivation. They are content with the social relationships they develop on the outside. Finally, there is the "bookworm" or "grind." People of this type devote all their energy to getting top grades. As a result, they often graduate with honors but fail to achieve the social development acquired by the average college graduate. People who fall into this category are often the first to admit later in life how they failed to get much out of college. Since many jobs require a fair amount of social facility, such people often find themselves inadequately equipped to deal with others.

Those who do participate in extracurricular activities, however, often develop appreciably on the social side during their four years of school. In dealing with others of their own age, they frequently become more sociable, develop more tact, become more aggressive, and acquire traits of leadership. A girl elected president of her sorority, for example, is confronted with responsibilities that are entirely new to her. She is naturally anxious to show up well in the eyes of other members of the group and therefore takes particular pains to do the best job she can. In the course of shouldering these responsibilities, she often matures perceptibly, acquiring new poise, learning how to handle the more difficult people, and developing the kind of infectious enthusiasm that sparks an organization.

Participation in athletics—contact sports in particular—often fosters the development of competitive spirit, cooperation, and ability to serve as an effective member of a team. One who has a tendency to "hog the show" is frequently batted down rather quickly by teammates.

People who reach college at a younger age than their classmates often experience problems of adjustment. Such people often have difficulty gaining acceptance on the part of their older associates. Older students frequently have a tendency to "write them off," taking the view that they are not old enough to appreciate their thinking or to engage in their activities. Inability to compete successfully with one's contemporaries in college—either academically or socially—can have a marked effect on the individual's behavior. Some may develop feelings of inferiority that remain throughout life. If this turns out to be the case, they may have a tendency to underestimate their real abilities and may lack the confidence necessary to achieve up to their potential.

EFFORT

The subject of the amount of effort expended should be introduced after the discussion of extracurricular activities, so that applicants will be not quite so likely to relate effort to grades. In other words, first talk about all the academic factors such as subject preferences, grades, and college boards before the discussion of extracurricular activities. Only after the latter have been thoroughly explored is the question of effort brought up. This should be introduced with the question that appears on the Interview Guide: "How conscientious a student were you? Did you work about as hard as the average person, a little harder, or perhaps not quite so hard?" If an individual seems to have difficulty with this question, help him or her to become more definitive: "Well, how many hours a day did you study on the average and what time did you normally get to bed at night?"

Information developed in this area can provide excellent clues to both intellectual level and motivation. If a candidate obtained good grades in a school with high academic standards without working unduly hard, possession of good mental ability can be assumed. On the other hand, if no better-than-average grades were obtained in a school with questionable academic standards despite unusual effort, there would seem to be some question about the level of mental ability. The latter individual, however, can be given credit for strong motivation. It is not unusual for such a person to say, "I really had to work for everything I got. I certainly burned a lot of midnight oil. In fact, I used to be envious of my roommate who was always able to get things twice as easily as I could."

When interpreting grades in terms of the amount of effort expended, it is also necessary to factor in the amount of time spent on extracurricular activities as well as time spent on part-time jobs. People with average grades in a good school who have devoted a great deal of time to student activities or to financing their own education of course deserve credit for their over-all accomplishments. Such people often develop social skills and work habits that stand them in good stead later in life. Moreover, people who crowd in a great many activities, do a considerable amount of part-time work, and also manage to make good grades are usually the kind of people who have learned to organize their time effectively. Normally, they work on a specific schedule and do a considerable amount of planning.

SPECIAL ACHIEVEMENTS

Interviewers should be alert to the possibility that certain individuals may have attained achievements beyond those of most of their classmates, and such achievements may provide additional clues to mental ability, specific aptitudes, and leadership strength. Some individuals are basically modest and may not reveal this type of information unless they are specifically asked to do so. Hence, when a liberal arts student indicates that she made top grades in college, the interviewer should ask her if she made Phi Beta Kappa. A top technical student should similarly be asked if he achieved any academic honors, such as Tau Beta Pi or Sigma Xi. People achieving such honors are normally those who possess both high mental ability and strong motivation.

If asked about special achievements in high school, an

applicant may say that she won the mathematics prize, the physics prize, or the oratorical contest, thus revealing the possible existence of special aptitudes. Likewise, it is good to ask an athlete if he was ever elected captain of a team. Again, responsibility of this kind fosters the development of leadership traits. In the case of persons elected to the student government or to the presidency of the student body, the interviewer has a right to assume that such individuals were popular with their contemporaries and probably possessed some degree of leadership ability. Of course, school politics are responsible for the fact that some people are elected to class offices, but the people involved usually display some traits that set them apart from the crowd. At the very least, they are ordinarily liked by others, have a genuine interest in people, and have developed an ability to get along amicably with people on all levels.

In the development of education information, interviewers should make certain that they get all the information about high school (subject preferences, grades, extracurricular activities, and effort) before permitting applicants to discuss their college experiences.

TRAINING BEYOND THE UNDERGRADUATE LEVEL

Where the application blank indicates graduate training, interviewers explore this area immediately after getting the complete description of the college experience. Even in the case of those who do not have graduate training it is good to ask, "Did you ever give any thought to going to graduate school?" A question such as this frequently provides clues to the strength of the individual's theoretical drive. A person may say, for example, "I had enough of studying in college; I'm not the academic type, you know.

As soon as I finished college I wanted to do something practical where I could earn some money."

Except for the fact that they usually do not ask about extracurricular activities, interviewers explore graduate training in much the same way that they carried out the college discussion, concentrating on subject preferences, grades, amount of effort involved, and any special achievements. In some graduate schools, grades are either satisfactory or unsatisfactory, but other schools give letter grades, insisting that courses counted for graduate credit must be at a B level or better. In such a case, it is interesting to learn whether the graduate student obtained mostly B's and a few A's or made practically a straight A record.

Special attention should be devoted to the individual's thesis or dissertation. Even though the applicant's field may not be very familiar to the interviewer, the latter can still ask the individual about the problems she encountered and how she went about solving such problems. Evidences of creative ability may be revealed here, particularly in cases where the candidate solved most of her own problems rather than relying upon her sponsors. It is also good to ask about the extent to which the research findings may be expected to make a contribution to the field. In some cases, individuals publish articles in technical journals even before they are awarded their degree. In evaluating graduate training, again consider the academic standards of the school. A Ph.D. from some schools means a great deal more than it does from others.

Consideration of postgraduate training should not be confined to formal courses taken with a view to getting a master's or doctoral degree. Many people take special courses of one kind or another, including extension work, correspondence courses, and company-sponsored courses. Moreover, many such courses are taken at night, after putting in a full day on the job. Such attempts to improve oneself frequently provide clues to perseverance, aspiration, and energy level. In going to school at night individuals often extend their capacity for constructive effort. Many courses taken in the evening also equip people to turn in a better performance on their jobs.

After-hours courses may also reflect an individual's attempt to broaden his horizons. Sensing a lack of cultural background, he may take courses in history, art appreciation, or government. In a sense then, the selection of evening courses may tell as much about a person as the kind of elective courses selected in college.

HOW WAS EDUCATION FINANCED?

The interviewer will have acquired much of this information as a result of having discussed the applicant's early jobs under work history. But it is good to reconsider such information mentally while discussing the applicant's educational background. As indicated above, awareness of the fact that applicants worked their way through school may cast a different light on the kind of grades they received or on the extent of their participation in extracurricular activities. Individuals who have to work their way through school by carrying out part-time jobs frequently develop greater maturity and motivation than people who did not have to earn any of their college expenses. When individuals help finance their own education, they usually appreciate it all the more and try to get the most out of it. In the course of this experience, they frequently develop sound work habits, perseverance, and resourcefulness. On the other hand, people whose parents pay for their entire education may become accustomed to having things too easy. In fact, they may suffer a rude shock when they do finally get out into the world and find it necessary to earn their own living. Certainly in those cases adjustment to industry will be more difficult than for people who have already learned to earn their own way.

Scholarships are awarded to certain individuals as a means of financing part of the educational expense. In this case, it is important to know whether the scholarship was awarded on the basis of previous academic achievement or on the basis of economic need. The latter of course represents less of a factor in the individual's favor than the former.

Many people will say that if they had it to do over again they would borrow money rather than work so hard while going to college. They seem to feel that they missed a great deal by not being able to participate in extracurricular activities, for example. All things considered, the greatest overall development probably comes to the student who tries to maintain some kind of balance with respect to academic work, extracurricular activities, and part-time jobs. Too much concentration on any one of the three at the expense of the others usually has some retarding effect on the overall growth of the individual.

When the interviewer concludes the discussion of education, the entire experience is mentally evaluated in terms of the extent to which it has equipped the person to handle the job under consideration. In making this evaluation, formal courses in high school and college, training acquired while in military service, special company-sponsored courses, extension work, and correspondence courses are of course all included. Then the interviewer considers whether or not the applicant has the specialized training that the job requires, whether the applicant has developed the necessary skills, and, equally important, whether or not the applicant has developed the kind of thinking demanded for the job in question. Many job descriptions indicate simply that the incumbent should be a college graduate. This usually implies a certain degree of cultural background, the ability to think logically and to reason from cause to effect, and the ability to get along successfully with other people on the college level.

In evaluating the factors mentioned above, the interviewer naturally takes into consideration all major achievements such as grades, participation in sports, membership in clubs, offices held, and any special effort involved in financing education. How much the individual benefited from the educational experience is also considered. Did the applicant look for the easiest way out by selecting the easiest possible major course of study and by taking snap courses as electives? Or was a reasonably difficult major course of study and electives undertaken, designed to develop a broad cultural background? Is there any indication that the individual became so interested that additional unrequired reading was done? Was any really significant research work accomplished in connection with graduate studies? Answers to questions such as these help to cast the educational experience in its true perspective.

Obviously, too, the interviewer will evaluate the educational history in terms of resulting clues to abilities, personality traits, and motivation. Particular interest should be paid to those clues that supply further confirming evidence to support interpretive hypotheses which were established in the discussion of the applicant's work experience. It is to be expected, in addition, that the interviewer will have picked up some new clues to behavior that did not come to light during the earlier discussion. For the most part, these new clues will have added to the understanding of the candidate. At the same time, some of the newer clues again provide only tentative hypotheses. For example, the interviewer may have noted that the individual's extracurricular activities in school were confined to such "loner" activities as chess, hiking, and coin collecting. Suspecting that the individual may possibly fall into the trait constellation of introversion the interviewer will look for further confirming evidence in subsequent areas of the interview and will probe specifically for the possible existence of such traits as oversensitivity, lack of confidence, lack of tough-mindedness, and the like.

Finally, the interviewer must take the long view with respect to traits that the candidate developed while in school. In the case of older people it is probable that they have grown and developed considerably since school days. For example, they may have been quite immature as students but may have caught up with their chronological age group in this respect long since. The simple fact of not working hard while in high school and college need not mean that such candidates do not work hard today. Experience has nevertheless shown that people are seldom able to "change their spots" entirely as they grow older. In other words, if their performance in school reflected serious, deep-seated shortcomings, there is a good chance that vestiges of these shortcomings still remain with them as part of their makeup today.

PRESENT SOCIAL ADJUSTMENT

After completing the discussion of applicants' education, interviewers begin to explore current social adjustment. As will be noted below, outside interests and hobbies are the primary means relied on to determine the extent to which applicants are reasonably well-adjusted socially. As in the case of all the other interview areas, this discussion can also provide many clues to emotional adjustment, motivation, personality traits, and even abilities. In particular, the resulting information often brings into focus such factors as sociability, intellectual breadth, and intellectual depth. Obviously, discussion in this area is usually less significant in the case of young men and women just out of college than with somewhat older people. In talking with young people about their extracurricular activities in college, interviewers will already have learned a great deal about their social adjustment.

Interviewers lead applicants into this area by means of a simple question concerning interests and hobbies. Such a question as, "Well, now, what are some of the things that you like to do for fun and recreation outside of work?" will usually launch this discussion very effectively. And much of the information developed in this area may provide confirming evidence of clues to abilities and personality developed earlier in the interview.

Sports

Since the United States is very sports-conscious, many applicants will be found to participate in such sports as golf, tennis, handball, racquetball, and softball. Many others will jog several miles every day. Participation in sports obviously represents an asset, since most sports participants try to keep in good shape physically. A healthy person may have fewer absences from work and may be able to devote more energy to the job. Sports activity also provides clues to energy level. People who are able to engage in sports that are physically demanding, after working a full day on their jobs, certainly have a high level of energy.

A discussion of sports may also provide an indication of an individual's competitive spirit. A finding of this sort is meaningful because a competitive spirit represents an important aspect of leadership.

It is important to note whether sports tend to be carried

out alone or at best with one other person, such as backpacking, jogging, weight lifting, and the like. Individuals who tend to devote themselves exclusively to these kinds of "loner" activities, often have an inclination to be shy and somewhat introverted. Because such activities, moreover, do not give them much *practice* relating to others, individuals whose interests are limited to such pursuits are often lacking in poise and social facility. At the other end of the spectrum, individuals who participate frequently in team sports get a greater opportunity to sharpen their social skills and to learn what adjustments have to be made in performing as a member of a team.

Community Involvement

As in the case of sports, community involvement also offers an opportunity for practice in social situations. Activities associated with a church, local government, or various community clubs, not only provide practice in getting along with people, but may very well offer opportunities for leadership. Such activities, moreover, often reflect the type of person who takes their community responsibilities seriously and care enough to get involved. More often than not, such people reflect the attributes of a solid citizen and tend to be people of good character.

Interviewers should give particular attention to the extent to which women returning to the work force have participated in community activities. Because such woman have often spent several years at home raising their children, they often have relatively little relevant work experience. Many such women are extremely talented and these talents often show up in their participation in community affairs. Some women acquire valuable experience heading fund drives or serving as an important officer in various clubs. Many such responsibilities require a good level of intelligence, judgment, the ability to plan and organize, and the ability to persuade others to their point of view.

At the same time, interviewers should be on the alert for people with a strong social drive. When people devote themselves almost exclusively to such activities as fund drives, hospital work, YMCA work and helping out with the scouts, they may be sincerely motivated by a strong desire to help other people. Should this turn out to be the case, interviewers will be alerted to the possibility that such individuals may possess some of the assets and shortcomings frequently found in people fitting the description of the social-drive trait constellation.

Reading

Here, as in all other areas of the interview, every effort should be made not to put words in an applicant's mouth. Such a leading question as, "Do you enjoy reading?" or "Do you read much?" pushes the applicant to say "Yes." On the other hand, an open-ended question such as, "What about reading? Do you have any opportunity at all to read or do other activities leave little time for this?" sets the stage for an objective response. In response to such a question, applicants do not feel embarrassed to admit that they do not read very much.

The extent to which people read provides excellent clues to intellectual depth and breadth, particularly if the reading ranges over a number of areas and includes some books of a more serious nature, such as biographies and philosophy. As soon as an applicant professes an interest in reading, then, interviewers should ask about the kind of books he or she likes to read as well as the number of books the individual reads per month. Remember, we make every possible attempt to *quantify* information. Some people may profess to be avid readers but when asked to tell how many books they read per month they may reply "Oh, at least one book every month." Such a person would not qualify as an avid reader in the minds of most interviewers.

In asking about kinds of books read, it is also interesting to note whether or not an individual's reading habits reflect unusual intellectual curiosity. This may represent an important clue, since people with a high degree of intellectual curiosity are more likely to be creative in their thinking.

Experience has shown that brighter people tend to read more than people with no more than average intellect. Thus, if interviewers have picked up a number of earlier clues to high-level mental equipment, they will find additional confirming evidence of this ability in people who do a considerable amount of reading. This is not to say that all bright people read. In particular, engineers and other technically oriented people often concentrate so much on technical subjects in college that they have little time for the humanities. As a consequence, many such technical people have not had a real opportunity to develop good reading habits. At the same time, it should be a matter of interest to the interviewer as to whether or not technical people try to keep abreast of new developments in their fields by reading the various journals.

Interest In the Arts

An appreciation of music, painting, dance, the theater, etc. may reflect breadth as well as a good cultural background. Again, experience has shown that people with a good cultural background bring another dimension to the decision-making process. In sharp contrast to those who have difficulty "seeing the forest through the trees," people with good cultural backgrounds often find it possible to put things in proper perspective. In view of the long hours that many top-level managers spend on the job, it is often surprising to find how many of them *do* have an appreciation of the arts.

In discussing interest in the arts, interviewers should not be satisfied with such a comment as: "Oh, I like music very much." Rather, they should probe for the type of music enjoyed as well as the individual's favorite composer. Such probing often reveals whether artistic interest are superficial or quite deep-seated.

Energy Level

High energy level, vigor, and stamina, obviously represent extremely important assets. In fact, few people attain genuinely high vocational achievement unless they possess these important qualities in some abundance. Given a reasonable degree of intellect, educational training, and personality effectiveness, the degree of energy and stamina a person possesses may account in large part for his or her ability to win promotions over associates.

By the time interviewers have reached this stage of the discussion, they will, of course, have acquired numerous clues to individuals' energy level and stamina. For example, a man may have been able to work long hours over a protracted period of time without showing any serious effects. Or, a woman may have secured her college degree by going to night school over a period of 6 or 7 years while carrying on a full-time job during the day.

If interviewers are not certain of an applicant's amount of energy at this stage of an interview, they may ask specifically about this by saying, "How would you describe your energy level—as average, somewhat above average, or perhaps a little below average?" Most younger people like to think that they have an above average energy level.

Hence, if they admit that they have no more than an average degree of this important quality, they may have even less than that amount. Other clues to lack of energy may be reflected in an applicant's tendency to take the easy way out, to procrastinate, to be unwilling to make present sacrifices for future gains, and to reflect a rather phlegmatic general manner.

Mental Review of Present Social Adjustment

Just as interviewers mentally review other areas of the interview upon completing them, so should they try to determine what the discussion of outside interests has told them about a given individual's social adjustment. Do interests reflect a "loner" who seems to have no friends and is not an altogether cheerful or happy individual? Such findings *may* provide clues to lack of emotional adjustment. The latter shortcoming may also be reflected in people who "bite off more than they can chew" and who spread themselves so thin that they find it difficult to marshal all of their energies and focus them appropriately on a given task.

People with good social adjustment are normally those who enjoy the companionship of others, who participate in enough activities so their lives are relatively full, who are capable of deriving genuine satisfaction from achievements, and who do not take things so seriously that they worry unduly.

EEO CONSIDERATIONS

1. Make sure that educational standards (high school graduation, for example) established for selection of new employees are consistent with the educational attainment of employees already working on those jobs in the

plant or office. An artificially established educational standard may screen out a disproportionate number of minorities, and this is unfair (and cannot be defended) if some of the workers already on the job do not meet the new standard. (New educational requirements can only be established if the technology changes.)

2. Hard and fast grade requirements, such as a B average, are difficult to defend. Many factors affect grades, such as an outside job, an inordinate number of extracurricular activities, or the academic standards of schools attended. Do not be overly critical of low grades before giving an applicant a chance to explain.
3. Even if educational requirements can be defended, an organization must consider the extent to which additional recruitment may be necessary to provide a sufficient number of qualified minorities and women to meet its EEO commitments.
4. The effect of educational requirements on the handicapped must also be considered. Many handicapped people have not been able to obtain a formal education because of their inability to attend classes due to architectural barriers. In such cases, try to determine if the individual has obtained an informal education that is in any way comparable through self-study or other means.
5. Do not ask questions about marital status, children, arrangements for taking care of children while working, or health.

CHAPTER 13

Mental Ability, Motivation, and Maturity— A First Consideration

The interviewer is required to search for so many traits and abilities that it seems justified here—at the risk of some redundancy—to point out that three factors take precedence over all others. These factors may be referred to as the 3 M's—mental ability, motivation, and maturity—the level of importance in that order.

If an applicant is bright mentally, highly motivated to succeed, and mature emotionally, he or she undoubtedly represents a good candidate for some kind of job in any given organization. The specific job for which such a person is qualified, of course, depends upon such secondary factors as relevance of work experience, educational background, specific aptitudes, and temperament.

In this chapter, then, we shall point out the reasons why mental ability, motivation, and maturity loom so importantly in the evaluation of any candidate. And we shall review the major clues which help to identify these three factors, bringing together material from a number of the previous chapters.

Just as mental ability, motivation, and maturity represent the three most important factors to be identified in selecting an employee for industry, so do they also represent the three most important requisites to be considered in selecting students for college. This will be discussed in some detail at the end of this chapter.

MENTAL ABILITY

As implied above, mental ability probably represents the single most important factor to be considered in any evaluation of a candidate for a higher-level position. Despite this seemingly obvious fact, many highly placed managers in industry have been observed evaluating candidates for important positions without making any real effort to determine the individual's intellectual level or to give appropriate weight to that important factor. The reason for this omission may lie in the fact that most managers have not been trained in interviewing techniques and therefore do not know how to judge a candidate's mental capacity.

Yet, mental ability represents the *power* factor, in the sense that it means the individual's ability to acquire new information, to generate new ideas, and to solve complex problems. And in determining the *potential* for ever-increasing responsibilities, we must again give major consideration to the level of the individual's mental capacity.

Keep in mind, too, that there are some jobs which cannot competently be performed by a person who is not really bright—such jobs as demanding research positions, engineering design, and high-level management.

It is equally important to identify the intellectual factor in candidates for less intellectually demanding jobs—jobs that have a fair amount of routine detail, such as laboratory control work, some types of engineering testing, and door-to-door sales. Most really bright people, placed in a job that is routine and not at all intellectually challenging, become quickly "fed up" and leave. Obviously, therefore, it is necessary to staff such jobs with people whose intelligence is no better than average or perhaps even slightly below average.

Although aptitude tests represent the best means of establishing the individual's intelligence, most companies are still not equipped to give these tests, and many organizations shy away from them because they are afraid of being accused of unfair employment practices. In many cases, such fears are of course groundless, but they nevertheless represent some deterrent as far as the use of aptitude tests is concerned. Consequently, it becomes all the more important *to be able to identify mental ability without giving additional tests.* Actually, an applicant's mental ability can be quite accurately assessed by means of a comprehensive interview, *provided the interviewer is well-trained and has developed a broad frame of reference, in the sense that he or she has evaluated many hundreds of people and can thus compare a given applicant's qualifications against those of many others seen for that same type of job.* Although clues to mental ability have been brought to light in several of the preceding chapters, it will perhaps best serve our purposes if these clues are pulled together and presented again here.

High School and College Grades in Relation to Effort Required to Make Such Grades

Although grades per se are not a reliable indication of mental ability, they become significantly more reliable when considered in the light of the amount of effort the individual expended in order to get these grades, particularly if the academic standard of the school attended is factored into this equation. Thus, if people attained relatively high grades in schools with acknowledged high academic standards without having to expend a great deal of effort, it can be assumed that they are reasonably bright individuals. In sharp contrast, if students are not able to obtain better-than-average grades in schools of questionable academic standards, despite a great amount of effort and long hours of study, they are quite probably somewhat limited intellectually. (Refer to Chapter 12 for a more complete discussion of this subject.)

College Board Scores

Most individuals 25 or younger will have taken SATs (Scholastic Aptitude Test) during their senior year of high school, will have been informed of their scores, and will undoubtedly remember them still. Actually, Scholastic Aptitude Tests are made up of two separate tests—*verbal* and *quantitative,* or numerical. A perfect score on each of these tests is 800. In our attempts to identify a given individual's mental abililty, we must consider the *combined score* resulting from both of these tests. Thus, if a person obtained a score of 575 on the verbal test and 625 on the numerical test, the combined score is 1200.

Most colleges today look for a certain minimum combination score on the SATs to qualify for college entrance. And the level of this minimum required score tells us a good bit about a given college's academic standards. Many of our most prestigious colleges and universities require a minimum combined score of at least 1300, although some other colleges require no more than a combined minimum score of 1000.

Since most mental ability tests are made up of verbal and numerical items, the combined score on an individual's SATs represents quite a good indication of intellectual level. The table below represents a distribution of the combined scores on two SAT's for the high school senior populations.

Combined Test Score	*Interpretation*
1400–1600	Excellent
1150–1400	Above average
850–1150	Average
600–850	Below average
Below 600	Poor

As pointed out in Chapter 12, however, the above distribution includes many people who did not make it to college. Therefore, the distribution on the college population is much higher. In fact, a combined score of 1000 represents a rather marginal score for a college graduate. Scores ranging higher than this, of course, reflect higher mental ability—the higher the combined score, the brighter the individual.

Graduate Record Examination Scores

A person applying for graduate study leading to a master's or a doctoral degree in most of the better colleges and universities will be required to take the Graduate Record Examination. A perfect score on this examination is 800 but, since the test is appreciably more difficult than the Scholastic Aptitude Test, relatively few people make scores in the 700s on this test. A minimum score of at least 500 represents a requirement for entrance at most of the better schools. Scores ranging above 500, of course, reflect higher-level mental ability—the higher the score, the brighter the individual.

In talking with people who have done graduate work—or have even applied for graduate study—it is often helpful to ask them about their score on the Graduate Record Examination. Practically everyone who has taken this examination will remember the score because it is pivotal in gaining admittance to the university of his or her choice.

Quality of Response to Depth Questions

Although interviewers should be alert to the quality of the applicant's responses throughout the discussion, they should give extra attention to certain items appearing on the Interview Guide, particularly to achievements, development needs, and factors of job satisfaction (under Work History). Interviewers should be equally alert in examining the quality of applicants' responses to why they liked or disliked academic subjects in high school and college.

The areas identified above—perhaps more than any of the others—require a great amount of concentration, analysis, and in-depth thinking on the part of the applicant. Hence, responses in these areas should be carefully evaluated in terms of the extent to which they reveal analytical power, perception, self-insight, and intellectual breadth and depth. Obviously, analytical power, perceptiveness, and perspective are directly related to a favorable degree of mental ability.

Achievements Reflecting Mental Ability

High academic achievement such as election to Phi Beta Kappa (liberal arts student) or Tau Beta Pi (engineering student) normally reflects high-level mental ability. Of course, there is the occasional student who attains these high honors by dint of inordinate effort rather than because he or she is particularly bright, but such persons are few and far between. Hence, it can usually be assumed that a person who has attained either of these two scholastic honors has very good mental capacity.

Because certain academic courses require a rather high

degree of abstract thinking, people who like and do well in such courses as philosophy, logic, thermodynamics, and differential equations are usually relatively bright. It is equally true that demonstrated ability to handle intellectually demanding jobs represents a further clue to good intelligence. As noted earlier in this chapter, such jobs include important research positions, engineering design, and high-level management.

MOTIVATION

As important as intellect is, it cannot do the job alone. Unless individuals are motivated to utilize what they have, their overall achievement may not be particularly great and will most certainly be less than that of which they are capable. Moreover, many people with average intelligence coupled with high motivation attain a greater success than some other more intellectually gifted people who fail to make maximum use of what they possess. This is another way of saying that many people find it possible to compensate for something less than a brilliant mind by means of unusually strong motivation. As a matter of fact, high-level vocational achievement in certain areas may stem more from strong motivation than from any other single factor.

In view of the relationship of motivation to achievement, therefore, no evaluation of a candidate's qualifications is complete unless the degree of motivation has been identified and its relationship to overall achievement spelled out. In fact, motivation ranks almost as important as intellect as far as the candidate's qualifications are concerned.

As we did in the case of mental ability above, therefore, we have pulled together clues to motivation from various parts of the interview in order that we may treat this important factor here as an entity.

High Energy Level

There is a direct relationship between the amount of energy people possess and the achievement they are likely to attain. One needs only to look around in almost any business situation to understand the truth of this statement. The people at the top—those in important management jobs—will almost invariably be equipped with a great amount of energy. In fact, a highly placed person who does not have great energy will certainly represent a rather rare exception.

Energy appears to be largely inherited, with environment playing a secondary role. Thus, if people are born without a great deal of energy, they can do little about it. On the other hand, if they are equipped from the beginning with a high degree of energy, they possess an extraordinarily important asset, particularly if they learn to harness and focus that energy.

Since energy is so important to the prediction of success on a job, it seems surprising that there has been so little research effort expended in the direction of attempting to develop a valid and reliable measurement. If we could obtain as good an objective measurement of energy as we have of mental ability through intelligence tests, we would have a tremendously valuable tool for predicting behavior.

Well-trained interviewers—those with a broad frame of reference—can do quite an accurate job in assessing the candidate's energy level. They normally pick up clues to this important factor in all the interview areas. By means of adroit questioning, they can usually tell whether an applicant was able to handle certain enervating jobs without undue difficulty or whether such jobs actually seemed to have taken all the applicant's energy and stamina out of them.

Interviewers should be equally alert to the degree of

energy demonstrated during an applicant's educational experience. If a student was able to take a heavy academic load and still participate in many extracurricular activities or carry on an outside job, the evidence speaks for itself. Such an individual must have a high degree of energy.

It is furthermore helpful to note the kind of activities a person is able to carry out after completing a hard day on the job. Some people have enough energy left to participate in all types of physically demanding sports or to "moonlight" on another job. Other people appear to become completely "bushed" at the end of a normal work day.

Finally, interviewers can discuss the subject of energy quite directly, providing they have developed sufficient rapport. Such a discussion often results in additional important evidence.

Vocational and Educational Achievement in Terms of Mental Level

In an applicant whose mental ability has been assessed by the interviewer as not much better than average, there must be some other factor responsible for unusual vocational or educational achievement. That factor is almost invariably strong motivation. Many people have attained rather unusual success in industry on the basis of strong motivation as the primary factor. In fact, *in cases where other qualifications are reasonably good,* strong motivation is often the single most important factor in vocational success.

Some people make such maximum utilization of their rather modest abilities that they manage to do very well in high school and college. Such people are often referred to as "overachievers"—people who have attained a higher level of achievement in school and on the job than might have been expected of them in the light of their level of intelligence. Many of these people manage to do so well on their way up that they develop the philosophy that they can achieve anything at all providing they are willing to work hard enough. Unfortunately, that philosophy only works well until the individual is confronted with a task that is highly demanding intellectually. At that point, he or she often discovers that hard work alone is not enough.

Conditioned to Work

People who have developed successful work-habit patterns have become accustomed to working hard and expect to extend this type of behavior throughout the rest of their lives. In interviewing such people, it is easy to tell the extent to which they have become conditioned to work by probing for likes and dislikes on their various jobs, by noting the amount of overtime hours they regularly put in on many of their assignments, and by making observations about the kind of things which give them satisfaction.

Strong Drive for Achievement

People with strong motivation are normally those who "set their sights high." In the words of Ralph Waldo Emerson, they have a strong drive to "become." Motivated by a drive to "make something of themselves," they are usually willing to pay whatever price may be required as far as hard work is concerned.

Clues to high aspirations are most often brought to light during the discussion of *factors of job satisfaction* at the close of the discussion of work history. There it is frequently fruitful to ask candidates what level of job they expect to attain at the end of 5 years and then at the end of 10 years.

MATURITY

Some bright, highly motivated people fail because they lack *emotional maturity.* As discussed in previous chapters, the development of this important trait stems largely from environmental factors—the major influences which have been brought to bear on individuals from the time of their birth until the time of their appearance at the employment office. Just as in the case of mental ability and motivation, however, individuals have little actual control over the extent to which they mature emotionally. They are not able to select their parents; they have nothing to do with the early environment in which they were raised; for the most part, they have no choice of their teachers; and even their playmates during the early years have to be chosen on the basis of the immediate neighborhood in which they live.

Although most immature people have had very little to do with this lack of development, they nevertheless possess a shortcoming which very frequently stands in the way of success. This becomes immediately apparent when we go back to our earlier definition of emotional maturity: the ability to take the bitter with the sweet without rationalizing, the ability to acquire self-insight, the ability to exercise good judgment, the ability to establish reasonable vocational goals, and the ability to exercise self-control.

People who lack judgment, often make the wrong choice when confronted with important alternatives at critical stages of their lives. They may take the wrong kind of job, may leave a job for the wrong reasons, may select the wrong college major, or may do a poor job of planning their personal and financial affairs.

People who lack self-insight, do not know who they are or where they are going. This often means that the factors they tend to emphasize in their lives may not be appropriately related to success or achievement. They may not even realize the fact that they tend to rationalize their failures because they do not face up to their own shortcomings and hence are inclined to blame others for their difficulties. Furthermore, immature people are often self-centered, expect too much from others, and are too open in their criticism when things do not suit them.

Again, clues to emotional maturity should be brought to light in all the interview areas and have therefore been discussed in previous chapters. However, the factor of emotional maturity is so important that a certain amount of repetition seems justified and we are therefore summarizing some of these clues below.

Good Judgment

Lack of good judgment in leaving a given job, in selecting a major field of study, or in handling finances usually represents a sign of immaturity. Judgment is also a pivotal factor in deciding the type of job individuals desire, in terms of the extent to which that job realistically draws upon their ability and personality assets. Reasons for undertaking graduate study provide further clues to judgment, particularly in the sense that those reasons are consistent with goals and "make sense" in terms of previous educational background and work experience.

That judgment is directly related to maturity and that maturity is directly related to age will be found in the fact that insurance companies assess higher premiums for automobile insurance for males under the age of 25. (It is widely held that boys mature less rapidly than girls.) Many studies have demonstrated that young men often use poor judgment while driving a car, are sometimes inclined to be reckless, and pay too little attention to the consequences of their actions.

Demonstrated Ability to Put First Things First

Mature individuals have enough self-discipline that they are able to make themselves do the things that have to be done even if these things may not be particularly pleasant. Such people resist the temptation to do too much socializing in college, making certain that they get their homework done first. The ability to resist the temptation to buy a new car every other year in favor of saving for a down payment on a home also shows indications of maturity.

Reasonable Vocational Goals

When, in the discussion of factors of job satisfaction, it becomes apparent that people with very modest abilities aspire to positions which are way beyond their reach, it becomes clear that they have not recognized their limitations and learned to live with them.

In assessing the degree of candidates' emotional maturity, they must be compared with their chronological age group. Since maturity is a dynamic rather than a static factor, we normally develop more of this trait as we grow older. Hence, we do not expect a 19-year-old to be as mature as a 25-year-old, despite the fact that some 19-year-olds are far more mature at that age than some other young men and women of 25.

It can be noted in passing that there are at least two other forms of maturity—intellectual maturity and social maturity. Sometimes people brought up in homes where the father and mother are professionals develop more breadth and perspective than others of their age. Social maturity, on the other hand, implies an ability to handle oneself well in social situations, particularly with one's peers. Thus, the extremely shy person who finds it difficult to relate to other people of his or her own age is said to be socially immature.

IMPLICATIONS FOR SELECTION OF COLLEGE STUDENTS

Many colleges still do a relatively poor job of selection, as reflected in the attrition at the end of the first semester or at the end of the first year. In these times of rising costs when many institutions are struggling to remain solvent, inefficient selection creates an unnecessary demand for more classroom space, more laboratory facilities, and more dormitory space and puts an additional burden on the teaching staff. Moreover, students who fail to make the grade often lose confidence and never try again. This is something of a tragedy since many of those students are capable of doing college work but simply *were not ready at the time they applied for admission.*

Now, if we think of the college-admission situation in terms of the 3 M's discussed in this chapter, we find that the colleges have no problem dealing with the factor of mental ability. This is because most applicants today take the college boards, an examination which clearly determines whether or not a boy or girl is bright enough to do college work. But some institutions are modifying their ideas of fixed-minimum-score requirements, now realizing that certain individuals are capable of *compensating* for something less than a brilliant mind. As a matter of fact, even the prestigious colleges are discovering that a student does not need a combined score of 1300 or better on the SATs in order to handle the academic work competently. Accordingly, they are experimenting, taking in some applicants with lower scores, providing they have *something else* in abundance, usually athletic prowess, demonstrated leadership in extracurricular affairs, or perhaps unusual talent in music.

However, the colleges would be well-advised to look for that *something else* in the direction of unusually strong motivation and emotional maturity beyond the student's chronological years. Most students with good SAT scores who fail do so because they are not sufficiently motivated to study or are so immature that they cannot adjust to the college situation.

It seems quite clear that much of the attrition that takes place during the first year of college could be largely eliminated if the colleges would staff their admission offices with trained interviewers. These interviewers should not be so young, incidentally, that they have not yet had an opportunity to do a great deal of interviewing and hence to have acquired a broad frame of reference. The latter is important in enabling the interviewer to compare one applicant with many others that have been interviewed over the years.

Once the colleges were staffed with trained interviewers, they would be in a position to consider the all-important factors of motivation and emotional maturity, in addition to their current concentration on mental capacity. At that point, it would be perfectly logical to take some young people with lower SATs, provided these individuals possessed strong motivation and a high degree of emotional maturity.

CHAPTER 14

Terminating The Interview And Writing The Interview Report

With the completion of the third section of the Interview Guide, Present Social Adjustment, interviewers are ready to terminate the interview and subsequently to write the interview report. Under optimal conditions, the report of interview findings should be written immediately after completion of the interview. With interview data fresh in mind, interviewers should be able to write the report in a fraction of the time it would take should they wait several hours after finishing the interview. In this chapter, then, we will discuss the last two functions of the interview—terminating the interview and writing the report.

TERMINATING THE INTERVIEW

As noted earlier, it is occasionally permissible to terminate an interview before all the suggested background areas have been discussed. This is only done in cases where a predominance of negative information results from the early discussion. If after a discussion of the work history, for example, it becomes clearly evident that the candidate is not at all suited for the job in question, the interview may be terminated at that point. However, the interviewer should guard against snap judgments, making certain that the decision not to carry the interview any further is based upon adequate factual evidence rather than upon an emotional reaction to the individual concerned. There are occasions, too, when interviewer's impressions of a candidate may change materially after the first half hour of discussion, swinging from a rather negative impression to an entirely positive one. Hence, the accumulation of negative findings must be substantial in the case of an early interview termination.

In a well-designed selection program, applicants scheduled for the evaluation interview will already have been screened by preliminary interviews, application forms, aptitude tests, and reference checkups. For the most part, such applicants will represent likely prospects and will merit the complete interview. And the more likely a prospect the candidate seems to be, the more the interviewer needs to know, in terms of possible shortcomings as well as assets. Thus, early termination of an interview in which the findings are positive is never justified.

Since the vast majority of surviving applicants will get the full interview, termination will normally take place at the end of the discussion of present social adjustment. Termination, in the sense that we are using it here, involves more than the windup of the information-gathering aspects of the interview. It also includes the information-giving aspects. As noted below, every applicant should be given some information about the company and, in particular, about the job for which he or she is being considered.

Terminating the Unqualified Applicant

Even in the case where the applicant is to be rejected, a certain amount of information-giving should take place at the end of the interview. Directed toward the objective of public relations, this should be kept general. In other words, the applicant should be told about general factors, such as company organization, company policy, products manufactured, and the like—rather than about specific factors such as wages, hours of work, and employee benefits. The latter are important only in the case of an applicant who is to be offered a position. Five minutes will ordinarily prove sufficient to tell the unqualified applicant about the company. However, courteous and informative answers should always be given to any questions raised.

An attempt should always be made to terminate the interview on a positive tone. Such a statement as the following will often accomplish this objective, "Well, you certainly have a long list of impressive assets—assets that will stand you in good stead throughout your working life. And, at the same time, you seem to have some insight into the areas to which you should give your attention in terms of further development. I will discuss your qualifications with other interested persons within the company and will let you know the outcome within a day or two. Thank you very much for coming in; I certainly enjoyed talking with you."

Once the interviewer has decided to terminate the discussion, this should be done with dispatch. Otherwise, the conversation will deteriorate into meaningless chitchat. Hence, after a concluding statement such as the one noted in the paragraph above, the interviewer should stand up, shake hands, and escort the candidate to the door.

Rejection of applicants is always a difficult task at best and, as such, must be handled with care and finesse. First and foremost, applicants must be rejected in such a way that their feelings are not unduly hurt and their self-confidence is not undermined. In the second place, the company's public relations are at stake. In other words, rejected applicants should be permitted to "save face," so that they do not bear ill will toward the company. Because this task requires so much skill and finesse, many companies prefer to inform applicants of an unfavorable employment decision by letter. Actually, the latter means is almost uniformly used in the case of applicants for high-level jobs. A carefully worded letter not only represents an expression of courtesy but carries the implication of more thorough consideration. At the same time, the letter should be sent within a day or two after the interview, thus freeing the unsuccessful candidate to concentrate on other job possibilities.

Whether the applicant is informed of the unfavorable decision by letter or at the end of the interview, the reason for the rejection should be phrased in terms of the job demands rather than in terms of the individual's personal qualifications. The candidate should be given credit for his or her real assets but, at the same time, should be told that, in the interviewer's opinion, the job will not make the best use of the candidate's abilities. Instead of deprecating the individual's personal qualifications, this approach simply implies that he or she will probably be better suited in some other job with another company.

Another way to help a person "save face" involves a comparison with other candidates for the job in question, on the basis of experience and education. The person can be told, for example, "Although you possess many fine assets, there are one or two other candidates being considered for this job whose specific experience and training are somewhat more appropriate." Note that this statement makes no mention of personal characteristics such as ability to get along with people, willingness to work hard, or leadership traits. In general, it is far easier for an individual to face up to the fact that his or her experience or training does not quite fit the job than to admit that he or she does not qualify because of personal characteristics.

The more aggressive applicant may occasionally press the interviewer for further reasons as to why the job may not make best use of his or her abilities. In such a case, the temptation to inform the individual about specific test or interview findings should be resisted at all costs. The "feedback" of specific information of this kind represents a difficult task. Because it requires specific experience and training, it can lead to a discussion that may easily get out of hand. Hence, it is much better to keep the discussion general, elaborating on previous remarks. The interviewer might say, "As a member of the personnel department here I have a rather thorough knowledge of job requirements and, in my opinion, our current job openings are not likely to make the best use of your abilities. In fact, I have seen one or two other candidates whose experience and training are a little more appropriate."

Once in a while an individual will ask for vocational guidance. The applicant may say, "If your jobs will not make best use of my abilities, what kind of a job do you think I should look for elsewhere?" In answer to such a question, the interviewer should refer the individual to a professional vocational guidance counselor. Guidance requires a great deal more academic preparation than does interviewing. Moreover, interviewers are normally familiar only with the requirements of the jobs in their company. To do an adequate guidance job, the counselor must have knowledge of job requirements in a great many different fields. Hence, an applicant who expresses a desire for vocational guidance should be referred to a competent psychologist specializing in this field.

Terminating the Interview of the Qualified Applicant

Although the interviewer ordinarily has the authority to reject unqualified applicants, final responsibility for placing qualified candidates on the payroll usually rests with the head of the department to which the applicant is being referred. Even when the interviewer's decision is entirely favorable, this should not be communicated to the applicant. Rather, the interviewer should express real interest in the individual's qualifications, assuring the applicant that the department head will schedule a later meeting.

The information-giving aspect of the interview takes on even greater importance when the interviewer's decision is favorable. In these situations, everything possible is done to sell the candidate on the job. And the interviewer is in a unique position to do this. With the full knowledge of the applicant's abilities and qualifications in mind, the extent to which these qualifications apply to the job can be specifically pointed out. Where the decision is favorable, moreover, the interviewer should talk in terms of job specifics—earnings, employee benefits, and subsequent opportunities for promotion. In addition, company policies, products, and the organization's position in the industry can be explained. At the same time, the interviewer will be careful not to oversell the job, knowing that this might lead to eventual disappointment and poor morale.

COMPLETING THE INTERVIEW RATING FORM

This chapter provides instructions for recording interview findings on the Interview Rating Form found in the back of the book. To help interviewers summarize their thinking, moreover, the chapter also includes a cross-reference section, showing how possible clues from each of the major interview areas can be used to form judgments of the candidate's rating on traits of personality, motivation, and character appearing on page 3 of the Interview Rating Form.

The write-up of the case represents an important, integral part of the interviewing process. Experience has shown that, as the results are recorded, the interviewer's thinking crystallizes with respect to the applicant's qualifications. By the time the applicant leaves the room, the interviewer will normally have decided whether the man or woman is qualified for the job in question. But the write-up of the case represents an extension of this decision-making. In the process of recording the findings, the interviewer isolates out value judgments and hence is normally able to assign a more precise rating to the candidate's qualifications. The case write-up forces the interviewer to weigh all the relevant factors, and as a consequence he or she is usually in a much better position to decide whether the applicant's qualifications merit a slightly above-average rating, a well-above-average rating, or perhaps an excellent rating.

Because the recording of interview findings represents such an essential aspect of the entire process, the Interview Rating Form should be completed immediately after the candidate leaves the room. With all the essential facts still fresh in mind, the interviewer usually finds it possible to complete the form within 45 minutes. If this task is postponed, twice the amount of time may be required, and subsequently all the salient information may not be recalled.

In writing up the Interview Rating Form, use the space provided under each interview area for recording major findings pertinent to that area. Since the space is obviously limited, the interviewer will have to decide which findings in each area contribute most to understanding the applicant's behavior and overall qualifications for the job in question.

The recording of interview results should not be confined to facts alone, since many of these facts will already have appeared on the application blank. Rather, the interviewer should try to indicate his or her interpretation of these facts, in terms of the extent to which they may provide clues to the individual's personality, motivation, or character.

Personality and Ability Configurations

We have noted throughout the chapters on interpretation that interviewers—with proper training and practice—will normally know whether or not they wish to hire an applicant by the time that individual leaves the room. This is because they have been picking up clues to behavior throughout the discussion of work history, education, and outside interests and, by the end of the interview, have acquired sufficient hard, factual documentation to support an objective employment decision. Even so, reference to the personality and ability configurations detailed below should enable an interviewer to become more definitive with respect to the individual's make-up.

It is suggested that interviewers copy the personality and ability configurations shown in Exhibit 1 onto an 8½- by 11-inch card for easy reference at the end of all their interviews. This should permit them to decide, first of all, the extent to which an applicant possesses the three M's—listed as "primary qualifications." They should then check out the applicant on the "secondary qualifications," people skills, leadership potential, character, technical ability (if applicable), emotional adjustment, and sales aptitude (if applicable).

Exhibit 1 Personality and ability configurations.

Primary

Mental Ability	Motivation	Maturity
• Verbal aptitude • math aptitude • analytical power • perceptiveness • capacity to think critically • intellectual breadth and depth	• energy • willingness to work • aspirations • self-discipline • initiative • perseverance • personal standards	• judgment • reasonable vocational goals • self-knowledge • does not rationalize • aware of limitations • can make present sacrifices for future gains

Secondary

People Skills	Leadership	Emotional Adjustment
• tact • empathy • social sensitivity • cooperativeness • friendliness • sensitivity to the needs of others	• assertiveness • self-confidence • tough-mindedness • ability to communicate • enthusiasm • good organizer • "take charge" type of person	• ability to take pressure • reasonably cheerful outlook on life • not moody • not a worrier • does not experience marked "ups" and "downs"
Technical Ability	**Character**	**Sales Aptitude**
• math aptitude • academic preparation • analytical approach • creativity • capacity to think critically • attention to detail	• honesty • reliability • possessing value system	• assertiveness • self-confidence • tough-mindedness • gift of gab • infectious enthusiasm • sense of humor • extrovertedness • colorfulness • charisma

Reference to the personality and ability configurations also helps interviewers make a relatively quick assessment of an applicant's strengths and shortcomings. Some interviewers find it helpful, moreover, to use these configurations to complete the summary of assets and shortcomings of the Interview Rating Form immediately following the completion of the interview. Once having completed this summary, they work backwards in a sense, making certain that their write-up of work experience, education, and present social adjustment contains abundant documentation of the assets and shortcomings they have already summarized.

Writing the Work History

Data should be recorded chronologically, in much the same way as it is obtained during the interview. Thus, there should be a brief treatment of early jobs, followed by a discussion of postcollege jobs in chronological order. Because of space limitations, early jobs may be treated as a group rather than discussed singly.

The discussion should be primarily *interpretive*, drawing upon factual information to highlight clues to personality, motivation, and character. Obviously, it is impossible to draw off meaningful interpretations from every single fact presented, but clues to behavior should nevertheless be sprinkled frequently throughout the discussion of work history.

At the end of the work history discussion, the interviewer should be sure to indicate an evaluation of the applicant's work experience and its relevance in terms of the job under consideration. The following represents an example of how work experience should be recorded on the Interview Rating Form:

Early jobs (lifeguard, pressing apples, part-time farming) provided an introduction to work but did not seem to extend him to any great degree or to do a great deal for his development.

Worked two summers (forklift operator, testing carburetors) but did not find either job very interesting.

Enlisted in the Navy in 1963 just prior to taking exams that would have graduated him from college—apparently in a fit of anger because the college failed to extend a loan. This obviously reflected poor judgment, immaturity, quick temper, and impulsiveness. Did radar and missile electronics maintenance in the Navy and thus acquired relevant experience with electrical hardware. Elected to stay on 2 more years after 4-year enlistment "because I could earn $75 more a month and go overseas." This seems to reflect some lack of initiative in the sense that he took the path of least resistance. Did not have any significant leadership experience. Says he "does not like to offend people" and admits to a lack of confidence and mental toughness.

Now earning $11,500 at Crocker Electronics, doing testing work in the manufacturing section. Has enjoyed his work over the past year but now wants something "more professional" such as design or field engineering.

Although he does have some good electrical hardware experience, job history is not impressive for a man of 31, reflecting some lack of drive as well as some failure to make maximum utilization of his abilities.

After completing the write-up of the work-history area, the interviewer should assign a rating to this area by placing a check mark on the horizontal line that extends across the top of this area. Note that the horizontal line represents a continuum, in the sense that the check mark can be placed at any point on the line—directly over any of the descriptive adjectives or, for example, between "average" and "above average." The rating should be made in terms of the job that appears at the top of the form—the job for which the applicant is being considered. In cases where most of the interpretive comments are favorable, an "above average" rating would normally be expected. If the majority of comments are unfavorable, a "below average" rating would normally be indicated. Where favorable and unfavorable comments are about equally weighted in terms of their importance, an "average" rating would usually be made.

Writing Up Education and Training

As in the case of the treatment of the work history, educational data should also be recorded in chronological order. This means that initially there should be a discussion of high school followed by a treatment of the college experience. Any graduate experience should of course be recorded last.

Again, the recorded information should be largely interpretive, with a liberal use of factual data for documentation. Thus, actual grades and class standings should be noted here. Be sure to record extracurricular activities as well as the extent to which the individual seems to have applied himself or herself.

Here, as in the previous area, be sure to indicate names of schools, employers, and the like. This report should be sufficiently complete so that the reader does not have to refer to the application blank for additional information. An example of the manner in which the educational information should be recorded appears below:

> Did exceptionally well in high school, graduating third in a class of 458 and doing her best work in math and science. College Boards were 630 verbal (good) and 745 math (exceptional). Because she was very shy, Mary did not take part in extracurricular activities and did not date boys.

Studied very hard at Swarthmore—a top school—and made outstanding grades (3.7 out of a possible 4.0), winning election to Tau Beta Pi during her junior year and graduating magna cum laude. Mary majored in electrical engineering and enjoyed all of the more theoretically oriented courses such as thermodynamics, circuitry, and higher math—a strong clue to her ability to think in the abstract. Also enjoyed and did well in her design courses. Began to "blossom out a bit" in college, becoming more social and beginning to date more frequently. But she almost left college one semester because she was "upset over a relationship with a boy," again raising some question concerning her emotional adjustment.

Mary made an exceptional record at a top school and hence is unusually well trained academically. Obviously, too, she has superior intelligence both with respect to quantity and quality (analytical, perceptive, critical).

Once the interpretive comments have been recorded in this area, the interviewer should assign a rating on the line at the top, in accordance with suggestions discussed above in connection with the rating of work history.

Writing Up Present Social Adjustment

Interpretive comments in this area should be concerned primarily with value judgments as to the man's or woman's interests and overall social adjustment. Illustration of such comments appears below:

Interests fairly broad and somewhat intellectual—reads five or six books a month, likes to make her own clothes, has student license as a pilot, and enjoys listening to classical music.

Energy level is admittedly no better than average and, in truth may be somewhat less than average.

Pursues many of her activities by herself or, at best, with one or two other people. Admits that she does not have as much social facility as she would like. Overweight problem probably somewhat of a social handicap.

Seems something of a "loner" and not altogether happy, raising a question concerning her emotional adjustment.

Again, after recording the appropriate information in this area, the interviewer should assign a rating to the area by placing a check mark at the appropriate point on the horizontal line at the top.

Rating Personality, Character, and Motivation

Each of the fourteen traits listed under this area is preceded by a set of parentheses. This permits the interviewer to assign a rating to each trait. As in the case of ratings made in all the other interview areas, value judgments should be formulated in terms of the demands of the job for which a person is being considered. Using a five-point scale, the interviewer places a + in the parentheses to indicate the belief that the applicant has a high degree of the trait in question, an A+ if the individual is judged to have an above-average amount of the trait, an A in the parentheses if the applicant is judged to have an "average" or adequate amount of the trait, an A− if the applicant is thought to have a below-average degree of the trait, and a − if the individual is evaluated to be seriously lacking in that characteristic. If the interviewer is unable to decide about a given trait or, if the particular trait has no relevance in terms of the job under consideration, the parentheses is left blank.

In devising forms such as the Interview Rating Form, it is of course impossible to include all the traits of personality, motivation, and character that should be considered in evaluating applicant characteristics for a wide range of jobs. The fourteen characteristics listed on this particular form simply represent some of the traits which experience has shown to be most relevant in assessing applicants for high-level jobs in general. Other characteristics deemed of particular importance in a given case can be listed as representing either a strength or a shortcoming on Section V of the Interview Rating Form, summary of assets and of shortcomings.

In rating an applicant on traits of personality, motivation, and character, the interviewer is called upon to summarize his or her thinking, in terms of the variety of clues to these traits that have come to light as a result of the discussion of the candidate's work history, education and training, and present social adjustment. To take a specific example, the rating of the applicant as a "hard worker" will be based upon such considerations as the extent to which he seems to have applied himself on his various jobs, the amount of effort he gave to his studies in school, the extent to which he may have developed sound work habits as an adolescent, and his capacity for constructive effort as reflected in his outside interests or in his demonstrated ability to carry a heavy academic load in night school while working on a full-time job during the day.

The material presented below is designed to aid the interviewer in thinking through the various kinds of information that might be used to support a rating on each of the fourteen traits listed on the back of the Interview Guide. It is of course impossible to produce an exhaustive list of items that could conceivably merit consideration in rating an applicant for a given job on each of these traits. Hence, the questions appearing below under each trait are designed simply to stimulate the interviewer's thinking, in terms of the kind of positive and negative information that would ordinarily be factored into the rating of that trait. Items preceded by a minus sign represent examples of unfavorable findings with respect to a given trait; those preceded by a plus sign represent examples of favorable or positive findings.

Maturity

– Any tendency to rationalize failures?
+ Has she learned to accept her limitations and live with them?
– Chronic dissatisfaction with job duties and working conditions, reflecting an inability to take the bitter with the sweet?
+ Well-formulated vocational goals?
+ Worked during college summers to help pay tuition, even though parents could have afforded to pay total amount.
+ Responsible attitude toward her family?
– Effort in school confined only to those studies which he liked?
– Does he rationalize academic failures by blaming the school or the teachers?

Emotional Adjustment

+ Has she shown an ability to maintain composure in the face of frustration?
+ Has he been able to maintain his emotional balance and mental health in the face of trying personal circumstances, such as a protracted period of unemployment?
– Have there been problems with supervisors, teachers, or patents, which reflected a decided tendency to "fly off the handle"?

+ Is she able to deal with the shortcomings of subordinates calmly and patiently?
– Is he admittedly moody and inclined to experience more than the normal degree of ups and downs?
– Is she inclined to sulk in the face of criticism?
– Do current difficulties with peers seem to stem in part from his tendency to be sarcastic or hotheaded?
+ Is there considerable evidence that she does not allow her emotions to color her judgment?

Teamworker

+ Does he seem to have operated successfully as a member of a team, in connection with sports activities in school, community activities in the neighborhood, or group activities on the job?
– Is she strongly motivated to be the "star" of the team, taking more than her share of credit for accomplishments?
+ Does he seem to place the accomplishments of the group ahead of his personal feelings and ambitions?
– Did she have difficulty getting along with her associates while in the army or navy?
+ Does he have the degree of tact and social sensitivity necessary for the establishment and maintenance of good interpersonal relations with other members of a team?
– Does she show any pronounced tendency to be inflexible, intolerant, or opinionated?

Tact

+ Does the manner in which he phrased his remarks during the interview reflect tact and consideration for the interviewer?

− Has she talked disparagingly about minority groups?
− Has he made a number of remarks during the interview that have been unduly blunt and direct?
+ In discussing her relationships with subordinates, does she seem to have reflected genuine consideration for their feelings?
+ Is he sensitive to the reactions of others to the extent that he is able to structure his approach without antagonizing them?
+ Does she show any evidence of being a good listener?

Adaptability

+ Did he adjust easily to army or navy life?
+ Has she shown a liking for jobs involving contact with many types of people and diverse situations?
+ Has he shown an ability to handle a number of job assignments simultaneously?
+ Has she demonstrated the ability to move from one job to a completely different kind of job without undue difficulty?
− Was he unable to do well in certain subjects "because of the teacher"?
− Was she raised in a provincial small town atmosphere where there was relatively limited exposure to diverse situations and different types of people?
− Does his approach to a job reflect such a tendency to be a perfectionist that he has to do everything "just so"?

Tough-Mindedness

− Does she have a strong dislike for disciplining subordinates?

– Is he willing to take a stand for what he thinks is right?
+ Has she demonstrated an ability to make decisions involving people that, of necessity, work to the disadvantage of the few but have to be made for the good of the many?
– Is he insufficiently demanding of subordinates, in the sense that he is reluctant to ask them to work overtime or to "push" them to some extent when there is a job to be done within a certain deadline?
– Is she a product of a soft, sheltered, early work experience where there was little opportunity to become conditioned to the seamier side of existence?
– Does he give the impression of being too sympathetic or overly concerned about the feelings of others?
+ Is she willing to delegate responsibilities even though inadequate performance on the tasks delegated may reflect directly upon her?

Self-Discipline

– Has he shown a tendency to procrastinate unduly in carrying out the less-pleasant jobs assigned him?
+ In connection with her academic career, has she shown a willingness to apply herself diligently to those courses which she disliked?
– Did he fail to take full advantage of academic opportunities because he was not able to make himself "dig deeply enough" really to understand the subject?
+ Does she assume her share of civic responsibility, even though community activities in general do not appeal to her?
– Has he been so conditioned by a soft, easy life that there has been relatively little need to cope with difficult problems or situations?

+ Has she demonstrated a willingness to give first attention to those important aspects of a job which are perhaps of less interest to her?

Initiative

+ Has he demonstrated an ability to operate successfully without close supervision?
– Does she show a dislike for situations that have not been structured for her?
+ Does he reach out for ever-increasing responsibility?
+ Is there any evidence to indicate that she is a self-starter, in the sense that she does not have to wait to be told what to do?
– Does he seem to have fallen into a job rut, in the sense that he has been unwilling to extricate himself from a dead-end situation?
+ Has she demonstrated a willingness to depart from the status quo in order to accomplish a given task in a new and perhaps more efficient manner?

Perseverance

+ Did he show perseverance in college by completing his undergraduate work despite a lack of good scholastic aptitude?
– Has she changed jobs too frequently?
+ Once he starts a job, does he continue with it until it has been completed, resisting any tendency to become distracted?
+ Has she completed an appreciable portion of her college education by going to school at night?
– Does he find it inordinately difficult to complete tasks

on his own, such as correspondence courses where he does not have the stimulation of group effort?

– Is there evidence to support the view that she starts more things than she can finish?

Self-Confidence

– Was confidence undermined by an overly demanding supervisor who tended to be a perfectionist?

+ Does he reflect a realistic appraisal of his abilities and a willingness to take action?

– During the early years was she unable to compete successfully with those of her own age in athletics or in academic affairs?

+ Does his general manner reflect poise and presence?

+ Does she have sufficient confidence in her assets so that she is willing to discuss her shortcomings objectively?

– Has he been reluctant to take on additional job responsibility because of fear of failure?

– Did she limit her extracurricular activities in school because of a fear of lack of acceptance on the part of her classmates?

Assertiveness

+ Does his personality have considerable impact?

+ Has she done a considerable amount of participation in contact sports where aggressiveness represented an important requisite?

– Has he shown a tendency to let others take advantage of him because of lack of self-assertiveness?

+ Has she operated successfully in sales, expediting, or production supervision—types of jobs conducive to the development of personal forcefulness?

+ Is his history replete with evidences of leadership in school, on the job, or in connection with activities in the community?
– Does she tend to be introverted in the sense that she shies away from group activity?

Conscientiousness

+ Did he show conscientiousness in school by doing more than was actually required by the teachers, in order to satisfy his own standards?
– Does her record on the job reflect a tendency to let things slide?
+ Is he inclined upon occasion to work evenings and weekends, even though this is not actually required by his supervisor?
– Does she tend to be a clock-watcher?
+ Does he have high personal standards for his work?

Hard Worker

+ Has her history been such that she has become conditioned to hard work and long hours?
+ Did he get good grades in school despite limited mental ability?
+ Did she earn a relatively high percentage of her college expenses?
– Does his general manner seem phlegmatic, reflecting a possible below-average energy level?
– Has she shown a strong dislike of overtime work?
+ Has he had any experiences that may have extended his capacity for constructive effort, such as going to school at night while carrying on a full-time job during the day?
– Does she seem always to look for the easy way out?

\+ Does he seem to be in excellent health, reflecting a considerable amount of vigor and stamina?

Honesty and Sincerity

\+ Has she "come clean" during the interview discussion, in the sense that she has shown a willingness to talk about the unfavorable aspects of her background as well as the favorable aspects?

– Is there any evidence to support the view that he is exclusively oriented in the direction of personal gain, to the point that he does not develop strong loyalties to any organization or perhaps even to his own family?

\+ Is she willing to give credit where credit is due?

– Does he seem to derive satisfaction from the discussion of situations where he has been able to get the better of the other fellow or to "pull a fast one"?

– Does she have any appreciable tendency to exaggerate her own accomplishments?

– Does his story seem to be inconsistent in terms of other selection findings, such as information developed from the application form, the preliminary interview, the aptitude tests, or the reference check-ups?

After completing the ratings on the fourteen traits of personality, motivation, and character, assign an overall rating to this area by placing a check mark at the appropriate point on the horizontal line at the top. In making this rating, the interviewer will of course be guided by the preponderance of pluses or minuses, as the case may be. At the same time, the pluses and minuses should not be added algebraically, since certain traits obviously merit a greater weighting than others. For example, a minus rating on "honesty and sincerity" would undoubtedly be sufficient to outweigh plus ratings on all the other traits. Moreover, certain traits such as maturity, emotional adjustment, and willingness to work hard are more important to job success than traits such as tact, tough-mindedness, or personal forcefulness. In assigning an overall rating on this area, the interviewer must also be guided by the demands of the job for which the candidate is being considered. The trait of assertiveness, for example, would be given more weight in the case of a candidate being considered for production supervision than in the case of a person being evaluated for a job as office manager.

Writing the Summary of Assets and Shortcomings

Items listed under assets and shortcomings in this section of the Interview Rating Form should be concerned with the most important findings, in terms of the applicant's overall qualifications. And these items, for the most part, should in themselves represent a summation of a number of individual factors. For example, the interviewer would list as an asset an item such as "effective sales personality," rather than trying to list all the factors of which the so-called "sales personality" is composed—factors like aggressiveness, sense of humor, poise, presence, social sensitivity, and persuasiveness.

The summary of assets and shortcomings should include major findings from all the selection steps, with special emphasis of course on aptitude tests and interview results. Thus, in addition to principal interview findings, this section should include any available test results such as mental ability, verbal ability, numerical ability, mechanical comprehension, or clerical aptitude. Interviews should also combine test and interview findings in such a way that they summarize the *quality* of the applicant's thinking. Items concerned with quality of thinking would of course be expressed in such terms as: analytical ability, ability to plan and organize, criticalness of thinking, and intellectual breadth and depth.

In writing up the summary of assets and shortcomings, interviewers should select items of particular importance in terms of the job for which the candidate is being considered. Thus, in addition to listing appropriate items of ability, personality, motivation, and character, they should always note the relevance of the candidate's work history and educational preparation.

Writing the Overall Summary

In completing the overall summary on page 4 of the Interview Rating Form, the interviewer should write a brief description of the candidate's qualifications for the job in question. This takes the form of three paragraphs—the first paragraph devoted to a summation of the applicant's principal assets, a second paragraph which describes the most serious shortcomings, and a third paragraph in which interviewers seek to *resolve* the major assets and shortcomings in such a way that they show whether the assets outweigh the shortcomings or vice versa. And, in this third and final paragraph, interviewers show how they arrived at their overall rating. The three paragraphs of the overall summary will of course draw upon the summary of assets and the summary of shortcomings which appear above. Hence, there will be some obvious redundancy but every effort should be made to word the summary in such a way that the individual seems to "come to life" as a unique person. An example of an appropriately worded overall summary appears below.

Harry Ritter deserves great credit for what he has been able to make of himself in view of what he has had to work with. Without much in the way of early financial, educational or cultural advantages, he has managed to attain a very good record of achievement both in the army and at Elmer Electric. He has done this primarily as a result of his tremendous energy, his willingness to work hard and to put in long hours, and his ability to make maximum utilization of his abilities. In addition, Harry has some natural leadership ability as a result of his personal forcefulness, self-confidence and tough-mindedness. Finally, his experience with Elmer Electric represents a strong plus in terms of his ability to fit in here.

Negatively, Harry is not especially gifted intellectually, although his intelligence probably falls within the average range of the college population. Nor does he have a great amount of intellectual depth or breadth. Hence, he is more of a "doer" than he is a "thinker." The kind of a person who tends to push people a bit too hard, Harry needs to develop more tact and social sensitivity.

Harry Ritter's assets clearly outweigh his shortcomings —to the point that he represents a very good candidate for the first level of supervision in the manufacturing function. Actually, he has a rather ideal personality for production supervision in the sense that he is at his best when he can "put out the day-to-day fires" and move the "pieces out the door." Harry should be able to progress to the middle management level without much difficulty but it is somewhat doubtful that his intellectual capacity will carry him much beyond that point.

Making the Overall Rating

By placing a check mark on the line at the bottom of page 4 of the Interview Rating Form, the interviewer makes the final selection decision. In so doing, the interviewer weighs the evidence that has been accumulated from all the selection steps. Thus, not only the ratings made in each of the six major interview areas on the Interview Rating Form being considered but also all pertinent information that has been derived from the preliminary interview, the application blank, the aptitude tests, and the reference checkups is kept in mind.

In making the final rating, the interviewer will of course be guided by the extent to which the applicant's assets outweigh liabilities, or vice versa. Remember, no applicant is expected to possess all the qualifications listed in the worker specifications for a given job. The interviewer's task is to weigh the strength of the applicant's assets against the severity of his or her shortcomings. The interviewer must evaluate how much the candidate's shortcomings are likely to be a handicap in the job under consideration. And, at the same time, the interviewer estimates the extent to which the individual's assets should lead to a successful job performance.

The interviewer must remember, too, that assets of considerable strength may compensate for certain shortcomings. For example, in some cases strong motivation, relevant work experience, and good intellectual qualifications may compensate for below-average educational preparation. In such instances, an "above average" overall rating might be justified, despite the "below average" rating on education and training.

As pointed out earlier in this chapter, however, certain liabilities may be so damaging to the candidate's cause that they disqualify the individual regardless of the number of favorable ratings in other categories. An applicant decidedly lacking in honesty and sincerity, for example, or one exceedingly immature would undoubtedly merit a low overall rating despite the number of high ratings that may have been given in other important areas.

In assigning a final, overall rating, the interviewer thinks in broad terms. Does the person have the appropriate skills to handle the job? Is he or she willing to work hard and apply these skills? Has the candidate demonstrated ability to get along with people? Is he or she basically a person of good character? Has the candidate been sufficiently prepared academically?

Overall ratings are of course made in terms of the job demands. In other words, an overall rating of "average" means that the candidate should be able to turn in an average job performance, not much better and not much worse. Applicants rated "above average" should be able to turn in a good performance, while those rated "excellent" should, in the interviewer's opinion, be able to do a top-notch job.

The overall rating of "excellent" is normally reserved for applicants who have a great many assets and whose shortcomings are not at all serious. People rated "above average" are well-qualified individuals whose shortcomings, while a little more serious than the excellently rated person, are not serious enough to handicap them unduly. Candidates rated "average" are those whose assets and liabilities are about equally weighted. However, none of their shortcomings should be serious enough to keep them from turning in an adequate or average job performance.

Ideally, only those individuals with excellent or above-average ratings should be hired. In a tight labor market, however, it may be necessary to employ a number of applicants with only "average" qualifications. Candidates rated "below average" or "poor" should not be hired under any circumstances, both in terms of the good of the organization and in terms of the long-range benefits to the individuals themselves.

In making the final decision, the interviewer should be guided by one further consideration—the applicant's potential for further growth and development. Thus, although the candidate's qualifications for a given job may be only "average" at the present time, he or she may be a person of such potential that the candidate could one day become a most productive employee. The age of the individual of course represents an important factor in this connection.

FURTHER USES OF THE COMPLETED INTERVIEW RATING FORM

In the case of those individuals who are employed, the completed Interview Rating Form becomes an important part of the employee's permanent file. And since shortcomings have been carefully recorded, this information can become the basis for the employee's further development. Apprised of the new employee's developmental needs, supervisors can take immediate steps to help the employee beginning the first day of the job.

The completed Interview Rating Form also can provide the basis for follow-up studies designed to improve the selection procedures. The overall interviewer rating can be subsequently compared with performance on the job. Such follow-up information helps interviewers to identify their own interviewing weaknesses and makes it possible for them to make an effort to eliminate these weaknesses in their future discussions with other applicants. Moreover, follow-up studies of this kind enable the employment manager to evaluate the interviewing staff, in terms of both additional training needs and possible reassignment to other employment functions.

CHAPTER 15

How to Train Interviewers

That this book continue to sell as well as it does so many years after its orginal publication (1958) would seem to indicate that it is being used to *train* interviewers. If this is true, the book must be helping to meet a great need, since interviewers, by and large, receive far less formal training than do people for any other important position in business and industry.

In this third edition, therefore, the author has decided to share what he has learned about training interviewers over a lifetime of performing this consulting service—over 30 years of uninterrupted service in the case of some clients. Over the years, there has been an opportunity to try out a wide variety of training techniques in many different types of companies. The techniques discussed in this chapter, then, are the ones which have been found to be most effective.

LEARNING BY DOING

Interviewing involves a *skill* and, as such, can only be *learned by doing.* In much the same way that a person picks up any other skill, such as that of playing golf, skiing, or playing tennis, interviewers need someone who can *tell* them how to do it, *show* them how to do it, and *observe* while they do it. Interviewing is a very complex intellectual activity, and therefore can only be learned as a result of intensive training. Ideally, there should be no more than five participants in the training group and the training period should extend throughout a 5-day week. This provides an opportunity for the trainer to carry out two demonstration interviews and for each participant to conduct two practice interviews. The size of such a small training group, of course, represents a sizable per capita expense, but the rewards far exceed the costs.

As applied to interviewing, learning by doing involves the following steps:

1. The *telling* aspect involves a preliminary session during which the trainer discusses Parts Two and Three of *The Evaluation Interview.* This involves the *mechanics* of actually conducting the interview together with instructions for interpreting information brought to light.
2. The *showing* aspect is incorporated in the demonstration interviews. The trainer, of course, conducts these interviews with bona fide candidates, with the trainees observing and listening from an adjacent room.
3. The *observing* aspect involves practice interviews with bona fide candidates carried out by each trainee, with the trainer and the rest of the training group listening and observing from the observation room.

PHYSICAL FACILITIES

As implied by the above discussion, this training requires two adjacent rooms—an interview room and an observation room. The installation of a one-way mirror between the two rooms represents the best means of observation. When lights are turned out in the observation room, the observers cannot be seen from the interview room. Because the interview room is well lighted, the observers are able to get an excellent view of both interviewer and interviewee—even to the point of being able to see the slightest change in facial expression.

Interestingly enough, the presence of the mirror in the interview room represents no handicap at all to the interview itself. The interviewer's techniques for developing rapport are so effective that the interviewee normally forgets all about the mirror 5 or 10 minutes after the interview has begun. The size of the one-way mirror should be at least 3-feet wide and 3-feet high and should be installed about 2½ feet from the floor.

When the number of training sessions does not merit the installation of a one-way mirror, a closed circuit television setup can be installed as an effective substitute. Because observation in this case is limited to a 21-inch or 23-inch television screen, it is not always possible to perceive subtle changes in facial expressions. Moreover, closed circuit television requires a relatively large interview room, so that the camera can be far enough away from the interviewer and interviewee to get both in proper focus. Closed circuit television does have one distinct advantage. Tapes of each interview can be made during the course of the interview. Thus, interviewees can be invited to return at a later date to view their tapes if they so desire. Many trainees also regard this as a fine opportunity to improve their effectiveness in the interview situation. Because time does not permit for them to do this during the day, some trainees also like to stay on after hours in order to view their own performance. This gives them a better idea of what they need to do to improve their effectiveness in the second interview.

It goes almost without saying that a quality sound system is also important. The microphone can be placed in full view on the table between the interviewer and interviewee. Experience has shown that most interviewees soon forget all about the presence of the microphone, to the extent that this equipment in no way interferes with their ability to talk easily and spontaneously.

Finally, it is most important for the trainer to be able to communicate with the interviewer during the course of each practice interview. A simple, inexpensive intercom—purchased from any electronic equipment supplier—can provide this important link between trainer and trainee. The intercom has two units connected by a long wire (up to 60 feet) which is strung between the two rooms. The interviewer wears an earplug connected to the intercom unit in the interview room throughout the entire course of the discussion. The trainer uses the other unit, communicating comments and suggestions to the interviewer from the observation room. This equipment is extremely important during each participant's first interview, an interview during which the trainer normally has to provide a considerable amount of direction as well as questions designed to probe deeper for clues to behavior.

QUALIFICATIONS OF THE TRAINER

Academic preparation in psychology together with extensive experience as an interviewer represent an ideal background for one who is to serve as an interviewer trainer. Such a person should be knowledgeable in the area of human behavior in order to help participants interpret the interviewee's remarks throughout the interview. And, if the trainer has extensive experience interviewing applicants for a variety of jobs, that person brings a *broad frame of reference* to the training situation. In other words, the trainer with broad interviewing experience can compare the qualifications of any given applicant for any specific job with those of many hundreds of other applicants he or she has interviewed over a period of time. To cite an example, participants in the training group might evaluate an applicant as "brilliant" intellectually, whereas the trainer—with far more experience—might consider that candidate as "above average" but certainly not brilliant.

A bright, perceptive individual with appreciable interviewing experience but without extensive academic background in psychology can operate successfully as a trainer, *providing* that individual has been intensively trained as a trainer by a psychologist. The ideal trainer should also have experience as an instructor, since he or she must know how to maintain interest and rapport during a week of intensive and enervating activity. Finally, the instructor must be able to dominate unobstrusively, in order to maintain a very tight schedule.

COMPOSITION OF THE TRAINING GROUP

Any company should, of course, give priority to employment interviewers as the first group of people to be trained. It is a matter of interest, though, that the author now finds an ever increasing percentage of highly placed corporate managers in his training groups. One client, in fact, has specified that *all* of its managers must participate in the interviewer training, as an aid to their growth and development. All such managers are, of course, very busy people and sometimes find it difficult to take an entire week away from their day-to-day duties. Once they have completed the training, however, they usually find that all the sacrifice and hard work have been worthwhile.

Corporate managers and employment interviewers alike find that interviewer training sharpens their analytical skills with respect to the evaluation of people, provides them with much improved questioning techniques for developing information, and contributes to their understanding of human behavior. Interviewing skills also have a direct relationship to such managerial functions as feedback of appraisal information, disciplinary action with subordinates, and decisions concerning which of their people has the best potential for promotion.

One recently trained manager describes the application of his newly acquired techniques as follows:

> Successful managers sometimes tend to adopt a dominating style, causing subordinates and even peers to be reluctant to speak up at meetings and in one-on-one conversations. But I have found that techniques such as the laundry-list and 'why' questions, the calculated pause, reinforcement, the use of lead questions, and the conscious utilization of facial and vocal expression improve the free flow of information, interpersonal relationships, and the opportunity for better decision making. Managers are also frequently involved in discussions with subordinates relative to the status of various programs and projects in their area. I now find that techniques for getting the other person talking and controlling the discussion tells me more about that particular subordinate's organization and understanding of each particular project. They also help me, as the manager, to resist a tendency to take over ownership of the project from the subordinate. Finally, appraisals and career discussions are often too one-sided. Again, using techniques of getting the other person talking and controlling the conversation,

when appropriate, leads to a far more efficient discussion as well as more appropriate focus on the issue.

INTERVIEWEES FOR PRACTICE INTERVIEWS

Many professional people who train interviewers rely entirely upon the device known as role playing, as a means of providing trainees an opportunity to practice interviewing techniques. In such situations, participants in the training group frequently interview each other, with the trainer observing and making comments. This situation is obviously artificial and, although of course better than nothing, in no way represents a true interviewing experience. Although participants derive some benefit from this, the benefit is minimal indeed. Experience has shown that it is far better to provide trainees with an opportunity to interview *strangers*, in much the same way that they would be interviewing applicants for a job in their own personnel department. Hence, an interviewer training program that does not provide for bona fide interviewees is not likely to be very effective.

As mentioned earlier, the training week consists of twelve interviews, two conducted by the trainer and two carried out by each of the five participants. Since interviews on higher-level applicants normally extend over a period of 1¼ to 1½ hours and since postinterview discussions require at least 1 hour more, the time factor becomes exceedingly important. In order to fit twelve interviews into a 5-day week, it becomes necessary to carry out three interviews per day on at least 3 of the 5 days. Therefore, it is much better to use *young people* as interviewees for practice interviews. Since young people have less background to be evaluated, it is easier for the participants to complete their practice interviews in the time allowed. Moreover, it is just as easy to learn the appropriate techniques and interpretive skills by interviewing younger people as it would be by interviewing men and women with more background.

Source

Interviewees for bona fide practice interviews can be obtained from at least two sources: (1) newly hired employees and (2) students from local universities. When students are recruited from local universities, they are usually compensated (at least $25). Many students in their senior undergraduate year or in their last year of graduate school welcome the opportunity to get the interviewing experience, as a means of helping them to improve their effectiveness in job interviews taken just prior to graduation. When students are used as interviewees, someone should telephone them the evening before their appointment, reminding them of the time and place. A "no show" means that one participant will only get one practice interview.

Preparing Interviewees

Participating students are asked to complete the company's application form and to send this, together with any other material such as a résumé, to the instructor several days prior to the training session. They can be told that they will not only acquire good interviewing experience but may also be considered for job openings within the company, should their qualifications turn out to be appropriate for any current job openings. They should also be told, of course, that they will be taking part in the interviewer training program and that their interviews will be observed and perhaps taped.

Interviewees can also be told that they may learn more about themselves as a result of this experience, particularly since this type of interview is designed in such a way as to help them crystallize their thinking concerning their assets and to throw some light on those traits or abilities that need further improvement. When closed circuit television is used, interviewees can be invited back to view their own tapes.

When newly hired company employees are used as interviewees, they can be told that the interviewing experience may help them to clarify their vocational goals. All interviewees—company employees and students as well—should be invited to the observation room after the interview in order to meet the people who have been observing, several of whom may be important people in the organization. This provides such young people with a wonderful opportunity to ask the advice of seasoned managers concerning their near-term and long-term vocational direction.

Postinterview discussions should also be concerned with the kind of impression the interviewee made during the interview. This discussion should, of course, begin with favorable comments about the individual's background, such as indications of hard work, educational achievements, or the open, candid manner with which the person revealed his or her experiences. Once favorable comments have been made, members of the observation group should tactfully point out those aspects of the interview performance that could have been improved. They might point out, for example, that a given individual's performance was overly serious and without much enthusiasm. Another person might be criticized for failure to enunciate clearly and for "swallowing" some important words. Another person might be tactfully told that her discussion was too verbose and that too many of her responses tended to be anecdotal. Still another person may be told that he tended to "hide his light," in the sense that he was too modest about discussing his genuine achievements.

Care must be taken not to discuss factors which are beyond the individual's control. Obviously, no mention should be made of such shortcomings as below mental ability, poor mathematical aptitude, immaturity, or lack of emotional adjustment. On the other hand, it can be exceedingly helpful to suggest such company-sponsored courses as public speaking, assertiveness training, or courses designed to give additional product information, should such courses be deemed useful to the individual's further growth and development. The postinterview discussion can be very valuable to students in their preparation for job interviews that take place prior to graduation. Such discussions can be equally valuable to newly hired company employees since, as they progress within the organization, they will have to be interviewed by a variety of managers for the next higher level position.

THE TRAINING WEEK

The training week begins with a discussion of Parts Two and Three of *The Evaluation Interview.* Even though participants have had an opportunity to read the book prior to the session, they cannot be expected to put these techniques into operation simply as a result of reading about them. They need to have the techniques explained in detail and to be given a chance to ask questions. This normally consumes the entire morning of the first day.

The trainer next prepares the group for the first demonstration interview. The instructor coaches participants concerning what to look for in the demonstration interview, placing particular emphasis on (1) rapport-inducing techniques, (2) questions designed to probe for clues to behavior, (3) techniques of control, and (4) how to interpret the information developed. The instructor also reviews application data on the first person to be interviewed, giving particular attention to such factors as possible gaps in employment, high school and college grades, academic standards of schools attended, and the specific job for which the candidate has expressed an interest. As a result of the discussion of application data, a surprising number of hypotheses may be generated, hypotheses which the trainer will, of course, pursue during the demonstration interview.

Note-Taking

It has been found that note-taking by the interviewer in the interview room takes too much attention away from the inteviewer's attempt to practice the recommended techniques. Interviewers, therefore, do not take notes during their practice interviews.

The actual note-taking is done by participants in the observation room. It is suggested that they record interview data in outline form and write clues to behavior in the margin of the page. In so doing, they learn the analytical process of picking up clues to behavior and documenting their findings with hard interview data. Exhibit 2 provides an example of note-taking on a small portion of one individual's work history and education.

At the conclusion of the interview, observers pass along their notes to the interviewer—notes which that person then uses as a basis for writing the report.

The trainer collects the notes about the person interviewed from the various participants and studies them that evening. One set of notes may reveal abundant, well-organized interview data but very few clues to behavior. Another set of notes may reveal many clues to behavior but insufficient interview data as a basis for such clues. Notes

Norman Metler

	I. Work History
	A. A&P grocery clerk
	1. Started at the age of 16
Hard worker	– worked 3 summers full time and 25 hrs. a week during the regular school yr.
thrifty	– regarded as responsible
early signs of maturity	2. Saved $3500 by the time he was ready for college
	B. Inland Steel
	1. Summers after freshman and soph. yrs. at college
hard worker perseverance	2. Worked as laborer – very hot, dirty but stuck it out 2 summers because of the good money ($10/hr.)
people skills	3. Invited back 2nd summer because of "willingness to work and ability to get along with everyone"
	C. Thomas Moor College
	1. 3rd summer
1st glimmer of leadership	2. Worked on college-sponsored gov't grant
	3. Noise-level strike
good attention to detail	4. Supervised 4 H.S. students – enjoyed leadership responsibility
Computer experience	5. Worked on computer – enjoyed the detail

Exhibit 2 Sample interview notes.

II. Education
A. H.S.
1. Good scholastic record — graduated in upper 1/3 of class
2. SAT's
Verbal 510 (only fair)
Math 590 (good)
3. Liked math, physics
4. Disliked English, history
5. Elected pres. of sr. class
6. Admits he studied harder than the average student
7. H.S. considered to have only fair academic standards
— didn't offer calculus
B. Thomas Moor College
1. Majored in bus. admin.

probably not highly intelligent

not very verbal
popular
people skills
leadership

can be returned to the participants the following morning and used as a basis for improved note-taking in connection with subsequent interviews.

The First Demonstration Interview

The trainer conducts the first interview, with the trainees observing and listening from the adjacent room. In this interview, the instructor places special emphasis on *mechanics*—rapport-inducing techniques, probing questions, and techniques of control.

As noted above, the interviewee is invited into the observation room at the end of the interview to meet the observers and to get their reaction as to how he or she came across. Most interviewees also like to pose questions about their near-term and long-term vocational goals.

Once the interviewee has departed, participants are asked to rate that individual on the fourteen traits that appear on the bottom of the back of the Interview Guide. This exercise is carried out for two purposes: (1) to provide a common understanding of each of the traits listed on the Interview Guide and (2) to teach the trainees that they must provide hard interview data as a basis for their ratings on each of the traits.

Writing Reports

During the evening of the first day, moreover, the trainer completes the write-up of the demonstration interview, using the Interview Rating Form found in the back of the book. The trainer has copies made of this interview report for each of the participants as a model for the reports they will write on their own interviews, and discusses the report with them the following day. The trainer emphasizes that report writing represents an extension of the interpretation process, pointing out that interviewers normally find it possible to become more *definitive* in their evaluation and overall ratings as they record interview data and clues to behavior. They also learn to disregard opinions for which they do not have adequate documentation.

Role Playing

Most interview trainees will have had little or no experience performing in front of a camera or being observed from an adjacent room. Nor will they have had any experience being on the other end of an intercom setup where they are required to listen to comments and suggestions during a normal interview discussion. For these reasons, it is good to do a little role playing as a first exercise on the morning of the second day of the training week. Participants, in pairs, occupy the interview room—equipped with camera and lights—role playing as an interviewer and an interviewee. The interviewer, equipped with the electronic earplug, runs through the lead questions which all participants have been told to memorize verbatim prior to the session. In pauses that occur between questions, the trainer makes suggestions and comments from the other room, comments having to do with facial expression, vocal intonation, and the like. The "interviewee" in this situation, makes no responses at all. Once the "interviewer" has had an opportunity to run through the lead questions and listen to the trainer's comments, the two participants change chairs, in such a way that the former "interviewee" now becomes the "interviewer." As a consequence of this kind of role playing, participants find it much easier to conduct their first practice interview.

Practice Interviews

The person assigned to conduct the first practice interview is selected by deciding which of the participants appears to have been the most comfortable with the lead questions during the role playing exercise. Practice interviews are scheduled throughout the week—usually two or three each day—until each participant has had an opportunity to conduct two practice interviews. As noted above, each interview is conducted with a bona fide candidate. In cases where the interviewee is a college student, emphasis at the end of the interview is placed on the specific type of job for which that person seems best qualified. That particular discussion, of course, is continued in the observation room with all participants after the interview has been completed. In cases where the interviewee is a newly hired company employee, the discussion considers which type of position that individual might most logically aspire to as a next step in his or her progress within the organization.

The participant writes a report on the person whom he or she has interviewed. This means that only two or three members of the group will be required to write reports on any given evening. Reports completed during the evening are read to the group at the beginning of the following day and suggested changes made. These reports are viewed in the light of how much documentation is provided to support evaluations.

Instructor's Role During Practice Interviews

While observing the interviews, the instructor carries out running comments to the observing group, pointing out clues to behavior and indicating those things that the interviewer is doing well, as well as those things that need to be improved. The trainer also writes a critique of the interviewer's performance during the course of the interview. During the postinterview discussion, the instructor reviews the critique, with particular emphasis on factors that need to be improved during the second interview.

During each of the practice interviews, the instructor also communicates with the interviewer by means of the intercom. The trainer's comments are normally concerned with reminding the interviewer to lubricate, maintain control, use appropriate facial and vocal expressions, and to use the questions on the Interview Guide verbatim. The instructor also provides the interviewer with questions which enable that person to probe more deeply for clues to behavior. Should an interviewer forget to probe for the "why" of subject preference in high school, for example, the trainer can bring this to his or her attention, with the thought of generating possible clues to analytical ability.

The trainer may have to give rather frequent direction during the first interview but is normally required to give much less help during each person's second interview. The instructor communicates *only when the applicant is talking*, in order to avoid awkward pauses. The instructor also tries to keep comments short, often limiting them to a word or phrase.

Written reports are destroyed at the end of the training week, except in the case of an outstanding college student who is being recommended for employment. In the latter case, the report goes to the manager to whom the college student is being recommended.

Time Scheduling

The training is so intensive that an 8:00 A.M. to 5:00 P.M. workday will normally be necessary. The first 1½ hours of each day can be reserved for discussion of reports written the previous evening. Interviews can subsequently be scheduled at 9:30 A.M., 1:00 P.M., and 3:00 P.M. This, of course, represents a very tight schedule, and this is the reason why all interviews must take place at the time originally allocated.

THE BOTTOM LINE

By the end of the week, each participant will have carried out two interviews and have observed ten others. During each person's first interview, primary attention will have been focused on the *mechanics*—rapport-inducing techniques, probing techniques, and techniques of control. By the time each participant's second interview takes place, that person will have conducted one interview and have observed four others. As a consequence, the mechanics of the interview will normally have become part of the individual's unreflective behavior by that time—to the extent that, in the second interview, he or she will be free to concentrate on the interpretation of the candidate's remarks as they occur.

By the end of the training, each participant will also have written two reports. Most people profit greatly from the critique of their first report and do a much better job the second time around. Finally, each trainee will have participated in the evaulation of twelve candidates. This provides the beginning of a *frame of reference*, in the sense that they can compare new people they interview with the twelve they have already seen. As participants interview more and more people on their own, their frame of reference becomes increasingly broad, enabling them to become gradually more definitive in their evaluation of applicants for employment or, for that matter, current employees being considered for promotion.

APPENDIX 1

Interview Guide

INTERVIEW GUIDE

Name__________________Date________Interviewer__________________

1. WORK HISTORY

a. Duties?

b. Likes?

c. Things found less satisfying?

d. Conditioned to work?

e. Level of earnings?

f. Reasons for changing jobs?

g. Any leadership experience?

h. Number of previous jobs?

i. Achievements? "What did you learn about your strengths as a result of working on those jobs? Did you find, for example, that you worked harder than the average person, got along better with people, organized things better, gave more attention to detail—just what?"

j. Development needs? "Did you get any clues to your development needs as a result of working on those jobs? You know, we all have some shortcomings and, the person who can recognize them, can do something about them. Was there a need to acquire more self-confidence, more tact, more self-discipline—to become firmer with people—just what?"

k. Factors of job satisfaction? "What does a job have to have to give you satisfaction? Some people look for money, some look for security, some want to manage, some want to create—what is important to you? (Do you prefer a job that is structured or unstructured? theoretical or practical? with a fair amount of detail or without much detail?)"

l. Type of job desired?

(page 1)

2. EDUCATION AND TRAINING

a. Best and poorest subjects?

b. Grades? "What about grades? Were they average, above average, or perhaps a little below average?"

c. College boards? "What were your college board scores?"

d. Extracurricular activities?

e. Effort? "How conscientious a student were you? Did you work about as hard as the average person, a little harder, or perhaps not quite so hard?"

f. Special achievements?

g. Training beyond the undergraduate level?

h. How was education financed?

3. PRESENT SOCIAL ADJUSTMENT

a. Interests and hobbies
Sports
Community involvement
Reading
Interest in the arts

b. Energy level "How would you describe your energy level—as average, above average, or perhaps a little below average?"

c. Overall social adjustment
"Loner," introspective, seemingly not very happy
or
Meets people easily, considerable group involvement, has many friends, cheerful outlook on life.

4. PERSONALITY, MOTIVATION, AND CHARACTER
(+, A+, A, A−, −)

( ) a. Maturity
( ) b. Emotional adjustment
( ) c. Team worker
( ) d. Tact
( ) e. Adaptability
( ) f. Tough-mindedness
( ) g. Self-discipline
( ) h. Initiative
( ) i. Perseverance
( ) j. Self-confidence
( ) k. Assertiveness
( ) l. Conscientiousness
( ) m. Hard worker
( ) n. Honesty and sincerity

(page 2)

APPENDIX 2

Interview Rating Form

INTERVIEW RATING FORM

Name____

Interviewed for___________________________________

Interviewer________________________Date___________

I. WORK HISTORY	Above Avg.	Avg.	Below Avg.

(page 1)

II. EDUCATION AND TRAINING	Above Avg.	Avg.	Below Avg.

III. PRESENT SOCIAL ADJUSTMENT	Above Avg.	Avg.	Below Avg.

(page 2)

IV. PERSONALITY, MOTIVATION AND CHARACTER
(+, A+, A, A−, −)

Above Avg.	Avg.	Below Avg.

( ) 1. Maturity
( ) 2. Emotional adjustment
( ) 3. Teamworker
( ) 4. Tact
( ) 5. Adaptability
( ) 6. Tough-mindedness
( ) 7. Self-discipline
( ) 8. Initiative
( ) 9. Perseverance
( ) 10. Self-confidence
( ) 11. Assertiveness
( ) 12. Conscientiousness
( ) 13. Hard worker
( ) 14. Honesty and sincerity

V. SUMMARY OF ASSETS

SUMMARY OF SHORTCOMINGS

VI. OVERALL SUMMARY

VII. OVERALL RATING

Excellent	Above Avg.	Avg.	Below Avg.	Poor

APPENDIX 3

Illustrative Reports of Interview Findings

INTERVIEW RATING FORM

Name Harry Mantz
Interviewed for Shop Operations, Manufacturing
Interviewer Dorothy Stewart Date 3/4/83

I. WORK HISTORY	Above Avg.	Avg.	Below Avg.
	X		

Harry worked on his father's sod farm from a very young age, doing hard manual work and spending long hours (dawn to dusk, 6 days a week) in the field, thus developing excellent habits of hard work.

While in college, he returned to the farm two summers and spent two summers on scientific research projects under the auspices of the college and funded by government grants. He found that he could handle the detail with a high degree of accuracy but did not like this aspect of the work and found the laboratory "altogether too confining." He did get some practical work experience with computers, however.

After graduating from college in 1981, he wanted to go to the University of Michigan to get a degree in optical engineering but decided that he could not afford this.

Harry joined Pratt & Whitney June 1981 and was assigned the Manufacturing Training Program. In his first assignment as a production control specialist he learned a great deal about the jet engine and enjoyed his association with people.

In his second assignment as a supervisor, Harry ran into problems with the union because of his quick temper and tendency to be blunt and tactless at times. Harry showed mental toughness, assertiveness and self-confidence in "pushing people to put in a good day's work" but became involved in some fifteen grievances. But he learned from experience and discovered ways to work with the union steward to get the job done. Harry "loved" this assignment and derived genuine satisfaction "getting the parts out the door."

In his third assignment in process control, he missed the lack of supervisory responsibility but worked hard and earned a job appraisal rating of 9 out of a possible 10. Even so, his manager criticized him for being overly independent, impulsive, and not a very good team worker.

Now in his fourth assignment, Harry finds information systems technically challenging but misses exposure to people and finds the work a bit too detailed and confining. He also realizes that he is much more practically than theoretically oriented.

After completing his manufacturing training program in June, Harry hopes to take a leave of absence in order to get his master's degree in optical engineering at the University of Michigan. In the light of his lack of

(continued)

theoretical orientation and seeming lack of genuine interest in optical engineering, this appears to be an inappropriate aspiration and raises some question about his judgment and maturity. He seems more interested in simply getting a master's degree than anything else.

Harry's work experience is impressive for one of his age. He has demonstrated terrific energy, willingness to work hard, ability to motivate people, and leadership potential. He is a bit of a "bull of the woods" but seems to be modifying this aspect of his personality.

II. EDUCATION AND TRAINING	X Above Avg.	Avg.	Below Avg.

Harry made an excellent record in high school, graduating 11th in a class of 276. But he candidly admits that he studied a lot harder than the average student in order to make these grades. His SATs: math 615; verbal 580 (both good). He had few extracurricular activities because he had to hurry home after school to work on the farm.

Harry attended David Elkins College because he received a full tuition scholarship. This raises some question about the maturity of judgment because of the relatively low academic standards of that institution. But he took full advantage of his opportunities, carrying a double major in math and physics and graduating cum laude with 165 credits when 120 would have been enought to graduate. Again, he worked inordinately hard, regularly studying until 1:00 a.m. to 2:00 a.m. on most weekdays. His more theoretical studies such as advanced physics and math gave him a lot of trouble. His comment that "David Elkins has very high academic standards" would seem to reflect some lack of critical thinking. Harry was very active in college, serving on the student council, being elected to positions of leadership on several clubs, and taking part on several intramural athletic teams.

Harry's educational experience abundantly reflects his ability to make maximum utilization of his talents. His mental ability is "good" but clearly not outstanding. He had trouble with the more highly theoretical subjects and had to work extremely hard to make his grades in a school with rather mediocre academic standards. Even so, he is reasonably well trained.

III. PRESENT SOCIAL ADJUSTMENT	X Above Avg.	Avg.	Below Avg.

Interests are quite varied (volleyball, hiking, jogging, piano playing, basketball) but not very deep or intellectual. He does very little reading except text books and his musical interests are rather shallow.

energy level appears to be unusually high.

(continued)

has a lot of poise, meets people easily, appears to have many friends, and seems to be an altogether happy person. Harry is the kind of a person who does not let disappointments bother him very much. He has demonstrated the ability to "roll with the punches." Hence he seems to be well-adjusted, emotionally and socially.

IV. PERSONALITY, MOTIVATION AND CHARACTER
(+, A+, A, A−, −)

X		
Above Avg.	Avg.	Below Avg.

(A) 1. Maturity
(+) 2. Emotional adjustment
(A−) 3. Teamworker
(A) 4. Tact
(+) 5. Adaptability
(A+) 6. Tough-mindedness
(+) 7. Self-discipline
(+) 8. Initiative
(+) 9. Perseverance
(A+) 10. Self-confidence
(+) 11. Assertiveness
(+) 12. Conscientiousness
(+) 13. Hard worker
(+) 14. Honesty and sincerity

V. SUMMARY OF ASSETS

Outstanding motivation
- high energy
- very hard worker
- strong self-discipline
- excellent perseverance
- excellent initiative

Good (but not excellent) mental ability
- good math aptitude
- good verbal aptitude

Strong leadership potential
- assertive
- self-confident
- tough-minded
- "take charge" person
- infectious enthusiasm
- communicates well

Well adjusted emotionally
- can take pressure
- cheerful outlook
- does not let things get him down

SUMMARY OF SHORTCOMINGS

Not as mature as some of his age
- vocational goals not well thought out.
- knowledge of self leaves something to be desired

Something of a "shooter from the hip"
- impulsive
- makes some decisions too fast

Overly independent
- stubborn at times
- bit inflexible
- too blunt and direct
- not always tactful

Quality of intellect leaves something to be desired
- not a critical thinker
- not much intellectual depth or breadth
- has difficulty thinking in the abstract

(continued)

VI. OVERALL SUMMARY

Harry Mantz is a "natural" for the manufacturing function. He has the assertiveness, self-confidence, and mental toughness so important in leadership; he has strong practical interests; he is productionminded in the sense that he likes to get things completed quickly; and he has demonstrated the ability to motivate people. Harry is much more at home on the shop floor than he is in the laboratory. He has energy "to burn," is an uncommonly hard worker, and has learned to make maximum utilization of his generally "good" basic abilities. Harry is also well-adjusted emotionally.

Negatively, Harry tries so hard to get things done quickly that he has become something of a "shooter from the hip," making some decisions too quickly and being a bit impulsive at times. Not yet as mature as some persons of his age, moreover, his judgment sometimes leaves something to be desired and his vocational goals are not well thought out. Harry can also be overly independent and a bit stubborn when he feels that he is right. Finally, he is not strongly analytical or critical in his thinking.

In summary, Harry is "barking up the wrong tree" in his desire to go to the University of Michigan to get a degree in optical engineering. He does not have the theoretical drive, the penchant for detail, the analytical power, or the creativity to make a significant contribution in engineering. On the other hand, he is *very* well equipped for a career in shop operations. In fact, he fits the latter mold to a "t." In terms of an assignment in shop operations, his assets far outweigh his shortcomings—to the extent that he merits a relatively high rating for that position. In shop operations, Harry has good potential for advancement to the next two levels of supervision. (For a purely technical assignment would be much less favorable.) Harry should be brought into the personnel department for counseling.

VII. OVERALL RATING	Excellent	Above Avg.	Avg.	Below Avg.	Poor
		X (for shop operations)			

INTERVIEW RATING FORM

Name ___Ruth Horton___

Interviewed for ___Information Systems Analyst___

Interviewer ___Edward Harting___ Date ___3/15/83___

I. WORK HISTORY	Above Avg.	Avg.	Below Avg.
	X		

Ruth had a series of restaurant-related jobs (Sambos, Chili Parlor, Burger King) starting as a dish washer at the age of 15, and gradually acquiring positions of more responsibility. She showed good maturity and self-discipline by saving enough money to buy a car of her own and still have $3500 left at the time she was ready for college.

Worked for Steak and Ale all through college—full-time summers and 30 hrs. a week during the regular school year. This reflects great energy, stamina, and willingness to work hard. She progressed from waitress to hostess. The latter job, in particular, provided an opportunity to develop good people skills as well as a higher degree of sophistication. Wages and tips amounted to about $7 an hour and helped to pay for college expenses.

Selected for the Information Systems Management Program at General Dynamics in June 1982, despite her lack of relevant experience and education. Her willingness to accept this position even though she did not have the technical skills possessed by the other trainees reflects her self-confidence. She evidently adapted very quickly to her first assignment as a programmer, readily picking up the computer languages and adjusting well to the confinement and detail which is so much a part of this job. She also showed good initiative in working on her own to develop a new system, with very little guidance from others. That she was so quick to grasp the new technology would seem to reflect good mental ability. Her job appraisal rating was a 5 out of a possible 6 with special commendation for her hard work, ability to get along with others, and initiative.

Since January 1983, Ruth has been working on her second training assignment in manufacturing systems. Again, she seems to be acquiring the necessary skills for this job quite rapidly. But she recognizes the need to develop better organization and planning skills as well as the need to do a better job of sorting out details as to priority and importance. She has been praised by her supervisor for her analytical skills but also told that she should become more assertive and tough-minded in "standing up" to her customers.

Although Ruth did not have any relevant work experience prior to coming to General Dynamics, she seems to have made good progress on ISMP. Her entire work experience reflects excellent habits of hard work, perseverance, initiative, as well as good mental ability. She would have received a higher rating still in this area if she had made more of any effort to have obtained experience relevant to her field of study during the summers she was in college.

(continued)

II. EDUCATION AND TRAINING	Above Avg.	Avg.	Below Avg.
	X		

Ruth made an excellent record in high school, graduating 22nd in a class of 575. She seemed to do this quite easily, considering that she was working 25 hours in a restaurant. Her college board scores were: math 710 (outstanding) and verbal 630 (very good). Ruth feels that she studied a great deal in H.S., placing her studies ahead of outside activities. Actually, she had little time for the latter because of her part-time job. Her high school experience reflects a degree of maturity beyond her years.

Accepted by Haverford, a college with extremely high academic standards, Ruth majored in economics and did well in all of her subjects. She graduated in the top 20 percent of her class—an excellent record indeed in view of the fact that she worked 30 hours a week on an outside job. She greatly enjoyed her more analytically demanding courses, such as calculus, philosophy, and the more theoretical courses in economics.

Ruth's fine academic record in a top school, her high SAT scores, and the fact that she was able to fit in a 30-hour-a-week outside job provide abundant evidence of high-level intellect. She is exceedingly well-trained in economics but did not take any computer-related courses. Obviously, too, her academic record provides additional evidence of her energy, stamina, and willingness to work hard.

III. PRESENT SOCIAL ADJUSTMENT	Above Avg.	Avg.	Below Avg.
		X	

Ruth has been so busy working and going to school that she has not had much time to develop many outside interests. But the interests she does have reflect her fine intellect and her broad cultural education. She reads 3 or 4 books a month, primarily concerned with biography and history. And she likes to listen to classical music (Bach, Mozart, Brahms).

When time permits Ruth enjoys model building, some such models taking as many as three months to complete. This hobby obviously requires perseverance and great attention to detail.

Despite her busy life, Ruth seems to have many friends and to be well-adjusted socially. But she has never had much in the way of leadership experience, either in school or in the community. She says: "This is still to come and I plan very definitely to seek it out."

(continued)

IV. PERSONALITY, MOTIVATION AND CHARACTER

(+, A+, A, A−, −)

X		
Above Avg.	Avg.	Below Avg.

(+) 1. Maturity
(+) 2. Emotional adjustment
(+) 3. Teamworker
(+) 4. Tact
(+) 5. Adaptability
(A−) 6. Tough-mindedness
(+) 7. Self-discipline
(+) 8. Initiative
(+) 9. Perseverance
(A+) 10. Self-confidence
(A) 11. Assertiveness
(+) 12. Conscientiousness
(+) 13. Hard worker
(+) 14. Honesty and sincerity

V. SUMMARY OF ASSETS

Superior mental ability
- learns quickly
- articulate
- perceptive
- problem solver
- intellectual breadth and depth

Outstanding motivation
- great energy
- very hard worker
- self-discipline
- sets high standards

Mature
- good judgment
- sets goals
- can make sacrifices
- good self-knowledge

People skills
- tact
- empathy
- sensitive to needs of others
- friendly

Character
- honest
- reliable
- high values

Assets relevant to systems work
- high math aptitude
- attention to detail
- perseverance
- excellent analytical skills

SUMMARY OF SHORTCOMINGS

Needs develoment of leadership
- needs to become more assertive
- needs more mental toughness
- could use more infectious enthusiasm

Lack of relevant experience and training

(continued)

VI. OVERALL SUMMARY

Ruth Horton seems to "have it all together." In fact, she seems to have just about everything that she needs for a successful career in information systems work. She is very bright; she has a high math aptitude; she gives excellent attention to detail; she has high standards; and she possesses strong analytical skills. Conditioned to work at an early age, Ruth has a high degree of energy and is an extremely hard worker. She is also mature beyond her years. Ruth's work as a hostess in a restaurant has enabled her to develop good people skills. In all of her jobs, she seems to have been able to get along well with peers and supervisors alike.

Ruth's shortcomings are not particularly serious. If she wants to become a manager, however, she will need to develop more assertiveness and mental toughness. She is well aware of these development needs and seems determined to do something about them. Ruth's lack of more relevant work experience and education probably represents a further shortcoming. But she is so bright and picks up new information so quickly that lack of relevant experience and training should not handicap her unduly.

In summary, Ruth's assets *far* outweigh her shortcomings in terms of qualification for a career in systems work. She has a large number of important strengths and such shortcomings as she has are well within her control to eliminate. Ruth is capable of eventual promotion to positions of appreciable responsibility in her field. General Dynamics is fortunate to have her.

VII. OVERALL RATING	Excellent	Above Avg.	Avg.	Below Avg.	Poor
	X				

INTERVIEW RATING FORM

Name George Anton
Interviewed for Engineering Training Program
Interviewer Andrew Corning Date 3/24/83

I. WORK HISTORY	Above Avg.	Avg.	Below Avg.
		X	

George worked two summers while in high school on a construction crew as a mason's helper, a job secured for him by an uncle. This involved extremely hard work, wheeling wheelbarrows of cement to the bricklayers. That he "stuck it out" all summer and returned to the same job the subsequent summer demonstrates stamina, perseverance, and willingness to work hard.

During the summer following his freshmen year in college, George worked for Bethlehem Steel as a metallurgical observer. This job was secured for him by his father, an employee of the firm. The job was highly relevant to his college major of metallurgical engineering. The indications are that George adapted well to the schedule of swing shifts and got along well with the people. Understandably, he found the repetitive nature of data collection unchallenging.

The following two summers George worked for Alcoa as a metallurgical trainee. Again, his father seems to have played a major role in getting him this job. George was praised by his supervisor for his energy, enthusiasm, and ability to get along with people. But, as his engineering duties became more complex during the second summer, he found it more difficult to understand the projects to which he was assigned. He decided as a result of that experience that the job was too research oriented and that he preferred work involving more practical application. His job appraisal that summer listed "weak technical skills" as a shortcoming. It seems significant, too, that Alcoa did not make him a permanent job offer at the time he graduated from college. This came as a shock and a disappointment but George apparently did not let it get him down, suggesting good emotional adjustment. Even so, the experience at Alcoa raises questions about his mental ability and technical strength. The candid manner in which George discussed this situation during the interview, however, underscores his complete honesty.

Hired by Rocket Engineering in July 1982, George has been assigned to the Engineering Training and has been working on failure analysis. He finds this "too theoretical" and hopes to get a job with more practical orientation for his next program assignment. His manager rated him high on effort and interpersonal skills but has called attention to "certain technical flaws" which the manager believes stem from lack of better academic training.

George's work experience reflects strong motivation, good people skills, and relevant metallurgical experience prior to his employment by Rocket Engineering. But, because all of his jobs have been secured for him by relatives,

(continued)

he has not had much of an opportunity to develop much initiative. And his technical ability appears to be weak. That George hopes one day to become an "engineer-manager" shows that he is not really aware of his limitations and suggests some degree of immaturity.

II. EDUCATION AND TRAINING			X
	Above Avg.	Avg.	Below Avg.

George made a good record in high school, graduating in the top 25 percent of his class. He candidly admits, though, that he had to work "a lot harder" than the average student in order to make these grades. His college board score was good in math (575) but rather poor in the verbal area (480). George made a letter in football but was not otherwise active in extracurricular affairs. He says: "I was very shy at that stage of my life and didn't have many friends but I have changed a lot since then."

George attended Hopetown College, an institution with questionable academic standards. He showed poor judgment in selecting a very difficult major (metallurgical engineering) and sticking with the major even though he did not really enjoy it and had to study extremely hard in order to make good grades, a further reflection of his immaturity. (George is evidently inordinately influenced by his father who is himself a metallurgical engineer and strongly persuaded his son to follow in his footsteps) George deserves great credit for doing as well as he did in college (3.0 out of a possible 4.0), but he really "took it out of his hide" in so doing. He says: "I regularly studied until 1:00 A.M. or 2:00 A.M. and pulled my share of all-nighters—usually one a week."

George demonstrated terrific motivation in college. But the extent to which he had to work in order to make good grades in college with below average academic standards—together with his low college board scores—suggests lack of good mental ability. It seems quite apparent, too, that he is not really well-trained technically.

III. PRESENT SOCIAL ADJUSTMENT		X	
	Above Avg.	Avg.	Below Avg.

George has devoted so much of his time during the past several years to study that he has not had time to develop many outside interests. Such interests as he has are understandably nonintellectual. George has never been at all interested in reading. He says: "I like to read magazine articles about hunting and fishing, but I almost never read a book. Books have too many pages to get through." George's attitude toward reading is quite typical of his view of music and the other arts. He definitely lacks intellectual breadth and depth.

On the positive side, though, Gorge has developed socially to a very considerable extent since his high school days. He has overcome his shyness to the extent that he meets people a lot easier and now seems to have quite a number of friends.

(continued)

There has never been any question about George's energy. He has not only worked hard all his life but has always made a point of keeping in shape. Even today, he jogs 4 or 5 miles a day and plays basketball at least once a week.

IV. PERSONALITY, MOTIVATION AND CHARACTER

(+, A+, A, A−, −)

Above Avg.	Avg.	Below Avg.
	X	

(A−) 1. Maturity
(A+) 2. Emotional adjustment
(+) 3. Teamworker
(+) 4. Tact
(A+) 5. Adaptability
(A−) 6. Tough-mindedness
(+) 7. Self-discipline
(A−) 8. Initiative
(+) 9. Perseverance
(A−) 10. Self-confidence
(A) 11. Assertiveness
(+) 12. Conscientiousness
(+) 13. Hard worker
(+) 14. Honesty and sincerity

V. SUMMARY OF ASSETS

Superior Motivation
- boundless energy
- extremely hard worker
- self-discipline
- perseverance
- high work standards

Excellent people skills
- tactful
- empathetic
- cooperative
- social sensitivity

Excellent character
- extremely honest
- very reliable
- genuine

Some prior relevant experience in metallurgy

SUMMARY OF SHORTCOMINGS

Not very strong mentally
- poor verbal aptitude
- can't think in the abstract
- not a critical thinker
- weak analytical skills
- little intellectual breadth or depth

Not very mature for age
- judgment in major decisions has not been good
- unrealistic vocational goals
- somewhat naive
- very dependent on father

Below Average technical ability
- does have good math aptitude, but:
- mediocre academic preparation
- not much analytical power
- does not really enjoy metallurgy
- not at all creative

Little leadership potential
- not self-confident
- lacks mental toughness
- not assertive
- does not communicate well

(continued)

VI. OVERALL SUMMARY

George Anton is in many ways a fine human being. He is extremely honest; he works inordinately hard; and he has learned to make maximum utilization of his modest abilities—to a far greater extent than most of the rest of us do. Once he got over his shyness in high school, George blossomed out socially, acquiring a rather pronounced ability to get along with people. Throughout all of his job and school experiences, he has earned a reputation for tact and sensitivity to the needs of other people. Unlike most other college graduates, moreover, George acquired some relevant experience in his chosen field of metallurgy as a result of his work during the summer months.

In view of the fact that he tries so hard, it seems unfair that George should be somewhat limited intellectually, at least in comparison with engineering graduates. He is not at all perceptive; he lacks analytical power; he is rather poorly prepared academically; and he has little breadth and depth. In short, he is somewhat limited both intellectually and technically. Unfortunately too, George has evidently been so dominated and influenced by his father that he has had relatively little opportunity to make his own decisions. Nor has he had much opportunity to develop self-confidence, assertiveness, or mental toughness. Again, due primarily to his father's domination, George has failed to acquire a normal degree of maturity. As a consequence, he really does not know who he is or where he is going.

In summary, George has many of the assets and shortcomings of the overachiever. He works so hard that he achieves more than might be expected of him in the light of his modest basic abilities. This kind of drive would carry him a long way in some types of work—but not in engineering. He simply does not have enough intellectual and technical strength to compete successfully with the average engineer. George Anton represents a sad case indeed. He has been trained in a field for which he has little potential and now it is almost too late to switch careers. He should never have been hired for the demanding engineering work found in Rocket Engineering. His best bet is to try his luck with a less sophisticated company where the competition would not be so difficult.

VII. OVERALL RATING

Excellent	Above Avg.	Avg.	Below Avg.	Poor
			X	

INDEX

Abusive discharge, 6
Academic record (*see* Education)
Adaptability, 267
Adjustment, social (*see* Social adjustment)
Affirmative action, 19, 21–22, 73
  (*See also* Equal employment opportunity)
Age, questions as to, 29–30
Age Discrimination in Employment Act of 1967, 19
Analytical capacity, 173
Applicants (*see specific entries, for example*: Education; Mental ability; Social adjustment; Trait constellations)
Application forms, 70–72
Aptitude tests, 77–80, 237
  state employment service, use by, 79–80
  transportability of, 78–79
  validity generalization of, 78–79
Arts, interest in, 231–232
Assertive personality, 168–170, 173, 270–271
Athletics, participation in, 219, 228–229
Automobile industry, 3–4
  retraining of workers by, 11

Balance in control of interview, 127–130
Behavior (*see specific entries, for example*: Maturity; Motivation)
Bethlehem Steel Company, 14, 26
Blocking of questions, 116–118

Calculated pause as interview technique, 94–95, 196
Campus interview, 74–76
Casual remarks of applicant, clarification of, 113

Children, questions as to, 27–28
Civil Rights Act of 1964, 4, 18, 20–21, 77
(*See also* Equal employment opportunity)
Coca-Cola Company, 24
College admissions, 248–249
College boards, 215–218
interpretation of scores, 238–239
in selection of college students, 248–249
College education (*see* Education)
Community involvement, 229–230
Comprehensive introductory questions, 102–105
assumed consent, 104–105
memorization, 104
reminding applicants of omitted parts, 111
Conditioning to work, 185–187, 244
Conscientiousness, 173, 271
Consent of applicant in obtaining references, 76–77
Constellations, trait (*see* Trait constellations)
Control of interview, 125–140
appropriate coverage in, 127
balance in, 127–130
by chronological development of information, 137
economy of interviewer's time in, 131–132
equal employment opportunity considerations, 140
by exhaustion of each interview area, 137–138
by follow-up questions, 115–116
importance of interviewing manner in, 135–136
by interruption, 133–135
with Interview Guide, 132–133
necessity of, 126–132
with older applicants, 138
pacing in, 139–140
penetration of candidate's basic reactions, 130–131

Control of interview (*Cont.*):
with recent graduates, 138–139
by systematic development of information, 137
techniques in, 132–136
with trained applicants, 39–45
"why" questions in, 42–43
Conversation:
calculated pauses in, 94–95, 196
interruption of, in control of interview, 133–135
Critical thinking, 174

Data evaluation (*see* Interpretation of information)
Demonstration interview, 292
Depth questions, 240
Descriptive versus evaluative information, 130–131
Direct observation in interpretation of information, 156–157
Direct questions, softening of, 121–122
Discharge:
abusive or wrongful, 6
of marginal workers, 6–8, 15
Discrimination (*see* Equal employment opportunity)
Do-gooders, 170–172
Double-edged questions, 120–121, 199

Earnings, 43–44, 187–190
Education, 208–227
achievements, academic, 221–222
college boards, 215–218
interpretation of scores, 238–239
in selection of college students, 248–249
discussion of: chronology of, 210
structuring, 209–211
effort expended in obtaining, 220–221

Education (*Cont.*):
equal employment opportunity considerations, 233–234
extracurricular activities, 218–220
financing of, 224–227
follow-up questions on, 112–113
grades, 213–214
Graduate Record Examination, 239–240
graduate training, 222–224
interpretation of information, 151–152
overachievers, 215, 243–244
recording, 261–262
special achievements, 221–222
structuring discussion, 208–211
subject preferences, 211–213, 240–241
(*See also* Mental ability)
Educational Testing Service, Princeton, N.J., 215
Emotional adjustment, 174, 265–266
Emotional maturity, 173, 245–246
(*See also* Maturity; Social adjustment)
Employee relations personnel, worker specifications for, 61–64
Employment at will, 6–9
and marginal workers, 6–8
Employment service, 79–80
Employment tests (*see* Aptitude tests)
Energy level, 232–233, 242–243
Equal employment opportunity (EEO), 4–5, 17–33
affirmative action, 19, 21–22, 73
and compliance during Reagan administration, 22
age, questions as to, 29–30
Age Discrimination in Employment Act of 1967, 19
benefits of, 25–26
children, questions as to, 27–28
Equal employment opportunity (EEO) (*Cont.*):
Civil Rights Act of 1964, 4, 18, 20–21, 77
costs of, 4–5
education and, 233–234
Equal Pay Act of 1963, 18–19
Executive Order 11246, 19–21
health, questions as to, 31
industry's reaction to regulations, 24–25
interview considerations, 26–33, 105–106, 124, 140
legislation and executive orders, 17–21
marital status, questions as to 27
race and national origin, questions as to, 29
reasons for, 22–24
reference checks, 32–33
Rehabilitation Act of 1973, 20, 31
religion, questions as to, 28–29
veteran status, questions as to, 32
Vietnam-Era Veterans' Readjustment Assistance Act of 1974, 20, 32
work force quality improvement and, 25–26
work history, discussion of, 206–207
Equal Employment Opportunity Commission (EEOC), 18, 19
Equal Pay Act of 1963, 18–19
Evaluation interview (*see* Interview)
Evaluation of information (*see* Interpretation of information)
Executive Order 11246, 19–21
Executives (*see* Management personnel, worker specifications for)
Extracurricular activities, 218–220
Extroverts, 163–165

Facial expressions of interviewer, 95–97
Feedback interview, 8–9
Females (*see* Minorities)
Final interview:
  essential aspects of, 86–87
  leads for, provided by preliminary selection steps, 82
Finance personnel, worker specifications for, 59–61
Firing (*see* Discharge)
Follow-up questions, 107–124
  to clarify casual remarks of applicant, 113
  to control interview conversation, 115–116
  direct, softening, 121–122
  double-edged, 120–121, 199
  equal employment opportunity considerations and, 124
  function of, 111–116
  for further work and education information, 112–113
  laundry list, 116–118
  note-taking and, 122–124
  open-ended comments and, 109–110
  probing, kinds of, 116–122
  to quantify information, 115
  to remind applicant of omitted parts of introductory questions, 111
  for shortcomings and assets, 44–45
  to support early established hypotheses, 113–115
  talking applicant's language, 110
  "why," 118–120
  work-related comments and, 110–111
Ford, National Development and Training Center, retraining of employees at, 11
Foreign competition, 3–4
Friend and Fuller, et al. v. Leidinger, Fulton, Thorton, and Fionegan, 78

Garino, David T., 24
General Electric Company, 98
General Motors, 11
Goals, vocational, 247–248
Grades, school, 213–214
Graduate Record Examination, 239–240
Graduate training, 222–224

Handicapped, hiring of, 20, 31
  (*See also* Minorities)
Hard worker, 271–272
Health, questions as to, 31
Honesty, 272–273

Information:
  balance in, 127–128
  chronological sequence of, 137
  descriptive versus evaluative, 130–131
  interpretation of (*see* Interpretation of information)
  quantifying, 115
  unfavorable, playing down, 147–148
Initiative, 173, 269
Intelligence (*see* Mental ability)
Internal consistency of information, 146–148
Interpretation of information, 143–174
  assets and liabilities of applicants, organizing, 152–153
  by cataloging of clues, 151
  clues to mental capacity, searching for, 153
  complexities of, 144–145
  contrasting applicant's history with job specifications, 155–156
  by determining whether applicant is telling truth, 146–148
  by direct observation, 156–157
  education, relevance in, 151–152
    (*See also* Education)

Interpretation of information (*Cont.*):
- hypotheses based on leads from previous selection steps, 161
- by inference, 157–160
- internal consistency of information, 146–147
- on Interview Rating Form (*see* Interview Rating Form)
- masking reactions by interviewer, 150
- objectivity, 145
- as ongoing process, 150
- process of, 149–153
- relevant information, 153–154
- trait constellations (*see* Trait constellations)
- trait descriptions, 172–174
- unfavorable information, 147–148
- unrealistic personal standards of applicants, 148–149
- veracity of information, determining, 146–148
- work history, relevance in, 151–152

Interruption, 133–135

Interview:
- allocation of time to, 67, 129–130
- calculated pause as technique in, 94–95, 196
- campus, 74–76
- control of (*see* Control of interview)
- demonstration, 292
- equal employment opportunity considerations, 26–33, 105–106, 140
- facial expressions in, 95–97
- feedback, 8–9
- final, essential aspects of, 86–87
- functions of, 88–89
- length of, 67, 129–130
- lubrication as technique in, 195
- note-taking during, 122–124

Interview (*Cont.*):
- philosophy of, 87–88
- playing down unfavorable information, 100–102
- practice (*see* Practice interview)
- preliminary (*see* Preliminary interview)
- question and answer technique in, 90–91
- questions (*see* Questions)
- rapport in (*see* Rapport, developing)
- reference checks in (*see* Reference checks)
- reinforcement in discussion of assets, 195
- small talk in, 92–94
- terminating, 250–255
- time factors in, 67, 129–130
  - economy of interviewer's time, 131–132
- unfavorable information, playing down, 100–102
- voice in, 97–99
- (*See also specific entries, for example*: Education; Work history)

Interview Guide, 132–133, 137

Interview Rating Form, 255–278
- adaptability, 267
- assertiveness, 270–271
- conscientiousness, 271
- education and training, 261–262
- hard worker, 271–272
- honesty and sincerity, 272–273
- initiative, 269
- maturity, 265
- motivation, 263–265
- overall rating, 275–278
- overall summary, 274–275
- perseverance, 269–270
- personality, character, and motivation, 263–273
- personality and ability configurations, 257–258
- self-confidence, 270
- self-discipline, 268–269

Interview Rating Form (*Cont.*):
  social adjustment, 262–263, 265–266
  summary of assets and shortcomings, 273–274
  tact, 266–267
  team worker, 266
  tough-mindedness, 267–268
  uses of, 278
  verbal rating, 275–278
  work history, 258–261
Interviewers, training of (*see* Training of interviewers)
Introductory questions (*see* Comprehensive introductory questions)
Introverts, 166–167

Jackson, Reverend Jesse L., 24
Job history (*see* Work history)
Job specifications (*see* Worker specifications)
Judgment and maturity, 246

Labor relations and worker specifications, 61, 63–64
Laundry-list questions, 116–118
Leadership experience, 193
Lippman, Thomas W., 10–11
Lubrication:
  in discussion of assets, 195
  as technique for developing rapport, 99–100

Management personnel, worker specifications for, 50–52
Marginal workers, 6–8, 15
Marital status, questions as to, 27
Maturity, 173, 235–236, 245–248
  college admissions and, 248–249
  emotional, 173, 245–246
  intellectual, 247
  of judgment, 246
  and priorities, ability to set, 247
Maturity (*Cont.*):
  rating, 265
  social, 247
  and vocational goals, reasonableness of, 247–248
  (*See also* Social adjustment)
Mental ability, 88, 235–241
  achievements reflecting, 240–241
  aptitude tests and, 237
  average, unusual educational achievements and, 243–244
  college admissions and, 248–249
  college board scores and, 238–239
  in effort required to make grades, 237–238
  Graduate Record Examination scores and, 239–240
  in response to depth questions, 240
Military service, 177–178
  (*See also* Veteran status, questions as to)
Minorities:
  affirmative action, 19, 21–22, 73
  education and, 233–234
  equal employment opportunity (*see* Equal employment opportunity)
  recruiting, 70
  work history and, 206–207
Motivation, 235–236, 241–244
  achievements in terms of mental level, 243–244
  college admissions and, 248–249
  conditioned to work, 185–187, 244
  drive for achievement, 244
  energy level and, 242–243
  interpretation of information, 241–244
  rating, 263–265

National origin, questions as to, 29
Note-taking, 122–124, 289–292

Office of Federal Contract Compliance Programs (OFCCP), 19, 20
Open-ended questions, 109–110
Organizing ability, 173–174
Outplacement, 10, 34–36
(*See also* Retraining workers; Trained applicants)
Overachievers, 215, 243–244

Pagues v. Mississippi State Employment Service, 78
Pauses, calculated, as interview technique, 94–95, 196
Performance appraisal, 8–9
Perseverance, 269–270
Personnel services, worker specifications for, 61–64
Philip Morris Inc., Seven-up unit, 24
Physical examination, 81–82
documentation of, 81–82
Planning ability, 173–174
Practice interview, 293–294
instructor's role during, 294–295
interviewees for, 285–288
preparing, 286–288
sources of, 286
Preliminary interview, 72–77
campus interview, 74–76
reference checks, obtaining permission for, 76–77
Prial, Frank J., 11
Probing questions, 116–122
Production supervisors, worker specifications for, 55–57

Questions:
as to age, 29–30
as to children, 27–28
comprehensive introductory, 102–105
assumed consent, 104–105
memorization, 104
reminding applicant of omitted parts, 111

Questions (*Cont.*):
depth, quality of response to, 240
direct, softening of, 121–122
double-edged, 120–121, 199
follow-up (*see* Follow-up questions)
as to health, 31
as to marital status, 27
probing follow-up, 116–122
as to race and national origin, 29
and reference checks (*see* Reference checks)
as to religion, 28–29
softening of direct, 121–122
as to veteran status, 32
"why," 42–43, 118–120

Race, questions as to, 29
Rapport, developing, 90–106
calculated pause as technique for, 94–95
comprehensive introductory questions in, 102–105
equal employment opportunity considerations and, 105–106
facial expressions of interviewer in, 95–97
lubrication as technique in, 99–100
small talk in, 92–94
unfavorable information, playing down, 100–102
voice of interviewer in, 97–99
Reading, 230–231
Readjustment Assistance Act of 1974 (*see* Vietnam-Era Veterans' Readjustment Assistance Act of 1974)
Recruiting, 69–70
(*See also* Affirmative action)
Reference checks, 32–33, 80–81
discrepancies between application information and, 81
obtaining permission for, 76–77
Rehabilitation Act of 1973, 20, 31

Reinforcement:
as technique for developing rapport, 99–100
as technique in discussion of assets, 195
Religion, questions as to, 28–29
Research and development personnel, worker specifications for, 52–55
Retraining workers, 11–12
quality of people selected for, 12–13
R. J. Reynolds Industries, Inc., Heublein unit, 24

Salary, 43–44, 187–190
Sales personnel, worker specifications for, 57–59
Satisfaction, job, 201–204
Scholastic Aptitude Tests (SATs), 215–218
interpretation of scores, 238–239
in selection of college students, 248–249
School (*see* Education)
Selection:
application form, 70–72
Bethlehem Steel Company study, 14, 26
costs of poor, 13–15
physical examination, 81–82
preliminary steps, 66–82
(*See also* Preliminary interview)
ratio of applicants to number of jobs to be filled, 69
recruiting, 69–70
screening techniques, 66
Self-confidence, 174, 270
Self-discipline, 173, 268–269
Self-evaluation, 200–201
Sincerity, 272–273
Small talk, 92–94
Social adjustment, 227–233
arts, interest in, 231–232
community involvement, 229–230
Social adjustment (*Cont.*):
discussion of, 227–228
energy level, 232–233
mental review of, 233
reading, 230–231
recording, 262–263
sports, 219, 228–229
(*See also* Emotional adjustment)
Social sensitivity, 173
of employee relations personnel, 63
Sports, participation in, 219, 228–229
Stamina, 232–233, 242–243
State employment services, 79–80
Subjects, academic, 211–213, 240–241
Supervisors:
in performance appraisal, 8–9
worker specifications for, 55–57

Tact, 266–267
of employee relations personnel, 63
Team worker, 174, 266
Technical personnel, 52–55
Technology, 10–13
Termination of interview, 250–251
for qualified applicant, 255
for unqualified applicant, 252–254
Tests (*see specific tests, for example*: Aptitude tests; Scholastic Aptitude Tests)
Time allocations in interviews, 67, 129–130
economy of interviewer's time, 131–132
Tough-mindedness, 173, 267–268
Trained applicants, 9–10, 34–36
controlling interview of, 39–45
earnings, discussion of, 43–44
identification of, 36–37
probing for shortcomings of, 44–45
taking advantage of skills of, 38–39

Trained applicants (*Cont.*):
"why" questions for, 42–43
Training, recording, 261–262
(*See also* Education)
Training of interviewers, 8–9, 279–296
composition of training group in, 283–285
demonstration interview, 292
importance of, 16
learning by doing in, 280
note-taking in, 289–292
physical facilities required in, 281–282
practice interview (*see* Practice) interview)
qualifications of trainer in, 282–283
role playing in, 293
time schedule in, 295
training week in, 288–295
writing reports in, 292–293
Trait constellations, 161–172
for assertive personalities, 168–170
for do-gooders, 170–172
for extroverts, 163–165
for introverts, 166–167
Trait descriptions, 172–174

Unemployment, 12
Unfavorable information, playing down, 147–148
Unions, 61, 63–64
United Auto Workers (UAW), 11
United States Employment Service (USES), 79

Validity generalization, 78–79
Veteran status, questions as to, 32
(*See also* Military service)
Vietnam-Era Veterans' Readjustment Assistance Act of 1974, 20, 32
Vigor, 232–233, 242–243
Voice of interviewer, 97–99
Vocational goals and maturity, 247–248

Wages, 4
(*See also* Earnings)
"Why" questions, 42–43, 118–120
Women (*see* Minorities)
Work history, 175–207
achievements, 194–197
assets, discussion of, 195–197
changing jobs, reasons for, 190–193
conditioning to hard work, 185–187, 244
development needs, 197–201
diligence, 185–186
discussion of, structuring, 176–178
dissatisfactions, 183–185
duties, 179–181
earnings, 187–190
equal employment opportunity considerations, 206–207
factors of job satisfaction, 201–204
follow-up questions on, 112–113
interpretation of relevance of information, 151–152
job satisfaction, factors of, 201–204
job situation in mind, 204–205
leadership experience, 193
military service, 177–178
number of previous jobs, 193–194
of older applicants, 138
reasons for changing jobs, 190–193
of recent graduates, 138–139
recording, 258–261
relevance of prior jobs, 178–179
satisfactions, 181–183
self-evaluation technique, 200–201
shortcomings, discussion of, 198–199

Work history (*Cont.*):
supervision, degree of, 187
type of job desired, 204–205
working conditions, 186–187
Worker specifications, 47–65
application form and, 70–71
building of, 47–49
contrasting, 155–156
for employee relations personnel, 61–64
for finance personnel, 59–61
labor relations and, 61, 63–64

Worker specifications (*Cont.*):
for management personnel, 50–52
for personnel services, 61–64
for production supervisors, 55–57
for research and development personnel, 52–55
for sales personnel, 55–57
for supervisors, 55–57
Work-related comments and questions, 110–111
Wrongful discharge, 6

ABOUT THE AUTHOR

Richard A. Fear, a personnel consultant for some of the nation's largest corporations, is a past vice president of The Psychological Corporation and is now serving as senior consultant with the Selection Systems Division of Mainstream Access, Inc., a New York–based career development consulting firm. He has trained several thousand interviewers in this country and abroad and is coauthor of *Jobs, Dollars, and EEO*. The second edition of *The Evaluation Interview* was named the most outstanding human resource management book of 1973 by the American Society for Personnel Administration.